Peacock

THE CLAIMS OF THE CHURCH OF ENGLAND

THE CLAIMS OF THE CHURCH OF ENGLAND

By

CYRIL GARBETT
ARCHBISHOP OF YORK

HODDER AND STOUGHTON LIMITED
ST. PAUL'S HOUSE, WARWICK SQUARE,
LONDON, E.C.4

First printed June, 1947
Reprinted - July, 1947
Reprinted November, 1947

Made and Printed in Great Britain for Hodder & Stoughton, Limited, London,
by Wyman & Sons Limited, London, Reading and Fakenham

INTRODUCTION

I FIND it difficult to describe this book. It is not a history of the Church of England, though it has history in it. It is not a textbook about its administration and organisation, though it gives some account of their working. It is not a programme of Church Reform, though reform is frequently mentioned. Nor is it a book of reminiscences, though I am afraid it contains a considerable amount of personal experience and recollections. It is an account in broad outline of the nature, the work and the claims of the Church of England as they appear to-day to one who has been a member of it since his baptism over seventy years ago, and has served it as one of its ministers for nearly fifty years. I make no pretence to have written an impartial and objective study, for I have written as one who is profoundly thankful that, through parentage and reasoned conviction, he belongs to the Church of England.

Reason by itself is as rarely a cause for membership of a Church as it is for citizenship of a State. More often than not both are due to parentage and place of birth. This was certainly so in my own case. I was born in a country vicarage[1]; my father was a clergyman of the Church of England. He came of an Evangelical family, and his two elder brothers were leaders of the Oxford opposition to the Tractarian Movement. He himself was a broad churchman, and had been greatly influenced by the writings of Frederick Denison Maurice. He accepted most of the more advanced results of the Higher Criticism of his days. He hated intolerance and held that lack of charity was a greater sin than doctrinal error. In his teaching he dwelt on the Majesty and Holiness of God, and on the obedience and reverence that He claims from His children. I am sure he never had the slightest doubt about the position of the Church of England and of the place of its clergy in the life of the nation. My mother belonged to a military and somewhat Evangelical family. Her grandfather had resigned his post as Commander-in-Chief at Madras rather than order the customary salute to a Hindu idol. But at some time early in her life she had been influenced by the Tractarians. As a

[1] Tongham, Surrey.

child I noticed her reverence and devotion, the little curtsey she made as she entered a church, the time she spent on her knees in private prayer, her daily reading of the Psalms and Lessons—a practice she continued, only interrupted by rare illness, until the day before her death at the age of ninety. The beauty and kindness of her face were a true expression of her love and goodness; for her sympathy and unselfishness had no limit. While my father's churchmanship was largely intellectual, my mother's was more devotional. Through their example and teaching they gave me my first lessons in churchmanship, and this was strengthened and deepened by the village church and its worship. It was a modern church of comparatively little interest or beauty, but both it and the churchyard were kept in perfect order. The services, though simple, were extremely reverent, and not so long as to be irksome to a child. So at a very early age the worship of the Church became a natural part of my life.

But this unreflecting and inherited churchmanship could not continue forever. Both at school and, later, at Oxford, I met many who rejected or criticised all that hitherto I had accepted unquestioningly about the Church of England. I read books written by those who ridiculed its claims and denounced its past. Like most young men, I enjoyed argument, and I rushed gladly into the fray against all who attacked the Church. But this forced me to think out for myself the grounds for my churchmanship, and most of the reasons which convinced me then have been strengthened and reinforced by experience. To-day there are many who reach manhood without any previous experience of churchmanship; some of them go through life without feeling the need of God and His Church; but others—through hunger of soul, or the influence of friends, or the attractiveness of worship, or a sense of their own weakness and sinfulness—will wish to join one of the Christian Churches, but they are hesitant and uncertain as to where they should make their spiritual home. This book may lead some of these to join the Church of England. It is true they will find in it no ordered and systematic argument, but a description of what the Church of England stands for, the work it has done and is doing, and its great opportunities for service in the future. At one time it was usual for the protagonist of a Church to advance its claims by exposing and denouncing the errors and limitations of other Churches. Few now follow this un-Christian method; instead they attempt to commend their own Church by speaking of the special gifts and blessings given to it by God and which they wish others to share. I have attempted to follow this better way.

In the pages of this book there will be found some of the reasons for acceptance of the claims of the Church of England. Here I only re-state them in a few sentences—first and foremost because it is the historic Catholic Church of this land, rejecting the claims of the Pope, and appealing to Scripture and the teaching of the ancient fathers for the justification of its faith: in doctrine and worship it is scriptural, catholic and reasonable. It has toleration and comprehensiveness, a consistent appeal to sound learning, and a combination of authority and freedom which are not possessed to such a high degree by any other Church in Christendom. Its fruits are seen in the holiness of so many of its members, both living and departed, in its influence for good on the nation, in its expansion overseas, and in its work for Christian re-union. And, finally, the character and spirit of the Church, its parishes, ministers and buildings, covering the whole land, give it unrivalled opportunities for the conversion of England.

If this statement of faith in the Church of England stood by itself it would rightly appear presumptuous and self-satisfied. It must be read and understood in the light of two qualifications which I hasten to make. Not the most devoted member of the Church has a right to claim it is perfect. It has often sinned, sometimes through arrogance; sometimes through worldliness; sometimes through self-complacency and slothfulness; often it has failed to use the great opportunities given to it by its place in the nation—there are chapters in our past history on which we should look with shame, and for which we should ask forgiveness; and there are still many blemishes and inequalities in our Church which hinder its work. The older I grow the more intensely I feel the necessity for Church Reform. We talk of it, we discuss it, we report on it, but year after year passes and little is done. But it is not necessary for me to emphasise the sins and failures of the Church; there are already too many, both within and without the Church, who never cease from proclaiming them both loudly and exhaustively. It is more useful (and possibly more original!) to speak of the

7

causes for thankfulness which exist for the life and work of our Church. But it needs greater holiness, greater zeal in its evangelisation, both at home and abroad, greater boldness in its witness against social injustice, and greater determination to remove abuses and anomalies in its structure.

And the second qualification I would make is that loyalty to the Church of England should not prevent us from recognising fully the work which God has done and is doing through other Christian Churches. I should indeed be sorry if anything I have written seemed to ignore or to depreciate the work both of the Free Churches and of the Roman Catholics. The Free Churches have won for Christ multitudes who have been neglected by the Church of England, and the Roman Catholic Church in many of the poorer parts of our seaports and towns, as well as in remote villages of Lancashire and Yorkshire, ministers faithfully to those who would never accept nor even listen to our Church. Devotion to the Church of England should not prevent us from gladly recognising that to other Churches also the Grace of God has been given, that they often bear witness to truths which we have forgotten, and sometimes succeed where we have failed. In these days of world-wide paganism we should dwell on the Christian faith and morals we hold in common, rather than on the unhappy causes for our divisions.

So I send forth this book with the hope and prayer that it may strengthen some who are already members of the Church of England, and that it may help others who are not its members to think more sympathetically of its nature, its work and its claims.

I am very grateful to the Reverend G. A. Ellison, recently my domestic chaplain, for reading through both the typescript and the galley proofs, and for making many useful criticisms and suggestions : and to my Secretary, Miss Steele, for typing and often re-typing somewhat illegible MSS.

CYRIL EBOR:

CONTENTS

CHAPTER

1. CATHOLIC AND REFORMED - - *p.* 13

2. THE FAITH OF THE CHURCH - - *p.* 31

3. THE WORSHIP OF THE CHURCH - *p.* 49

4. THE CATHEDRALS AND CHURCHES OF
   THE CHURCH OF ENGLAND - - *p.* 73

5. THE BISHOP AND " THE BISHOPS " - *p.* 93

6. THE PAROCHIAL CLERGY - - - *p.* 125

7. THE LAITY - - - - - *p.* 159

8. THE CHURCH AND STATE - - *p.* 181

9. THE CHURCH AND PEOPLE - - *p.* 203

10. THE EXPANSION OF THE CHURCH OF
    ENGLAND - - - - - *p.* 225

11. TOWARDS THE REUNION OF CHRISTEN -
    DOM - - - - - - *p.* 245

12. YESTERDAY AND TO-DAY - - · *p.* 265

13. TO-MORROW - - · - - *p.* 285

9

DEDICATION

IN PIAM MEMORIAM PATRIS ET MATRIS
CAROLI ET SUSANNÆ GARBETT
QUI CUM EXEMPLO TUM DOCTRINA
ITA ME PUERUM INSTRUXERUNT
UT ECCLESIÆ ANGLICANÆ CONSTANS
INSERVIRE STUDUERIM

I

CATHOLIC AND REFORMED

English Churchmen are often unduly apologetic for their Church. With our national habit of self-depreciation they see more easily its defects than its strength. Persistent and carping criticism of the Church of England by those who are either its commissioned officers or its communicant members injures it more than any attacks by its open foes. No thoughtful Churchmen will deny the existence of anomalies and defects which should be dealt with as soon as possible. But recognition of the necessity of reform should not lead to forgetfulness of the true greatness of our Church, both Catholic and Reformed, and of the special contribution which God has called it to make to the Church throughout the world. Uncompromisingly the Church of England is the Catholic Church in this land, set free from subjection to the Church of Rome.

I

CATHOLIC AND REFORMED

A N intelligent foreigner would find it very difficult after only
a few months in this country to give a clear and concise description of the Church of England. He would probably have
started on his inquiries with the presupposition that it was
Protestant, but he would soon discover that its services were
very different from those of any reformed Church on the Continent. He would hear in its Creeds a statement of belief in the
Holy Catholic Church, but he would find that many of its
clergy and its laity called themselves Protestant. He would be
surprised at the great variety in the manner of celebrating the
Holy Communion, in some churches with the utmost simplicity,
in others with all the splendour of a rich ceremonial. He would
find it was an episcopal Church, but he would discover that
some of its members were always criticising " the bishops."
He would be perplexed at the controversies of which he would
read in the Church Press and confused by the different descriptions of members of the same Church as " Anglo-Catholic,"
" Evangelical," " Central," " Liberal." Impatient at so many
apparent contradictions he might be tempted to follow the example
of a French Roman Catholic and describe the Church of England
as " admitting every doctrine which can be called Christian ; it
rejects, however, on the one side Socinianism and on the other
what it calls the corruptions of Rome, and yet we can find within
it both Socinians and those who hold all Roman doctrine."[1]

With a fuller knowledge of the Anglican Church he would
have formed a very different conclusion. He would have found
that its apparent contradictions were due to the fact that it was
both Catholic and Reformed. No judgement on it would be
accurate unless full account was taken of this. And in addition
to it being both Catholic and Reformed he would discover it had
two other characteristics which give it an unique place among
the Churches of Christendom : it appeals to sound learning,

[1] Dictionaire de Theologie Catholique. Vide Article " Anglicanisme."

and it practises a wide and charitable toleration. In other Churches one or more of these characteristics can be found, even in a higher degree than in our own Church, but in no other Church are present all four—Catholic, Reformed, Sound Learning and Toleration.

1. CATHOLIC

The Church of England is the ancient Catholic Church of this land. The word Catholic was originally used to describe the universality of the Church in all places and among all men, but later the term was applied to the soundness and primitiveness of its teaching as contrasted with the novelties of some of the heretical sects. When Christendom became divided the Catholic Church could still be recognised by its continuity with the past and by its possession of the ancient Scriptures, Creeds, Sacraments and Apostolic Ministry. " As the main body of the sea being one, yet within divers precincts hath divers names, so the Catholic Church is in like sort divided into a number of distinct societies, every one of which is termed a Church within itself"[1]

The Church came to England with the missionaries from Rome and from Scotland. St. Augustine with his missionaries converted the south-east of England and founded the Sees of Canterbury, Rochester and London. The missionaries from the north converted Northumbria and penetrated to the Midlands. The zeal of Wilfrid brought the converted kingdoms under the spiritual supremacy of Rome, which gave to the English Church a discipline and cohesion which it would never have gained from the Scottish missionaries. Later with the Norman Conquest the Church was strengthened both in discipline, morals and administration by being brought again into closer communion with the rest of the Western Church which had its centre in Rome. There is no question but that in the Anglo-Saxon and in mediæval days the Church of England was the Catholic Church of this land.

From this ancient and mediæval Church there has never been any complete break. At the Reformation there was indeed a breach with the Pope: the importance of this was great as ultimately it meant separation from the rest of Western Catholicism, but neither kings, bishops nor people intended to cut

---

[1] Richard Hooker, " The Laws of Ecclesiastical Policy," Book III Chapter I.

themselves off from the Holy Catholic Church and to substitute for it a new Church. They claimed that they were only removing that which was unknown in the early undivided Church and contrary to the teaching of the Scriptures and the Fathers. Bishop Jewel of Salisbury, in his " Apology for the Church of England," asserted : " We have planted no new religion, but only have renewed the old that was undoubtedly founded and used by the Apostles of Christ and other holy Fathers in the primitive Church." During the changes made in the reigns of Henry, Edward, Mary and Elizabeth the great majority of the clergy remained in their benefices until promotion or death. The bishops refused to accept the changes demanded early in Elizabeth's reign and were deprived ; but out of eight thousand beneficed clergy at least seven thousand accepted the new Prayer Book. Careful provision was made for the preservation of continuity by the consecration of Archbishop Parker by bishops who had all been duly consecrated. Equally significant evidence of the preservation of continuity is seen by the way in which, through all the changes of the Reformation, the machinery of ecclesiastical government remained unimpaired and in working order : " Through all this, the processes of ecclesiastical law had gone forward in the old way. Apart from the changes of constitution in certain cathedral churches consequent upon the suppression of the monasteries and from the creation of a few new dioceses, there are few alterations to be traced. The ordinary jurisdiction of bishops remained as in the past. Officials and vicars-general still exercised their delegated authority. In the official records of English dioceses for this period traces of contemporary changes are few and far between. Bishops were deprived of their sees and burned for heresy, but the business of diocesan administration founded upon centuries of long practice was not interrupted for a single day."[1]

This is confirmed by the evidence of a great mass of documents preserved in the Archbishop's Registry at York. I asked the archivist, the Rev. J. S. Purvis, to see how far these documents bore witness to continuity throughout the Reformation period. In reply he says : " So far as the record of business which normally passed through the Registry is any guide, it never occurred to ecclesiastical authority to suppose that any

[1] " The Reformation," by A. Hamilton Thompson, in " Essays Catholic and Critical," p. 361.

deep or general innovation was going on, or that any position had been reached so new or so removed from tradition that particular notice or anything in the nature of explanation or excuse was required. . . . It is possible to say with some confidence that although there were some clergy who did not accept the changes and reforms which were made in the order of the Church and of the services, and some who remained obstinately Roman in their allegiance, the majority of all ranks showed no breach of continuity, and it will be difficult, if not impossible, to gather evidence showing anything at all like a widespread belief amongst the clergy that a new Church had been formed, or that anything had happened further than an internal reform of itself by the ancient Church of England involving in essentials the rejection of a foreign control which had never been justifiably imposed. The administration, the machinery by which ecclesiastical authority functioned, shows clearly no sense of vital alteration at any time." It is also significant that before, during and after the breach with Rome successive Archbishops used in their legal documents the same term *Ecclesia Anglicana*. The repudiation of papal authority and drastic changes both in ritual and ceremonial did not break the continued and uninterrupted work of consistory courts, archdeacons, rural deans and the rest of the administrative instruments and machinery of the Church.

Dr. G. R. Owst in his book, "Preaching in Mediæval England," gives an interesting example of continuity. He is describing the various little devotional manuals and treatises which were in use at the end of the Middle Ages. They were supplies from the pulpit as well as an important supply for it.

They passed into countless homes and helped to create the English type of domestic piety ; they were handed on from one generation to another. "Sometimes the subsequent careful notes and scoring, the names entered by later hands in these very sermons and handbooks, seem to give almost tangible evidence of the continuity of use. Their influence stalks on silent, but wonderfully real and alive from generation to generation, troubling little about the noisy clash of theologians and parties without. For round the family board, and in the hearts of the peasantry, the Reformation meant no such break with the past as many would have us believe."[1]

[1] "Preaching in Mediæval England," by G. R. Owst, p. 280.

On one other occasion there was danger that the continuity of the Church of England might be destroyed. Under the Commonwealth episcopacy was abolished, the use of the Prayer Book made illegal, the cathedrals desecrated, and the clergy deprived of their benefices. The places of the dispossessed clergy were often filled by men with little or no training, " Tinkers, cobblers, saddlers, coachmen took on them the ministry of the Word."[1] In September, 1655, it was ordered that no Royalist was to be allowed " to keep in his house any of the ejected clergy as a chaplain or a tutor for his children, under pain of having his fine doubled : and no such clergyman was to keep a school, preach, or administer the Sacraments, celebrate marriage or use the Book of Common Prayer " under pain of a heavy fine or banishment. But with the Restoration the danger to the Church passed away. Exiled bishops returned to their sees, new bishops were consecrated, and the deprived clergy went back to their parishes. Ministers who had taken the place of the ejected clergy were compelled to resign unless they were episcopally ordained and promised to conform to the Prayer Book. The continuity of the Church had been threatened but it had never been broken.

But continuity of the Church as an outward organisation does not necessarily mean that it is Catholic. A Church to be Catholic must hold the Catholic Faith, treasure the Catholic Scriptures, administer the Catholic Sacraments, and retain the Catholic Ministry. The Church of England proclaims to all that it is Catholic. In its Creeds its members declare that they believe in the Holy Catholic Church. It prays for " the good estate of the Catholic Church, that it may be so guided and governed by thy good spirit, that all who profess and call themselves Christians may be led into the way of truth and hold the faith in unity of spirit, in the bond of peace and in righteousness of life." In the Bidding Prayer directed to be used before the sermon it exhorts the congregation to " pray for Christ's Holy Catholic Church, that is for the whole congregation of Christian people dispersed throughout the whole world and especially for the Churches of England, Scotland and Ireland." Its claim to be Catholic is proved by its acceptance of the three great Catholic Creeds, the Apostles, the Nicene, and the Athanasian :

[1] " A History of the English Church from the Accession of Charles I to the death of Anne," by W. H. Hutton, p. 167.

B

by its belief in the authority and inspiration of the Scriptures : by its faithful administration of the Sacraments ordained by Our Lord Himself as generally necessary for salvation, Baptism and the Holy Communion : and by its threefold ministry of Bishops, Priests and Deacons. At no time has it ever lost these distinguishing marks of the Catholic Church. Its possession of them unites it to the undivided Church of the early centuries and to the whole Catholic Church throughout the world to-day. While the Roman Church still refuses to acknowledge the Church of England as Catholic, the Eastern Churches are steadily moving towards the acceptance of its claim to be a living branch of the Catholic Church.

A member of the Church of England thus shares in the rich heritage of the Saints. By his baptism he is admitted to the holy fellowship to which Augustine, Aidan, Anselm, Hugh of Lincoln, Lancelot Andrewes and Bishop Ken belonged. He can glory in his membership of the communion of saints, and of the mystical body of Christ which includes the blessed company of all faithful people both living and departed.

The great contribution which the Oxford Movement made to the Church of the nineteenth century was its demand that its bishops, clergy and laity should never forget that the Church of which they were the officers and members was no provincial society or department of the State, dependent for its very existence on Parliament and the good will of the majority of citizens, but that it was the Catholic Church of this land and as such had an independent and supernatural life of its own. It recalled Churchmen to a sense of the wonder and mystery of the fellowship to which they belonged. It brought to light treasures in its public worship and in its devotional life which for long had been ignored. It revived practices of Catholic discipline which had been allowed for generations to rust. It called aloud to all to hear that the political and social privileges of the Church were as nothing compared to the splendour of its position as the Holy Catholic Church in this land of England.

2. REFORMED

But emphasis on the Catholicism of our Church must not obscure its Protestantism. The term Protestant has lately fallen somewhat into disrepute through its association with a narrow and militant form of religion, but Archbishop Laud did not hesitate to speak of the true Protestant religion established in the Church of England, and at the Coronation the King promises to maintain to the utmost of his power " in the United Kingdom the Protestant Reformed Religion established by law." It is only by ignoring the history of the last four hundred years that the Protestant and Reformed nature of our Church can be denied. It is a fact which some may regret, but which none can neglect. There was much in the methods and violence of the Reformation which most Anglicans to-day would deplore. The occasion which precipitated the break with Rome was the lust of an unscrupulous king and the political scheming of a Pope in the power of a rival sovereign. In the changes which followed the rupture with Rome much that was beautiful and edifying both in the actual churches and in worship was destroyed. The Church before and after the Reformation was compared by an Elizabethan divine to a garden before and after weeding, but unhappily with the weeds many valuable plants and flowers were plucked up and burnt. But when all this has been admitted the Reformation, in addition to its abolition of recognised abuses, gave to the Church four permanent boons of incalculable value, freedom from the Papacy, spiritual freedom for the individual Christian, freedom of access to the Scriptures and to their study, and openness and simplicity in its services.

From the days of St. Augustine the Church of England had been in full communion with the Pope and had accepted his spiritual supremacy. There were undoubted advantages in the existence of a spiritual power above all earthly monarchs. The ideal of a supernatural court of appeal was noble, and if it had been realised it would have done much for the cause of international justice. But the Papacy became increasingly political, it employed spiritual weapons to satisfy its temporal ambitions : and when spiritual weapons by themselves proved inadequate it used them to raise vast sums of money through the taxation of the clergy, and through the sale of benefices, dispensations and indulgences. The Papacy became a vast financial bureaucracy making sweeping demands upon Christendom. When Innocent IV fought Frederick " with the spiritual sword " we are told that " Everything spiritual, everything religious, become a means to one political end. The revenues and offices of the Church, its disciplinary and penitential system, its highest ideal of the Cross, its lowest pecuniary motives, its very sacraments were forged into weapons."[1] This was bitterly resented by the nations. In England frequent opposition had been offered to the Papal demands and Parliament had passed many Statutes to restrain Papal interference. There had been widespread indignation at the Pope's appointment of French and Italian nominees to vacant benefices. King and Commons alike were angered at the large revenues which he drew from this country, and the clergy groaned under a double load of taxation. Lawyers and litigants were both irritated by the appeals made from the national to the Papal Courts, they seemed to detract from the national dignity, and were invariably lengthy and costly. The repudiation of Papal authority was thus generally welcomed, however greatly disliked were some of the later phases of the Reformation. It did not leave the Church of England entirely free, for it transferred much of the authority of the Pope to the Crown, but once for all it delivered both Church and Nation from the incessant interference and exorbitant claims of the bishop of Rome. Since the Reformation the promulgation of the decree of Papal Infallibility has further widened the breach with Rome. Respect is paid by men of all Churches when the Pope speaks on behalf of the Christian conscience, but the authority which he then exercises is moral and spiritual and is recognised and accepted as such by the free choice of Christian men. The Church of England and the Eastern Churches stand for Catholicism without the Papacy.

The Reformation brought freedom to the individual as well as to the Church. This is not unfettered freedom, for the authorised minister of the Church only receives his commission after giving solemn undertakings both in the matter of doctrine and of worship, and the layman too is bound to accept loyally the faith and the rules of the Church to which he belongs. But he has freedom to enquire into the grounds of the faith he has accepted, to ask the reasons for it, and to request that it should be stated in an intelligent form to satisfy thoughtful men and women. And within wide limits freedom is given to both clergy and laity in matters of faith and practice. Where the Roman Church says " you must " the Church of England more often says " you may." It leaves much to the discretion of the individual. For instance it insists on the acceptance of the

---

[1] A. L. Smith, " Church and State in the Middle Ages," p. 228.

Bible as the inspired word of God, but the individual is not bound to any one special theory of inspiration. The clergy are given freedom in respect of marriage : in the Roman Church by their admission to the sub-diaconate young boys are pledged to lifelong celibacy, but in the Church of England each priest is free to decide for himself as to whether God has given him a vocation to marriage or to celibacy. The intending communicant must truly and earnestly repent of his sins making humble confession to Almighty God, but the manner of confession is left open to him : it may be made privately in his home, or it may be through sharing in the General Confession, or he may resort " to some discreet and learned Minister of God's Word, and open his grief : that by the ministry of God's Holy Word he may receive the benefit of absolution, together with ghostly counsel and advice." [1] In the minor matters of ceremonial the lay worshipper has almost complete freedom. In practice the note inserted in the 1549 Prayer Book is still operative " As touching kneeling, crossing, holding up of hands, and other gestures, they may be used or left, as every man's devotion serveth, without blame."

Freedom of access to the Scriptures is also one of the notes of the Church of England as a reformed Church. It would not be indeed correct to say that in pre-Reformation days the Bible was a completely closed book. Selections of it were read in the Church services. The Psalms seem to have been fairly familiar. Some books were known through rhyming paraphrases. Sir Thomas More in one of his most controversial writings declared " I myself have seen and can show you Bibles, fair and old written in English which have been known and seen by the Bishop of the diocese and left in the hands of laymen and women whom he knew to be good and Catholic people who used the books with devotion and solemness." But to the great majority of Christians the Bible was both a closed and forbidden book. It was in Latin and so could only be read by scholars, while the translations of it either in part or in whole were suspect as heretical productions. They were forbidden by the authorities ; when discovered they were confiscated and their owners subjected to severe penalties. With the issue of the Great Bible a new epoch started. Bible reading in public and private was encouraged. The reading of the Bible in the

[1] First Exhortation in the Order for the Holy Communion.

vulgar tongue at the Morning and Evening Services of the Church made the uneducated familiar with it; and the phraseology of the English version of the Bible became part of the common speech. To-day the Church of England is a Bible Church, accepting the Bible as the test of faith necessary for salvation, using it as the basis of its worship and teaching, and urging upon its children the necessity and value of the study and reading of the Scriptures. It has societies with large numbers of members which exist to provide intelligent and regular reading of the Bible. In the Authorised Version we have the perfect fruition of all previous attempts to render the Bible into the English tongue. It was perhaps the most valuable gift that the Church has ever conferred on the English people. Great as are its literary values, and for over three centuries it has moulded or influenced the noblest of our prose and verse, its religious significance has been greater still. "For nearly three centuries it has been the Bible, not merely of one sect or party, not even of a single community, but of the whole nation and of every English-speaking country on the face of the globe. It has been the literature of millions who have read little else, it has been the guide of conduct to men and women of every class in life and of every rank in learning and education. No small part of the attachment of the English people to their national Church is due to the common love of every party and well-nigh every individual for the English Bible."[1]

The worship of our Church is that of a Church which is reformed as well as Catholic. More will be said about this in a later chapter. Here it is only necessary to say that the public worship of the Church is open and intelligible. It is in the common language; it is open so that all can follow it or join in it, and its symbolism and ceremonies are intended to interpret and to make clear. The Lord's Supper is primarily a communion in which all partake, rather than a Mass conducted by the priest in the presence of a passive congregation.

3. THE APPEAL TO SOUND LEARNING

Bishop Creighton once claimed that the special distinction of the Church of England was that it appealed to sound learning.

---

[1] " Our Bible and the Ancient Manuscripts," by Sir Frederic Kenyon, p. 234, fourth edition.

The Reformation in this country took a different course to what it did elsewhere for it started with political changes, and later on when alterations were made in doctrine and worship the Reformers did their best to make them in accordance with the teaching of the Scriptures and of the early Fathers. It was this which steadied the movement and saved it from the violent disregard of the past which so often characterised it on the Continent. It was to sound learning that Cranmer appealed both in defence of the changes made in doctrinal statement and in framing the new forms of worship. Bishop Jewel in his "Apology for the Church of England" argues that an appeal to the Scriptures and the Fathers proved that the English Reformers were going back to the old Church. He claims to "show plainly that God's holy Gospel, the ancient bishops, and the primitive Church do make on our side . . . and that we have returned to the Apostles and old Catholic fathers ": and again "we are come as near as we possibly could to the Church of the Apostles and of the old Catholic bishops and fathers." Later on Richard Hooker in his "Ecclesiastical Polity " on a far grander scale stated constructively the case for the reformed Church of England as against both Rome and the Puritans. In doing this he appealed to reason, Scripture and tradition. Throughout the greater part of the seventeenth century the attacks made by both Roman and Puritan compelled the Church of England through its leading divines and scholars to defend its position by appealing to the Scriptures and the Fathers.

In the eighteenth century the necessity for the use of sound learning was required in a different direction. An attack was made not so much on any special form of Church government or doctrine as on all supernatural religion. In France and in England a number of brilliant writers launched a series of attacks on revealed religion and especially on the miraculous. The writings of the Free Thinkers and Deists caused widespread anxiety amongst orthodox Christians : their general position was that God has revealed Himself in Nature and that therefore no other revelation was necessary ; they held that sufficient knowledge of God could be obtained through the reason alone. Their arguments were countered and defeated by a number of Anglican Divines, the most famous among them were Butler, Berkeley, Paley and Warburton. They met Deists and Socinians on their own ground; they fought them with their weapons of reason, instead of falling back upon mere condemnations by authority. The result of the controversy was not merely the defeat of the rationalists, but the strengthening of the Church which had been challenged to think out afresh and to restate the grounds for its belief in revelation.

In the nineteenth century the attack on Christianity was renewed from various quarters. The criticism of received ideas on the nature, date and authorship of the books of the Bible ; the general acceptance of the theory of evolution ; and the advance in physical science all created new difficulties in the way of belief. There were many both among the clergy and laity who at once condemned these new views as opposed to Christianity, and demanded that those who held them should be censured as heretical, and if they were clergymen deprived of any benefices they might hold. But once again the better way was taken and an appeal was made to sound learning. Christian scholarship set to work both to answer the attacks and to restate the Christian position. The writers in " Essays and Reviews " in 1860 and in " Lux Mundi " in 1889 aimed at a new statement of religious and moral truth. They were representative of a whole series of able thinkers and writers—Maurice, Lightfoot, Westcott, Hort, Driver, Sanday, Illingworth and of many others who faced fearlessly the new problems and were confident that the truth learnt by reason could never be contrary to the truth of revelation.

In the last fifty years the challenge to Christianity has been insistent. This has been a period of amazing renaissance. The changes in thought have been immense. Greater discoveries have been made than in all the previous years since the coming of Christ. New fields of knowledge have been opened on every side. The Christian has found himself confronted with new and unexpected problems. The Church had the choice either of denouncing the new thought, wherever it was not immediately reconcilable with the accepted theology, or of examining it patiently and sympathetically to see if it did not throw fresh light on the old faith and would not help in its restatement. The Roman Catholic Church has adopted the first position, it has excommunicated or denounced its members who have accepted the new discoveries, and has discouraged any serious attempt to reconcile them with the old faith ; it has indeed a few eminent scholars like Baron von Hügel, Christopher Dawson, Alfred Noyes, Father D'Arcy and M. Maritain, whose writings have been of great help to many of all Churches. But even von Hügel was suspect, in a letter to Miss Maude Petre he tells how he has to face the possibility of expulsion or condemnation, and because of this " It is not necessarily cowardice or trimming if we look well around us before each step, if we plant our feet, very deliberately and slowly, alternately on the stepping stones between and around which roars a raging, deep, drowning stream."[1] He once told an Anglican friend that when he had written an article he was like a dog with a bone looking for some obscure Encyclopædia in which he might bury and conceal it from the inquisitive eyes of the authorities of his Church ! The difficulties of Mr. Noyes with his publishers and the threat of condemnation by Rome of his book on Voltaire are still recent. We owe to the Church of Rome many valuable books on worship, devotion and on moral theology, but it has given little help to those who feel the desperate need, either of answering the intellectual difficulties raised against the faith, or of restating it in the light of the best thought of our day.

The Church of England, true to its tradition, has adopted the other alternative. Its leading theologians have welcomed what is true in modern thought, they have criticised and attacked what is false in it, and while remaining loyal to its historic creeds they have sought to commend them in the terms and modes with which educated men are most familiar. Composite volumes like " Foundations," and " Essays Catholic and Critical," are in the direct succession of " Lux Mundi." We have many writers of distinction both clerical and lay who to-day are expounding the Christian faith. They are working in different fields—biblical, doctrinal, philosophical, ethical and historical ; but they are at one in their conviction that the faith can be commended to thoughtful men and women. Occasionally in their eagerness to explain, some have run the risk of explaining away accepted doctrine, and have made unnecessary concessions to their opponents ; but whatever mistakes they have made they have shown that it is possible to be both a Christian and intelligent. Their writings make a solid contribution to a reasonable faith. We make no claim that the Church of England stands alone in this respect ; it would be ungrateful to forget all that has been done in this way by the Presbyterian and Free Churches ; but alone among the ancient Churches, the Church

[1] Von Hügel's " Selected Letters," p. 168.

of England has consistently made this appeal to sound learning. Most of the writers referred to above would have been silenced if they had been members of the Roman Catholic Church. One of the services which the Church of England can render to Christendom to-day is to prove to the world that Catholicism can be progressive, to witness that Christianity has no fear of new discoveries, and to show that all truth, whether it is historical, philosophical or scientific, is a further revelation of the truth that is in God.

4. THE COMPREHENSIVENESS OF THE CHURCH

A Church which is both Catholic and Reformed and which has intellectual freedom is bound to be comprehensive. Within the Anglican Church are Anglo-Catholics, Evangelicals, Liberals and the great mass of English Churchmen who are content to describe themselves as Churchmen without any further label. In no other Church can there be found such various schools of thought. To the logically minded and to those who admire the strictly regimented systems of Rome or Geneva the position must seem quite intolerable. No one will deny that at times the presence of different parties within one Church causes inconvenience, and when controversy becomes acute, creates considerable scandal. Violent disputes over minor matters of ceremonial bring discredit upon the Church, while controversy when conducted with bitterness and lack of charity on major questions of doctrine or discipline hinders gravely its work. But the effect of these divisions is easily exaggerated by those who only know the Church from without. Men can belong to the different parties, hold different views on the Church and Sacraments, prefer different methods of worship and yet work happily together. Here I can bear personal testimony. For many years in the parish of Portsea, both as assistant curate and as vicar, I lived and worked with a staff of sixteen curates who had come from almost every theological college and whose views on many questions were very different; on no occasion were any of us conscious that difference in theological opinion or in preference over ceremonial was any obstacle in the way of our working happily and loyally together. When I left Portsea for the diocese of Southwark I found the different parties strongly represented with their own organisations and federations, there

were " advanced " churches with full ceremonial and there were
"low " or " evangelical" churches with a minimum of ceremonial.
But where there was true reverence and devotion I never felt any
difficulty in worshipping and preaching in an Anglo-Catholic
church in the morning and in an Evangelical church in the evening. I found that with two exceptions (one ultra Protestant and
the other ultra Anglo-Catholic) every parish was prepared to
support the diocese, and when there was a call for united action,
such as the raising of money for Church Extension, the clergy and
laity without distinction of party were ready to join in prayer, work
and sacrifice. In the diocese of Winchester, the overwhelming
majority of clergy and laity of all shades of thought were ready to
co-operate. And here in the diocese of York strife is non-
existent. This is generally true throughout the whole of England,
with the possible exception of two or three dioceses, divisions
which seem very serious on paper or on a party platform, or when
accentuated by some controversy, do not in actual fact hinder
Church life and work as gravely as might have been expected.

The different parties within the Church have each made some
valuable contribution to the fullness of its life. The Anglo-
Catholics have given it rich ideals of worship and of Churchmanship, and restored to it a deeper sense of the meaning of
the sacramental life : the Evangelicals have kept alive in it a
burning love for the conversion of souls and for the winning
of the world to Christ : the Liberals have witnessed to the
necessity of bringing all modern thought into the service of the
Master, and of using the intellect in the presentation of Christian
truth. Our Church would be infinitely the poorer if any one
of these parties were ostracised or expelled.

Through the presence of different parties in one Church we
have learnt the lesson of toleration. It was a long time before
Christians could tolerate religious differences or discuss them with
charity and courtesy. The violence of the language used by
the controversialists of the seventeenth century is almost incredible to us, though occasionally echoes of it still come from
some underworld. The cruelty displayed by the opposing
factions was hateful and utterly contrary to the teaching of
Christ. Toleration in matters of religion was regarded as a
sin. Calvin at the end of his life stated that there was nothing
in all his writings which he wished to retract, except a plea for
toleration which he had made at the age of twenty-five. Oliver

Cromwell, one of the most broad-minded men of his time, could not extend toleration to Anglicans, Roman Catholics or Quakers. Sir Thomas Browne was far in advance of his age when in his " Religio Medici " he wrote of the Roman Catholics " there is between us one common name and appellation, one faith and necessary body of principles common to us both : and therefore I am not scrupulous to converse and live with them, to enter their churches in defect of ours and either pray with them, or for them." Now confronted with the common danger of a militant paganism the shrill tones of domestic controversy are less frequently heard. Men holding different religious views are more ready to understand one another. There is reason to hope that before long mere toleration will be replaced by the love which should unite those who in the same Church are serving the same Lord.

The fact that within our Church there are found different views and practices should not be a cause either for reproach or for apology. The comprehensiveness of the Church of England is one of its most distinctive qualities. It is to-day the most liberal-minded Church in the world ; perhaps we might dare say it is the most charitable of all Churches. For as its members have grown in fellowship, so they have come to view with greater sympathy and respect communions other than their own. No longer do they cast reproaches at other bodies of Christians, but they look to see what they can learn from them. The Catholic and Reformed nature of our Church with its appeal to sound learning, gives us the hope that in God's good providence He may use it as one of His instruments for the healing of the wounds of a divided Christendom.

English Churchmen are often unduly apologetic for their Church. With our national habit of self-depreciation they see more easily its defects than its strength. Persistent and carping criticism of the Church of England by those who are either its commissioned officers or its communicant members injures it more than any attacks by its open foes. No thoughtful Churchmen will deny the existence of anomalies and defects which should be dealt with as soon as possible. But recognition of the necessity of reform should not lead to forgetfulness of the true greatness of our Church, both Catholic and Reformed, and of the special contribution which God has called it to make to the Church throughout the world. Uncompromisingly the Church of England is the Catholic Church in this land, set free from subjection to the Church of Rome.

II

THE FAITH OF THE CHURCH

The Church of England stands for both authority and freedom in matters of faith. It rejects both the autocratic authority which denies freedom of criticism and the licence which easily degenerates into anarchy. Its doctrinal position calls for intelligence, patience and humility. Intelligence so that God may be loved with the mind as well as with the heart; patience to search and to wait until the difficulties are removed and truth is made clear; humility to listen to and reverence the voice of Scripture and tradition.

II

THE FAITH OF THE CHURCH

SINCE the Reformation the doctrinal position of the Church of England has been criticised from two opposite directions. From one side it is attacked for vagueness and uncertainty in matters of faith, from the other for refusing to abandon what are described as obsolete and antiquated doctrines. Sometimes the demand is for greater authoritativeness in its statement of faith, sometimes for a larger freedom for its members and ministers in what they may hold and teach. There is, however, general agreement that some statement of belief is necessary. No society whether religious or secular can hold together unless its members are united by some common convictions and aims. A Church with no statement of faith could not exist. However brief and rudimentary it may be there must be some formula which its members must accept as a condition of membership, and to which they can refer as an authoritative statement of the doctrine held by their Church. Some such simple creed can be found in the earliest days of the Church. In a sub-apostolic insertion we read in the Acts that the Ethiopian eunuch declared as a preliminary to his baptism " I believe that Jesus Christ is the Son of God." St. Paul probably refers to a formula of belief when he wrote " If thou shalt confess with thy mouth Jesus as Lord, and shalt believe in thine heart that God hath raised him from the dead, thou shalt be saved." By the middle of the second century it is plain that simple creed forms were in use. The Creed was taught to the candidate for baptism, who had to learn it by heart and repeat it in the presence of his teacher before he was baptised. From these simple statements of faith have developed the Creeds and Confessions of the various Churches, some are of great antiquity, others are comparatively modern : some are brief, others of great length and complexity. All contain positive statements of belief, some in addition contain warnings against doctrines and practices which were regarded as erroneous.

31

Doctrinal Statements of the Church

The faith of the Church of England is stated in three sets of documents, the Creeds, the Prayer Book (including the Ordinal), and the Thirty-nine Articles. The reformers claimed that they were returning to the old religion of the primitive Church. They had no intention of creating a new Church, with special creeds of its own. It was, therefore, unnecessary for the Church of England to formulate new creeds or to draw up a new theology. It was sufficient to retain the old creeds of the early Church. Of these there are three. The Apostles' Creed is an enlarged form of the old Roman Creed which was in existence in the second century. It is a statement of belief in God the Father, in Jesus Christ His Only Son Our Lord, and in the Holy Ghost and His work in the Church, the communion of Saints, the forgiveness of sins, and in the future life. It is terse and practical in its statements. Its central portion is largely concerned with the historical facts of the birth, death and resurrection of Jesus Christ. It is our baptismal creed, for the acceptance of it is demanded of those who bring an infant for baptism and it is taught children when they learn their catechism. It is recited at Morning and Evening Prayer, and in the Visitation of the Sick it is directed that it should be rehearsed to those who are very ill. It is the simplest and most familiar of our creeds. It is the creed of millions, though it has never been used in the East. The Nicene Creed comes from the East; while the Roman was more interested in facts, the Eastern was more interested in doctrine. It does not ignore the historical facts, but it is mainly concerned with doctrinal statements. It is a theological creed making clear the Christian faith in the Deity of Our Lord " God of God, Light of Light, Very God of Very God, Begotten, not made, Being of one substance with the Father." This became by the end of the fifth century the baptismal creed of the East and eventually was accepted also in the West. From the sixth century it became the creed used at the Eucharist both in the East and the West. It is this use at the Holy Communion which has made it familiar to English Churchmen. It is the creed which more than any other unites Christians in the Anglican, Roman and Eastern Churches. Those who use it both as an expression of their Christian faith and as an act of worship cannot be very deeply divided. The Athanasian Creed is different in character. It is later than the other creeds ; it is the completed work of one hand (not St. Athanasius !), and not—like the Apostles' and Nicene Creeds—the outcome of the collective belief of the Church ; it has never been formally accepted by the Orthodox Church : and neither in the Roman nor in the Eastern Church has it been enjoined to be used at services attended by large numbers of the laity. It is a valuable theological document, but its language is too technical for popular use and the so-called damnatory clauses are always open to grave misunderstanding. Our Church, therefore, is in line with the rest of the Catholic Church in honouring the creed as an exposition of faith but in not insisting on its use at public worship. No formal decision has ever been reached by our Church to withdraw it from recitation at Mattins on the great Festivals, but in actual practice in the majority of our churches it is now rarely used in this way.[1]

The doctrine of the Creeds is supplemented by the doctrine set forth in " the Book of Common Prayer " and in the " Ordering of Bishops, Priests and Deacons." The Prayer Book contains the three Creeds and a useful and concise statement of faith in the form of questions and answers in the Catechism, in which a simple explanation is given of the teaching of the Church on the two Sacraments of Baptism and the Supper of the Lord. But all through the Prayer Book light is thrown on the doctrine of the Church. From its Orders for the administration of baptism and of Holy Communion we can gather more of the Church's mind on these Sacraments than from the formal statements of the Thirty-nine Articles. The language of devotion opens the door to mysteries which remains locked to clearcut definition. For one who has painfully studied the Articles on the Sacraments there are millions who have experienced and rejoiced in their inward and spiritual grace. From the Prayer Book too we learn the positive teaching of the Church on four[2] of the minor Sacraments—Confirmation—Penance—Holy Orders and Matrimony, which are states of life allowed in the Scriptures, " but yet have not like nature of Sacraments with

[1] In the Revised Prayer Book of 1928 its recitation was made optional on certain Festivals, " may " instead of " shall."

[2] While the Prayer Book of 1928 did not make any provision for the unction of the sick, it did so for the minister " laying his hands upon the sick person if desired."

Baptism and the Lord's Supper, for they have not any visible sign or ceremony ordained by God." In the Confirmation service we learn that by the laying on of hands "heavenly grace" is given. In the Visitation of the Sick, the teaching of the Church on confession and absolution is made more explicit. In the Ordinal, the Church's doctrine of the threefold ministry is made plain. In the Solemnisation of Matrimony the life-long union of Christian marriage "until death us do part" is proclaimed. We find in the Burial of the Dead the faith of the Church in the life to come, and in the Commination Service impressive witness to the necessity of public and national penitence. Everywhere in the Prayer Book the doctrine of the Church is expressed in devotion and worship. Through frequent use it gradually sinks into the mind, and the repetition of rites and ceremonies unconsciously and imperceptibly forms the doctrinal convictions of the worshipper more surely than hundreds of sermons and exhortations.

The laity as well as the clergy repeatedly affirm the doctrine of the Creeds and Prayer Book, but only the clergy are called upon to give their formal assent to the Thirty-nine Articles. These are in a different category to the Creeds and the Prayer Book, they have neither the antiquity nor the universality of the former, nor the devotion of the latter. They were drawn up at a time when it was necessary to define more fully the attitude of the Church to current controversies. They were issued in English as the Forty-two Articles in 1553, and were directed against the mistaken teaching and abuses of the mediæval Church and the errors of Anabaptists. In 1563 they were revised by Convocation and reduced to thirty-nine, Queen Elizabeth however struck out one Article which she felt might raise an obstacle to the Romanist party remaining in the Church. But after the Pope's Bull excommunicating the Queen the Article was restored and some minor changes made in 1571, when they were given synodical authority by Convocation as the Thirty-nine Articles which we now possess. The Articles are an excellent historical statement of the position the Church of England took up with regard to matters of controversy at the time they were composed. They are simpler than the lengthy confessions of faith which were drawn up on the Continent, and are more gentle and charitable in tone. They have none of the anathemas which the Council of Trent affixed to so many of its decrees : " anathema sit," " anathema sit " recurs again and again : or the fierce denunciation which for instance the Council of Pistoja at the end of the eighteenth century affixed to so many of its condemnations, *"falsa"* *" temeraria"* *"perniciosa"* *" scandalosa."*

But the Articles are not of the same permanent nature as the Creeds. Many feel that they are no longer suitable for clerical subscription. They deal largely with old controversies whose fires now burn very low. Some of the Articles are obscure and vague. Others have been partly rendered obsolete by the advance of modern thought. It would be impossible for any intelligent man to give wholehearted assent to every sentence in every Article. Until 1865 the usual form of subscription was " I do willingly and from my heart subscribe to the Thirty-nine Articles of Religion of the United Church of England and Ireland, and to the three Articles in the Thirtieth Canon and to all things therein contained." But in that year a revised and less stringent form was drawn up by the two Convocations and received the Royal Assent " I do solemnly make the following declaration, I assent to the Thirty-nine Articles of Religion and to the Book of Common Prayer and of the Ordering of Bishops, Priests and Deacons. I believe the doctrine of the Church of England as therein set forth to be agreeable to the Word of God and in public prayer and in administration of the Sacraments I will use the form in the said book prescribed and none other except so far as shall be ordered by lawful authority." By this new form assent is not formally given to each separate Article, but the affirmation is made that the doctrine as set forth in them is agreeable to the Word of God. At my own Ordination Bishop Randall Davidson, then Bishop of Winchester, made it plain that by our assent we were not committing ourselves to every individual Article, but to a general though loyal acceptance of the doctrinal position of the Church of England. I myself explain to my Ordinands that their subscription is an expression of loyalty to the faith of the Church, and that no man could honestly subscribe if he rejected belief in the supernatural, or held that either the Romans or the Puritans were right in their controversies with our Church. It would be a gain if a much simpler form of subscription were adopted, but this cannot be done without the general consent and the good will of all parties, which is impossible at present to obtain.

The Appeal to Scripture

For the justification of the statements in its Creeds and other formularies our Church appeals to the Scriptures. It is definite in affirming that all doctrine must be brought to this test. In the Sixth Article it is asserted " Holy Scripture containeth all things necessary to salvation : so that whatsoever is not read therein, nor may be proved thereby, is not to be required of any man, that it should be believed as an article of the Faith, or be thought requisite or necessary to salvation." The priest at his Ordination is reminded that he cannot by any other means compass work " pertaining to the salvation of man, but with doctrine and exhortation taken out of the holy Scriptures, and with a life agreeable to the same," and he is asked by the bishop " Are you persuaded that the holy Scriptures contain sufficiently all Doctrine required of necessity for eternal salvation through faith in Jesus Christ ? and are you determined, out of the said Scriptures to instruct the people committed to your charge, and to teach nothing, as required of necessity to eternal salvation, but that which you shall be persuaded may be concluded and proved by the Scripture ? " and to this he replies " I am so persuaded, and have so determined by God's grace." In an even more emphatic form the same question is put to a bishop at his Consecration, when he is asked if he will " maintain nothing " as well as teach nothing as required of necessity to salvation unless it can be concluded and proved by Scripture. In this insistence of the Reformers on Scripture as the test of what was claimed as necessary for salvation they were undoubtedly treading in the steps of the early fathers. " Do not " St. Cyril of Jerusalem says, speaking to catechumens, " do not believe me simply unless you receive the proof of what I say from Holy Scripture." " The source of error," writes Pope Leo " is that when men are hindered by some obscurity in knowing the truth, they run not to prophets, or apostles, or evangelists, but to themselves " they will not " labour in the broad field of Holy Scripture."[1] No doctrine or practice however useful or however ancient it may be can be taught as essential for eternal salvation unless it can be proved by the Scriptures. There are many pious opinions and customs which can be legitimately

[1] Bishop Gore, " Roman Catholic Claims," fifth edition, p. 68.

held and followed, but unless they are Scriptural they must not be regarded, still less taught, as necessary for salvation. This Scriptural test is the acid test, it applies to all new theories and practices which spring up in every age of intellectual activity : however eloquently urged and popularly demanded, they are not to be regarded as necessary to salvation unless they can be concluded and proved as such from the Scriptures.

But the Scriptures are the books of a Church. Before a single book of the New Testament was written the Church was proclaiming the Gospel. It was the Church also which collected the various books together and formed the New Testament. It is therefore natural that the Church should interpret and explain the Book, instead of leaving it solely to private interpretation. Tradition, which has been described as "the corporate memory of the Church of God," helps us to understand the Bible and to select its fundamental doctrines. A Canon of 1571 directs the clergy in their preaching to " see that they never teach ought in a sermon, to be religiously held and believed by the people except what is agreeable to the doctrine of the Old and New Testaments and what the Catholic Fathers and ancient bishops have collected from the same doctrine." The divines of the seventeenth century repeatedly appealed to tradition as expressed in the writings of the Fathers of the first centuries. Tradition was not a rival nor an alternative authority to the Scriptures, but it made clearer their meaning. And what was true of a number of theologians all working independently was even more so of a Council in which men assembled from different Churches and lands bore their witness to the doctrines which were accepted in their homes. The decrees of the Council were only valid in as far as they expressed the corporate mind of the Church. The Church therefore or even the individual Christian in doubt about the meaning of Scripture turns for enlightenment to the tradition of the Church. But even this is not always sufficient, there may have been disagreement between the Fathers, a clear tradition may be lacking, it is possible that later knowledge may show that an opinion once generally held was really due to mistaken exegesis or to incomplete knowledge. Reason must be used to weigh the opposed arguments and to decide on the conclusion.

Infallibility

The Church of England for its doctrine appeals to the Scriptures, to tradition and to reason. But this is a disappointing position for those who are looking for authoritative statements made by an infallible Church. They wish to escape from the responsibility of making their own decisions. In a world of conflicting voices they are eager that their perplexities and bewilderment should be brought to an end by pronouncements which remove all doubts. But our Lord never promised infallibility to His Church. He promised that the gates of hell and death should not prevail against it, and we read in the Fourth Gospel that He declared that His Holy Spirit would guide His disciples into all truth. We cannot find anywhere that He said that His Church might not temporarily fail before the forces of evil or might not sometimes fall into error. There is no text in the New Testament which justifies the assertion that the Church is infallible. Even in the first century a great part of the Church proved to be mistaken in its expectation of the immediate end of the world and the return of Christ in glory. And if no promise was ever given to the Church that it should be infallible, still less was it promised an infallible earthly Head or an infallible book. Frequently Popes have made from the chair of St. Peter statements which have been contradictory or proved subsequently to have been erroneous. Often too they have been silent when the Christian has been most in need of clear guidance. Nor is it possible to accept the Bible as an infallible guide : it was not intended to teach man history, science or philosophy. It is the inspired record of God's revelation of Himself to man. But its message is not automatic, it is clothed in the thought forms of ages far removed from our own, and is conditioned by the limitations of those who transmitted it, it is always golden treasure but sometimes conveyed in earthen vessels. The teaching of the Bible is best understood by those who listen to it with their minds as well as with hearts of simple devotion.

The demand for authority is often confused with absolute authority. Authority at its best respects the freedom of the individual, it guides and leads, only in the last resort does it command. Absolute authority crushes the individual, it destroys his initiative, it tends to make him an automaton. It commands

and man must obey in silence even if he is unconvinced. Our
Lord had supreme authority yet it is remarkable how He encourages His disciples to question Him, how sometimes He questions
them so as to stimulate their thought, how He leads them
rather than drives them into truth, how by parable and illustra-
tion He appeals to their reason and imagination instead of
suppressing their wills ; He treats them throughout as disciples
and not as slaves. It is this kind of authority, paternal and not
coercive for which the Church of England stands. By the
appeal to Scripture, tradition, and reason it aims at building up
its children in the truth. It encourages them to question. It
admits fully their right to ask the reason why. It is not indignant
or wrathful when in their search for truth its children take the
wrong path. It will not scold or anathematise but by love and
persuasion will do its best to help them to regain the right way.
It will listen patiently if any of its children claim to have found
some new light on ancient truth or to have heard the voice of
God speaking in some new movement. It will be ready to
learn, for it knows how often in the past the Church unwittingly
has silenced the prophets in their lifetime and only long afterwards honoured them with splendid sepulchres. And if this
spirit is attacked as easygoing and lax our reply will be " this
was the spirit in which the Master dealt with His disciples and
this is the spirit in which the Eastern Church of the early centuries
dealt with its members." The Greek Fathers " Conceive of
the doctrinal authority of the Church as a restricted thing—
restricted by Scripture. If it has to lay down dogmatic limits,
they must be justified by the necessity for defending the central
faith. And their Church was a broad Church which tolerated
many differences of minor belief and varieties of practice. And
intellectually life in the Church was a highly stimulating atmosphere in which enquiry was not quenched and there was plenty
of room to move."[1]

Fundamentals and Accessories

The Church of England through its threefold test of con-
formity to the Scripture, to tradition and to reason, distin-
guishes between those doctrines which it accepts, those which

[1] Bishop Gore, " The Holy Spirit and the Church," p. 181.

it repudiates as erroneous, and those which it regards as of secondary importance. The Anglican divines of the seventeenth century drew a clear distinction between what is primary and secondary in doctrine. " The distinction between fundamentals and accessories, or in the more usual language of the day between things necessary for salvation and things convenient in practice, is clearly drawn by Hooker and recurs constantly through the ensuing literature. The fundamentals are few and revealed, the accessories are indeterminate and more or less dependent on human invention. So Jeremy Taylor declares that the ' intendment ' of his discourse on ' The Liberty of Prophesying ' is that men should ' not make more necessities than God made which indeed are not many.' For Anglicans of the seventeenth century those few things were summed up conveniently in the Creeds, particularly in the so-called Apostles ' Creed."[1] On fundamentals the faith of the Anglican Church is clear, emphatic and uncompromising. It declares its belief in a personal God, the Father Almighty : in the Incarnation of His only Son, God of God, who died for our salvation, who rose again from the dead and who now reigns in glory : in God the Holy Ghost, the Lord and Giver of Life : in the Holy Catholic Church : in the forgiveness of sins : in the life and judgment to come. In its Catechism and its Articles it affirms that God gives, through outward and visible signs in Baptism and in the Holy Communion, inward and spiritual grace. These and other fundamental truths our Church holds with the whole of the Catholic Church both of the past and of the present. What the Scriptures and the ancient Fathers regarded as fundamental, so do we. The witness of our Church to the essential doctrines of the Christian faith is as bold, unmistakable and challenging as the witness of any other Church in Christendom. On the fundamental facts of the faith our Church speaks with one voice.

By the same threefold test our Church rejects certain doctrines as contrary to the Christian faith. Among these we find Arianism, with its denial that Jesus is truly God : and Pelagianism, with its teaching which encourages men to believe that they can obtain salvation by their own unaided efforts and merits. It condemns the mediæval doctrine of Transubstantiation on the grounds that it cannot be proved by Holy Writ,

[1] P. Elmer More in " Anglicanism," p. xxiv.

overthroweth the nature of a Sacrament, and hath given rise to many superstitions. It denies that men without being lawfully called can take upon themselves the office of public preaching or ministering the Sacraments in the congregation. Our Church is as clear in some of its negatives as it is in its affirmatives. The charge of vagueness in doctrine of primary importance is proved unfounded by reference to the authorised formulas of the Church.

This charge rises partly through the distinction our Church has always made between fundamentals and accessories. While its teaching is unmistakable on the fundamental doctrines of the faith, on secondary matters it is either silent or speaks with greater reserve and hesitation. A good example of this is given by Bishop Pearson writing on the Communion of Saints: "This communion of the saints in heaven and earth, upon the mystical union of Christ their head, being fundamental and internal, what acts or external operations it produceth is not so certain. That we communicate with them in hope of that happiness which they actually enjoy is evident; that we have the Spirit of God given us as an earnest, and so a part of their felicity is certain." So far the Bishop is speaking of fundamentals in this belief, but now he goes on to accessories: "But what they do in heaven in relation to us on earth particularly considered, or what we ought to perform in reference to them in heaven, beside a reverential respect, and study of imitation, is not revealed to us in the Scriptures, nor can be concluded by necessary deduction from any principles of Christianity."[1] There is a large number of matters both in doctrine and practice on which Scripture has given no clear teaching, and on which the Fathers are either silent or speak with different voices: these must not be regarded as necessary to salvation. There are pious opinions and customs which have helped millions; they are not only harmless but they aid devotion and make for the edification of those who hold or use them, but they must not be taught as fundamental and essential to the Catholic Faith. Many of the controversies which arise are due to the unwise championship of and the fierce opposition to views and practices which are accessories to the Faith and not inherent in it. On these matters every particular or national Church has the authority to give directions or to leave freedom

[1] Bishop Pearson, "Exposition of the Creed," p. 543. Bohn's Libraries.

to its members, provided it ordains nothing which is contrary to God's Word. On the other hand, no individual should of his private judgement deliberately break traditions and ceremonies of the Church which are not repugnant to the Word of God.

When we are dealing with profound mysteries we have no right to expect clear-cut definitions. The Church of England, possibly through the influence of Platonic philosophy, finds itself more in line with the Greek than the Roman Church in shrinking from the attempt to define where definition is really impossible. Bishop Talbot, in a Church Congress sermon in 1896, gave expression to what many Anglicans feel about the risk of over-statement and excessive dogmatism. "In that word definite," he asks, "is there not something which jars a little perhaps on ourselves and more on others? Definite, clear-bounded, within outlines firmly and plainly drawn, accurately weighed and measured out: are these quite words to be used without anxiety and without careful sense of risk about that which is from above, divine, tinctured with infinity and eternity? Is it so that we can plumb with our little lines the things which come out of the unfathomable depths of God and enter into the deep heart and mysterious life of man?"[1] We do not apologise for the fact that the Church of England is sometimes cautious and guarded, where other churches are dogmatic and outspoken. But this reverent hesitation and tolerant open-mindedness is confined to secondary matters, and does not impair its unflinching assertion of the great truths of the revelation of God in Christ.

Development in Doctrine

It may, however, be asked if the Church of England is always to be bound by ancient traditions and opinions, does it offer no room for development in doctrine? Is its statement of faith static and immovable, or is it possible for growth and re-adaptation in view of the great changes in thought and knowledge which have taken place since the first centuries of the Christian faith? This difficulty the Roman Catholic Church attempts to meet by the doctrine of development: it does not deny that there are many apparent additions to its doctrine,

[1] " Edward Stuart Talbot," by Gwendolen Stephenson, p. 103.

such as the treasury of merit, the immaculate conception of the Blessed Virgin, and the infallibility of the Pope, but it claims these were present in the Scriptures and in tradition, and fresh statements of doctrine made by the Church are not the introduction of new truths, but are due to growth and development from the original seed. This theory in its most extreme form as derived from Cardinal Newman has been used in support of Modernist doctrines which have called forth from the Papacy sweeping condemnation. But there are two fatal defects even to the more moderate Roman theory of development. Development is not always identical with progress, it may be movement in the wrong direction. Deterioration and degeneration are found in the history of institutions and ideas : there may be one-sided and unbalanced development which completely obscures or destroys the original germ. The historian sees in the development of the Roman Catholic Papacy an example of growth which is not true to type, and which has departed from its original form. And secondly, while the Roman Catholic claims that the doctrines of his Church are implicit in the Scriptures or in early tradition, he is usually unable to show that in them there is any trace of modern dogmas now to be accepted under pain of anathema.

There is, however, a legitimate development ; not indeed in the addition of new truths necessary for salvation, but in an ever-growing apprehension of the meaning of the old truths and in their explanation and re-statement in new and better forms of thought. There is the fact given, the eternal and unchanging truth ; but in the face of fresh needs and difficulties it is found that it has implications which had not been discovered before. And with new knowledge, new terms are often discovered in which the unchangeable truth can be presented to the understanding. We see this both in the New Testament and in the early Church. The first disciples beheld in Jesus the act of God ; they interpret it by speaking of Him to the Jews as the long-expected Messiah : St. Paul, in speaking of the same Christ to the Gentiles, uses the terms which they will best understand : the writer of the Fourth Gospel familiar with Alexandrian philosophy describes Him as the Word. The more the Church experiences the power of Jesus and the more it reflects on the glory and wonder of His Person, the more anxious it is to communicate its convictions in more adequate phraseology. We find this in the doctrine of the Atonement ; there has been no authoritative definition of the way in which redemption was wrought through the Cross, but there had been no hesitation in proclaiming it as a fact, and theologians of different centuries have sought to explain it in the language most appropriate to their contemporaries. Again in our own age there has been much development of eschatological doctrine. In the last century most Christians thought of heaven as above the sky, and hell as beneath the earth : these geographical interpretations of heaven and hell have now been abandoned, but the truth they conveyed that life here has eternal consequences of joy or loss remains unchanged. Only a century ago the verbal and literal inspiration of the Bible was held by the majority of Anglicans : the inspiration of the Bible is still their faith, but they would now say with the members of the Commission on Doctrine in the Church of England " that the tradition of the inerrancy of the Bible cannot be maintained in the light of the knowledge at our disposal."

The Diffusive Authority of the Church

How is legitimate to be distinguished from illegitimate development ? The Roman Church would say through the voice of an infallible Pope. But this method has been repudiated by the Anglican and Eastern Churches as opposed to the Scriptures, to primitive tradition and to reason. Many who reject the Pope would trust to the decision of a General Council, but there is no immediate hope of such a Council being held. Must, then, all re-statement be suspended until the distant date when a Council is held ? Must we, until then, be content by appealing with the Caroline Divines to antiquity, without reference to the great changes in knowledge and the revolutionary intellectual movements of our time ? To these questions the Church of England has an answer. No new doctrine, opinion, or practice may be accepted as necessary to salvation if it is opposed to the teaching of the Scriptures. But any new interpretation or theory must be freely examined by the light of the Scriptures, tradition and the best knowledge of the day. Reason, God's gift, must be brought to bear upon it. Argument, criticism and discussion by men who are both devout and learned followers of Christ, will gradually sift the true from the false. If it is mistaken it will soon be relegated to the vast lumber store of rejected theories. If it is true it will survive and slowly or swiftly win general acceptance by the Church. This is the work of diffusive judgement of the Church. It was this judgement to which the decrees of the great Councils had to be submitted before they became binding on the conscience of the Church. No Councils are held to-day, but the diffusive judgement of the Church still remains. It is a present reality ; it can express itself in hundreds of ways—through books, conferences, meetings, correspondence, appeals, resolutions, petitions—until at last a common mind is reached, which may be finally approved and formulated in an authoritative state-ment or canon by the bishops, the guardians of the faith, with the concurrence of the clergy in Convocation. If we indeed believe that God the Holy Spirit will guide His Church into all truth, we can trust and hope that He will reveal His mind on many of the difficult and perplexing problems which the latest Renaissance has brought to the faith of the Church.

The Church of England stands for both authority and freedom in matters of faith. It rejects both the autocratic authority which denies freedom of criticism and the licence which easily degenerates into anarchy. Its doctrinal position calls for in-telligence, patience and humility. Intelligence so that God may be loved with the mind as well as with the heart ; patience to search and to wait until the difficulties are removed and truth is made clear ; humility to listen to and reverence the voice of Scripture and tradition. Authority and freedom can only be held together at the cost of tension, but only by their union can a reasonable faith be won. George Tyrrell, when an unexcommunicated Roman Catholic, wrote " the compati-bility of freedom and authority, of science and revelation, is surely a most essential and fundamental Catholic principle. Its application is the perennial problem. The Church which solves it first will sweep the world into its net. So far, without attempting a logical synthesis, the Church of England has always preached, ultimately, respect for tradition and respect for conscience (moral and intellectual), it is perhaps she who seems more likely to win the race."[1]

[1] " Letters " p. 133.

III

THE WORSHIP OF THE CHURCH

Through ordered and regulated experiment the Church will gradually reach the form of worship which will best enable it to make its sacrifice of praise and prayer, and the worshipper to gain some clearer vision of God in His glory. But to leave such experiments at the complete discretion of the parish priest who is not necessarily a liturgist, will lead to hopeless confusion. The authorisation of such experiments must come from the diocesan bishops, but behind them there must be the concurrence of the Convocations.

III

THE WORSHIP OF THE CHURCH

WORSHIP is the primary duty of the Church. Through it the Church offers to God the best it possesses, and through it God reveals Himself and gives His blessing to His children. Public Worship lifts man from earth to heaven. It is the expression of the Church's faith in God and its response to His sovereignty and love. It is the act of a fellowship. And so that all may join with one voice in prayer and praise, and that the worshipper of to-day may be united with the worshippers of the past, the historic Churches have from the earliest days arranged their worship in set forms and in accordance with time-hallowed rules. Only by the use of such forms can the worship of the congregation transcend the idiosyncrasies and limitations of the minister who conducts it; and through the written word the noblest language can be employed in the sacrifice of prayer and praise.

The authorised worship of the Church of England is found in " The Book of Common Prayer and Administration of the Sacraments and other Rites and Ceremonies of the Church according to the Use of the Church of England." It is no new worship. It is expressly stated it is " of the Church," but it is according to the Use of the Church of England, which has availed itself of the right of every national Church " to retain, change and abolish ceremonies or rites of the Church ordained only by man's authority." The Book of Common Prayer was at the time of the Reformation substituted for the Breviary, the Missal, the Manual, the Pontifical, the Processional and other less important books which were used for the services of the Church. It was composed at a time when the English language was reaching the height of its splendour. It is a noble example of literature. The beauty of its prose is universally recognised, especially that of the Litany and the Collects. The Bible and the Prayer Book have done more than any other books to form the English language as we speak it to-day.

Phrases and terms from both have passed into common speech.

There is an impression in some quarters that the Prayer Book is no longer used in many of our churches. This is far from correct. Here and there are found eccentric and self-willed men who have practically banished the Prayer Book from their churches and who, contrary to the promise they made at their Institution, have substituted wholesale forms of prayer either invented by themselves or drawn from the service books of other Churches. There are such, but very rarely in a long experience have I come into contact with these individualists. There are changes, additions and adaptations of various kinds in almost every church, but in the majority of them the Prayer Book is substantially used, and a visitor without difficulty can follow the greater part of the service. The most important variations from the Prayer Book are unhappily in the service in which above all there should be uniformity, the Holy Communion : but even there in most of our churches both the order and substance of the Anglican Liturgy are found. In many of the churches in which there is considerable departure from the Order of the Holy Communion, the other forms of service are almost meticulously followed. Nor is it only in the British Isles that the Prayer Book is generally used : in many of the Provinces overseas in communion with the See of Canterbury there have been frequent revisions, but their worship is still substantially if not entirely based on the Book of Common Prayer.

There are three principles which run through the whole of our Prayer Book. (1) It is Scriptural. A great part of Morning and Evening Prayer is taken up with the recitation of the Psalms and the reading of the Lessons. In the opening exhortation one of the purposes mentioned for assembling and meeting together is for the hearing of God's Holy Word. A chief criticism against the mediæval forms of service was that they afforded no regular and orderly reading of the books of the Bible. This is the complaint in the Preface entitled " Concerning the Service of the Church " : " That commonly when any book of the Bible was begun, after three or four chapters were read out, all the rest were unread. And in this sort the Book of Isaiah was begun in Advent and the Book of Genesis in Septuagesima ; but they were only begun and never read through : after like sort were other books of holy Scripture read." So instead of this broken and haphazard reading of the Scriptures it was ordained that in future in the services of the Church there should be nothing read " but the very pure Word of God, the Holy Scriptures, or that which is agreeable to the same." In the Holy Communion there were provided readings from the Old and New Testaments, in the Ten Command; ments, the Epistles and the Gospels. Not only in the Psalms and Lessons do we find the words of Scripture, but they are used for the versicles and woven into the collects and prayers.

(2) It is open, for the services are drawn up so that the congregation can both understand them and join in them. Part of the older services were in the vernacular : there was a long Bidding Prayer in English and possibly, as sometimes to-day on the Continent, the Gospel was read in the vulgar tongue as well as in Latin. But the greater part of these services was in Latin, often recited quickly in a low voice by the priest, and the congregation stood or sat as the case might be without making any attempt to join in them. To quote again from the Preface, " Concerning the Service of the Church " : " Whereas St. Paul would have such language spoken to the people in the church, as they might understand, and have profit of hearing the same ; the service in this Church of England these many years hath been read in Latin to the people, which they under- stand not ; so that they have heard with their ears only, and their heart, spirit, and mind have not been edified thereby." The service of the Prayer Book is read and sung in the English tongue. It is intended to be said clearly by the Minister so that the people can hear it, frequently the direction occurs he shall say or read " in a loud voice." Opportunities too are given to the congregation to join in the service ; they are to say the Confession and Lord's Prayer " after the Minister," and as the service proceeds they are from time to time called upon to take their part in it. " Praise ye the Lord " is the invitation ; " The Lord's Name be praised " is their answer. " The Lord be with you " is the call with a loud voice, " And with thy spirit " is the reply.

(3) It is comprehensive, and this in two ways. The sources from which our Prayer Book is derived are many. Much of it consists of translations of the old Latin services and prayers, and a few prayers are translated from the Greek. In addition

Archbishop Cranmer did not hesitate to draw upon and to adapt the services used by the Continental Reformers. It has been stated that the representative character of the Book is its most prominent feature : " It has drawn from many sources : apart from the Bible, the old traditional Latin services of the English Church have provided by far the greater part of the contents : this is not merely true of actual bulk, but it is still more markedly true of the whole spirit and method of the Prayer Book : it has drawn also from other sources—Greek, Gallican, Lutheran and Swiss in their measure."[1] When therefore we take part in the Prayer Book services, we are joining our voices to those of a great multitude of worshippers of all lands and centuries ; in our own tongue we sing with the ancient Hebrews, pray with the Greek Fathers, recite the offices with our English forbears ; and make our own the prayers first drawn up by the Continental Reformers. And this is especially true of the Holy Communion service, in which the devotions of many Churches are assembled round the centre of it all, the very words spoken by Our Lord " in the same night that He was betrayed."

But there is another way in which the Prayer Book is comprehensive. It was drawn up to include different religious opinions. It is Catholic and Reformed, for it was hoped it would enable both those who clung to the old customs and the Puritans to remain within the same Church. The attempt largely failed, many of the Puritans seceded, whilst those who gave their allegiance to the Pope refused to use the Prayer Book or to attend the services of the Church of England. But this charitable and statesmanlike policy has left permanent marks on our worship. There are noticeable examples of this. The Words of Administration combine the Catholic affirmation " The Body of Our Lord Jesus Christ which was given for thee, preserve thy body and soul unto everlasting life " with the Reformed " Take and eat this in remembrance that Christ died for thee, and feed on Him in thine heart by faith with thanksgiving." It enables those who respectively hold the doctrines of the real objective Presence and the Receptionist to kneel side by side and hear these words without any violation of their conscientious beliefs. Within the same book we

---

[1] " A New History of the Book of Common Prayer," by Procter and Frere, p. 674.

find the general Confession and Absolution, as well as the private confession with the direct personal absolution. In the Ordination of Priests there is first the great Catholic commission " Whose sins thou dost forgive they are forgiven : and whose sins thou dost retain they are retained," followed by the Evangelical ex- hortation " And be thou a faithful dispenser of the Word of God and of His holy Sacraments." The attempt to include as many men as possible of different religious views in the one Church has given us the most comprehensive Prayer Book in Christendom.

Those who drew up the Prayer Book intended it to supersede all existing books and to become the one used in every church in the land. " And whereas heretofore there hath been great diversity in saying and singing in churches within this Realm : some following Salisbury use, some Hereford use, and some the use of Bangor, some of York, some of Lincoln ; now from henceforth the Realm shall have but one use." It was plain from this that Cranmer hoped that in every church exactly the same order of service would be followed. This was con- firmed by the Act of Uniformity in the first year of Queen Elizabeth's reign, in which it was enacted that severe penalties should be inflicted on any manner of Parson, Vicar or other whatsoever Minister who wilfully used " any other Rite, Cere- mony, Order, Form or Manner of celebrating the Lord's Supper, openly or privily, or Mattins, Evensong, Administration of the Sacraments, or other open Prayers than is mentioned or set forth in the said Book." (Open Prayer in and throughout this Act is meant " that Prayer which is for others to come into or hear, either in Common Churches or Private Chapels, or oratories, commonly called the Service of the Church.") It was a great ideal that in every church throughout the whole kingdom the whole nation should worship God in the same way, using the same prayers, and observing the same rites and ceremonies. If it had been realised it would have been an impressive demonstration of national unity in worship.

But from the outset this policy was doomed to failure. The Papalists and the Puritans refused to join in this worship, the one disliked it as new-fangled and heretical, and the other as superstitious. Coercion failed to crush the opposition. Within the nation there presently emerged different Churches, with their own worship in their respective churches and chapels. The attempt however to secure uniformity was very largely successful within the Church of England itself, for from the Restoration to the first quarter of the 19th century, with a few notable exceptions, the same service without additions, variations or omissions would have been found Sunday by Sunday in every church in the land. For nearly two centuries the Anglican Church presented a picture of almost complete uniformity in its worship.

This uniformity was partly the result of spiritual deadness. With the religious revivals which came from both the Evangelical and High Church parties, it was soon found that the existing services were not sufficient channels for the new spiritual life. The Tractarians at first were content with the demand that the whole Prayer Book should be faithfully and completely used. They defended their so called innovations by an appeal to it. Presently they felt the authorised worship of the Church was inadequate and they supplemented it by borrowing from the great treasure houses of devotion which belonged to the Churches of Rome and of the East. The parish priest also needed additional services and prayers. Some of these were provided by authority. But the demand remained far from satisfied. Moreover the revival of liturgical study revealed various defects and dislocations in a Liturgy which once too easily had been treated as incomparable, and the call for revision became insistent. As there seemed no way in which these demands could be quickly met individuals felt justified in taking action to change and modify the services of the Church in accordance with their own views, or those of the party to which they belonged. At the beginning of this century uniformity had vanished as a practical policy. While the Prayer Book was still almost universally accepted as the standard of worship and in most churches its services were faithfully rendered, there was hardly any church in which there were not some departures from it. Sometimes these were of minor importance, the shortening of the Dearly Beloved, the abbreviation or the complete change of the set Psalms and Lessons, the substitution of additional and modern prayers for the second part of the service, the introduction of hymns, the omission of the Longer Exhortation at the Holy Communion and other changes of a like character. Sometimes however the changes were more important, the omission of one of the Creeds, the transposition of the Prayers in the Holy Communion, sometimes alterations in the Canon itself, and the restoration of services deliberately abandoned at the Reformation.

It was extremely difficult for the authorities of the Church to deal with these changes. From a narrow and legalistic standpoint they were probably all equally illegal. According to a judgement of the Judicial Committee of the Privy Council in 1868 " it is not open to a Minister of the Church, or even to their Lordships in advising Her Majesty as the highest Ecclesiastical Tribunal of Appeal, to draw a distinction, in acts which are a departure from or violation of the Rubric, between those which are important and those which are trivial." They added that their Lordships are " disposed entirely to adhere " to an earlier decision of the Judicial Committee which laid down " In the performance of the services, rites and ceremonies ordered by the Prayer Book, the directions contained in it must be strictly observed : no omission and no addition can be permitted." The difficulty of the position is increased by the fact that every person ordained to the ministry has to make the specific declaration that " in public prayer and administration of the Sacraments I will use the form in the said Book prescribed and none other, except so far as shall be ordered by lawful authority." If the law is rightly interpreted above the Prayer Book must be strictly observed in every respect, on the other hand the clergy who have promised to use the said Book and none other have found themselves compelled by pastoral necessity to make various alterations and additions. The Report of the Archbishops' Commission on the " Relations between Church and State," characterises the confusion that has followed " No one obeys the law so construed. Not the clergy, since there is scarcely one of them who makes no change in the authorised forms of service. Not the bishops, who are charged to see that this impossible law is carried out. Worse still, by the Declaration, as interpreted by the Courts, every priest solemnly undertakes to do that which in fact none of them actually performs. No wonder discipline has suffered. No wonder the laity are uneasy. It is difficult to find temperate words to apply to such a state of things. The situation can only be described as deeply insincere." The statement undoubtedly exaggerates the position, it takes too seriously an opinion expressed in a judgement given nearly eighty years ago, it overstates the difficulties which have arisen, and it loses touch with reality when it describes the situation as " deeply insincere."[1]

[1] In a footnote the Commission attempts, somewhat unsuccessfully, to often the drastic nature of this statement.

But it affords useful evidence as to how gravely a number of the clergy and laity regard the present position.

An attempt had been made to meet it in two ways. No one is clear what is meant by " lawful authority," but it is maintained by many of the bishops that inherent in their office is a *jus liturgicum*, the right to allow variations from the existing Order and to authorise additional services. This right is by no means universally admitted. There are some who while they recognise the existence of this *jus* would exclude its operation from all the official services of the Church and hold that it can only be exercised over services which are not included in the Prayer Book. In any case the *jus* is clearly limited, the bishop has no power to authorise rites and ceremonies which are contrary to the teaching of the Bible and the Prayer Book. The permission he grants must be in accordance with the mind of the Church of England. It would be an illegitimate extension of his *jus* for an individual bishop to allow variations from the Prayer Book Canon, still more the substitution of some other Canon for it : though strangely enough some parish priests have no hesitation about their own right to do this. The careful and judicial exercise of a limited *jus liturgicum* has enabled bishops to regulate and control to some extent changes which somewhat euphemistically are described as " experiments in worship."

This position was however far from satisfactory. An attempt was made to improve it by incorporating a large number of the changes most desired in a new Prayer Book, the use of which would be entirely optional and which was not intended to supersede the Prayer Book so familiar to Churchmen. For many years bishops and clergy worked at this revision. At last it was complete and accepted by large majorities by Convocation and the Church Assembly. But the Book was in 1927 and 1928 rejected by the House of Commons, principally on the grounds that the new Revision authorised Reservation for the Sick and provided a new Canon as an alternative to our present Consecration Prayer. The House was also impressed by the opposition to the proposals from both the Evangelicals and Anglo-Catholics. The prospects of their bringing peace and order seemed very remote. It is easy to be wise after the event, but probably the decision to proceed by Measure was a mistake, this meant a debate in Parliament and the submission of members to the pressure of organised opposition. It might have been wiser to have asked for the Royal Assent to a Canon containing the proposed changes, though the King in giving or refusing this would have acted in accordance with the advice of his responsible ministers, and a resolution still might have been moved in either House asking the ministers to advise that the Assent should be withheld.

With the rejection of the Measure the bishops were in a most difficult position. It was impossible for them either to suppress or to treat as inconsistent with the teaching of the Church of England rites and ceremonies which they had just approved and for which they had found a place in the new Prayer Book. On the other hand deliberately to authorise the rejected Book would have been regarded as an act of defiance both to Parliament and the Law of the Land. Some would have wished for the Church to have asked for Disestablishment so that it might control its own affairs, but within the Church there would have been at that time little support for such a drastic demand. The bishops therefore fell back upon their *jus liturgicum* and resolved that in the exercise of it each bishop would be " guided by the proposals set forth in the Book of 1928 and will endeavour to secure that the practices which are consistent neither with the Book of 1662 nor with the Book of 1928 shall cease."

English common sense has prevailed and no attempt has been made to wreck this policy by an appeal to the Courts. By acting in accordance with it some practices which were inconsistent with the teaching of the Church of England have been brought to an end. Most of the forms of Prayer in the new Book are widely used, especially the additional prayers, the new collects and the occasional offices. The regulations on Reservation have been largely, though by no means universally, accepted. Very few parishes have adopted the whole of the 1928 Order of Communion, though considerable use is made of the new Prayer for the Church. But the position is not satisfactory and cannot be regarded as permanent. If at any time an appeal to the Courts resulted in the decision that the clergy were acting contrary to the Law in using additional Prayers and Offices and the bishops in sanctioning this, a grave crisis would at once arise which probably would only be solved either by Disestablishment or by the State acknowledging that the Church has the inalienable right to arrange its own worship. But while we are waiting for some method satisfactory both to the Church and State by which the Church can provide new services or vary the old, the demand for enrichment and alterations in its worship becomes irresistible. Men of all ecclesiastical parties are making changes in the services to meet pastoral needs. Under these circumstances it appears that the only course will be for the diocesan bishop to authorise services for optional and temporary use which previously have been approved by both Houses of Convocation. If experiment proves their value, later on steps should be taken either by Canon or by adopting the procedure proposed by the Church and State Commission to give them legal sanction. In the meantime though they would lack statutory authority, they would have behind them the spiritual and moral authority of the Convocations.

Ceremonial

The average worshipper is much more affected by changes in ceremonial than in ritual. The latter he only hears, but the former he sees. He may hardly notice a change in the words of the prayers, even though this may be of doctrinal significance : but he cannot fail to notice the introduction of lights, vestments or incense, or the ceremonial adopted by the officiating minister in conducting divine worship. It is natural therefore that there should have been more controversy over unaccustomed ceremonies than over the rites which they accompany. Often an incumbent has been able to change the whole character of the services and the teaching of his church without opposition, but the smallest variation in the accustomed ceremonial has at once called forth vigorous protests.

Some ceremonial is necessary. No orderly service can be conducted without a few simple rules. Where there are no written rules established custom takes their place. Ceremonial is not, however, merely utilitarian ; it is symbolic and expressive, conveying truths through the eye. Sometimes it is deliberately æsthetic, rather than utilitarian or symbolic, it is the offering in worship to God of all that is lovely in art. For God who is perfect beauty, should be worshipped in beauty as well as in holiness and truth. But ceremonial carries with it serious dangers. By a multiplicity of rules it may cramp and fetter the spontaneity of worship, we read of the " number and hardness of the rules called the Pie." It may degenerate into irritating fussiness, " Don't fidget " was the audible whispered injunction of Frederick Temple, Bishop of London, to two young curates who were in attendance on him at some service. It may also become so complicated that it obscures and confuses, instead of making clear.

In the Prayer Book Preface " Of ceremonies, why some be abolished and some retained," probably written by Archbishop Cranmer, we have the apologia for ceremonial changes which were made by the Reformers. Some were abolished " because the great excess and multitude of them hath so increased in these latter days, that the burden of them was intolerable " ; others because they were " so dark, that they did more confound and darken, than declare and set forth Christ's benefits unto us " ; but " the most weighty cause of the abolishment of certain ceremonies was that they were so far abused, partly by the superstitious blindness of the rude and unlearned, and partly by the unsatiable avarice of such as sought more their own lucre, than the glory of God, that the abuses could not well be taken away, the thing remaining still." But some ceremonies are necessary, for without them " it is not possible to keep any order or quiet discipline in the Church." If then ceremonies are necessary it is better to keep the old when they may be well used, rather than to adopt " innovations and newfangleness." Those which are retained are for discipline and order, they are " neither dark nor dumb ceremonies, but are so set forth, that every man may understand what they do mean, and to what use they do serve."

The ceremonial regulations actually set forth in the Prayer Book are very few. There is the much disputed Rubric on the Ornaments of the Church and the Ministers. There are here and there a few simple directions about standing and kneeling : the making of the sign of the Cross in baptism : the laying on of hands at Confirmation ; the position of the priest, the oblations, the manual acts at the Consecration, the covering of the consecrated Elements with a fair linen cloth and the consumption of any that remain, in the Holy Communion ; the giving of the ring in the Solemnisation of Matrimony ; the casting of the earth upon the body at the Burial of the Dead ; and in the Ordinal the delivery of the Scriptures and the imposition of hands. These are the chief ceremonial rubrics in the Prayer

Book. Obviously much had to be left to custom and common sense, and where there was an established custom not abolished by the new directions it should be followed, " the wilful and contemptuous transgression and breaking of a common order and discipline is no small offence before God."

With a few exceptions in the years that came after the Reformation there was an almost complete lack of ceremonial in the conduct of Divine Worship. The Elizabethan bishops had difficulty in persuading the clergy to officiate in surplices and not in their riding coats. Often until Archbishop Laud's time the Holy Table was a common table, moveable, and sometimes used for secular purposes. After the Restoration, there was greater seemliness and decency in the Church services, though little colour, symbolism or movement. But Canon Addleshaw says of the seventeenth-century liturgists " they paid great reverence to the altar, bowing to it when they came into church and when they went up to make their Communion. In the bare churches of the period the altar held the central place and at the Eucharist the eye would have been naturally carried towards it. It was covered with what the age called " a carpet," a covering usually of blue or crimson velvet falling in folds at the corners and embroidered on the front with the sacred monogram. On the altar were two candlesticks ; in the centre an alms basin embossed with a scene from the Gospels with the usually magnificently bound Bible and Prayer Book on each side."[1] It was not, however, until the middle of the nineteenth century that there arose a general movement in favour of a richer ceremonial. This was due to three causes : It was partly the result of the growth of the spirit of Romanticism which was affecting both literature and painting. It was an emotional reaction against the rationalism of the eighteenth century. " The romantic temper, with its sense of mystery, lent itself naturally to sacramentalism in theology. The growth of ritualism was certainly in part an outcome of the romantic love of colour, movement and pageantry."[2] It was also due to the wish of those who had been influenced by the Oxford Movement to assert the continuity of their Church with that of the pre-Reformed Church and its fellowship with the Catholic Church throughout the world. Old ceremonies were restored and new

[1] " The High Church Tradition," p. 52.

[2] " Development of English Theology," by V. F. Storr, p. 131.

ceremonies which had been admired on the Continent were transplanted. There were also many unconscious of the Romantic movement and largely indifferent to the theological implications of ceremonial who were anxious to introduce greater beauty and reverence into their worship.

At first there was a vehement outcry. The most harmless innovations were regarded as rank disloyalty. Small crosses embroidered at the ends of a black scarf were treated as sure signs of Roman tendencies and its wearer censured by a bishop. The fury of a mob was still further excited by the discovery of book markers embroidered with crosses. A cross over the altar caused " indescribable horror " to a good Protestant who visited Littlemore. Flowers on the altar were denounced as frippery. My father, the Vicar of a small country parish, who took the North End position to the close of his life, met with strong opposition when he abandoned the black gown, substituted alms bags for open plates, vested the choir in surplices, and most of all when he introduced an early morning celebration of the Holy Communion, on the first occasion of this the churchyard gates were closed with a placard bearing the inscription " This way to Rome at 8.30 a.m." In many parishes there were disgraceful riots and scenes of wild disorder. Most of the bishops denounced the changes (though Bishop Wilberforce came to my father's church and expressed approval of the surpliced choir). There were prosecutions which did nothing to arrest the movement which steadily permeated the whole Church.

Its results have been very great. There is hardly a church which has not been influenced by it. The whole standard of worship has been raised. In Evangelical churches the surpliced choir, the cross on the Holy Table, the coloured stole, the turning to the East, the regular early celebrations of the Holy Communion, and the processional banner are common. Sixty years ago any one of these changes would have caused a storm, now they have been accepted by many convinced Evangelicals without abandoning their distinctive views. In the great majority of the parish churches the East End position is adopted, there are frequent celebrations of the Holy Communion, the use of lights and often the wearing of plain or coloured vestments. In Anglo-Catholic churches every variety of ceremonial can be found, from a simple use to the full ceremonial, with incense, of an elaborate High Mass. Within a century nothing less than a revolution has taken place in the manner of conducting divine worship. This will be seen if we contrast the clergy of to-day with Anthony Trollope's description of the clergy of Barchester, who all belonged to the High Church school of thought: " They all preached in their black gowns as their fathers had done before them. They wore ordinary black cloth waistcoats. They had no candles on their altars, either lighted or unlighted. They made no private genuflections, and were contented to confine themselves to such ceremonial observances as had been in vogue for the last hundred years." When a newly ordained curate attempted to intone, it caused such perplexity that after the service Mrs. Grantley, the Archdeacon's wife, sent him some cough lozenges, assuming that he was suffering from a bad throat. The attempt was not renewed !

But the movement in favour of increased ceremonial has had two serious defects. The changes sometimes have been made against the wishes of the parishioners, great bitterness has been aroused, and many have left their parish church never to return to it again. This has been especially serious in the country districts, where there is only one church. In the town there is usually a choice of churches and in one of them the aggrieved parishioner can find a spiritual home. But in the country the chapel is usually the only alternative. Moreover many of the changes made have been without intelligence or principle. Often they have been due to the personal prejudices of the incumbent rather than to his liturgical knowledge. Fresh ceremonial, incredibly foolish, has sometimes found its way into the Church services ; possibly because the incumbent on a visit to the Continent was attracted by some custom which he did not understand, but thought he would like to reproduce it at home ; or possibly through some energetic and imaginative layman introducing some strange practice which he regarded as edifying. I had once to order a ceremonarius wearing court dress to desist from drawing a sword and pointing it at the Host during the Elevation ! But with further knowledge and research absurdities have been dropped, and the personal inventiveness of an imaginative incumbent plays a smaller part in the arrangements of Divine Worship. There is an increasing conviction that all ceremonial, whether simple or elaborate should be in accordance with recognised principles. There are two schools of thought on ceremonial. There are the strong advocates of the restoration of the old English use; this they claim would witness to our continuity with the pre-Reformation Church in this land, and also is preferable to the Roman on æsthetic grounds. The other school criticises the attempt to restore the Sarum use as sheer antiquarianism and labels it as " British Museum Ceremonial "; and urges that the present Roman use should be followed as more practical and as bringing the Anglican Church into line with the rest of the Western Church. There are many loyal Anglicans who have inherited from the early days of the ceremonial revival practices based on the Roman use, for at that time no other use was known. It would not be right to assume that those who follow completely or in part the Roman ceremonial are necessarily Roman either in doctrine or in general outlook.

The ordinary layman is not interested in the technicalities of this controversy : if a chasuble is worn he is not greatly concerned if it is full according to the English use, or short and tight fitting according to the Roman ; if candles are on the altar, he does not feel it makes much difference if there are the English two or the Roman six ; and if at the Eucharist there is incense, to him it is a secondary matter whether its use ends before the Prayer of Consecration, or whether the Roman practice is followed of continuing it throughout the Prayer. He is however angered and indignant if changes are made in the character of the service without any consideration of the views of the congregation. It is of vital importance if ceremonial is to attract and not to repel that it should not be forced upon unwilling congregations, that it should be intelligible and not " dark and dumb," and that it should not be so elaborate and fussy that it distracts instead of helping the worshipper. It is not practical to propose for our Church " a congregation of rites " with power to regulate : but a permanent committee of liturgical experts and parish priests, representing all schools of thought might do much by advice to prune eccentricities and to encourage ceremonial on sound lines.

Worship To-day

It is now possible to give some description of the worship which is found in the Church of England to-day. The most striking of all changes which have taken place in the last sixty years are to be found in connection with the Holy Communion. At the time of the Reformation Masses were frequent, but Communion was rare. The average layman only received Communion at Easter : even the lay brothers of various Orders communicated at considerable intervals. The Reformers aimed at the abolition both of private Masses and of non-communicating attendance and at the substitution of frequent Communion. " At least three times a year, of which Easter shall be one," was an advance on the Mediæval practice and was intended as a minimum. But the Reformers did not succeed in this, in most parish churches there were large numbers of communicants on Easter Day and often on Good Friday, but the opportunities given for Communion decreased and before long it became a rare act, reserved for some great Festival. In the beginning of the 19th century celebrations of the Holy Communion were infrequent both in cathedrals and parish churches. Usually they took place after Matins and were popularly known as " the Second Service " ; they were attended by a handful of devout people. There was no ceremonial, and often the Prayer Book service was seriously abridged, the priest omitting all that came before the Invitation. To-day it is very rare to find a church without a Sunday celebration, in many churches it is daily. There has been a remarkable increase both in the number of communicants and in the frequency of reception. The service is conducted almost everywhere with marked reverence and devotion : usually with some symbolism, from the coloured stole to complete vestments, and from the two lighted candles to incense, to distinguish it from the other services of the day.

Celebrations of the Holy Communion can be divided into two great groups, those which are solely or mainly intended for purposes of Communion, and those at which there are few or no communicants. The former are held in the morning, sometimes at noon, or now rarely in the evening. In the country the congregations are usually small, though they are often large in the town. These celebrations are conducted simply, with a minimum of ceremonial. The other group has its earlier services for Communion, and later in the day a High or Sung Celebration at which the sacrificial aspect of the Eucharist is emphasised, music and vestments with a rich ceremonial are used to make the service a great offering of praise and thanksgiving.

The congregation may be large, but there are very few communicants, possibly only the priest or at the most the three demanded by the Prayer Book. Many of those present have already communicated at the earlier hour, and use this later service as an opportunity for thanksgiving and for the pleading of the great Sacrifice and Oblation once offered for the sins of the whole world. While this choral Eucharist with few or no communicants is an attempt both to make the Eucharist the chief service of the day and at the same time to bring out aspects of it which are not so apparent at a quiet service of Communion, there are many who are doubtful if this is a desirable development. Two quotations in support of this statement may be given from writers who are in sympathy with the Anglo-Catholic movement. In " Liturgy and Worship," a publication of the Literature Committee of the English Church Union, Dr. Srawley writes " The separation of the Sunday Eucharistic worship into two distinct services, one for Communion early in the day, and another for worship and oblation (without communicants) at a later hour, is a compromise with which, however expedient it may be as an attempt to meet various stages of religious development and the conditions of modern life, many are beginning to feel that they ought not to rest content as a final solution."[1] Father A. G. Hebert of the Society of the Sacred Mission is even stronger " The late sung Eucharist, lacking the communion of the people, is a maimed rite : however beautiful and moving the service may be, the people are spectators at the liturgy, and not in the full sense partakers in it. . . . It can never be anything else till it becomes also a communion. The adoption of this arrangement may be pronounced without hesitation to be the great blunder of the Anglo-Catholic movement."[2]

An attempt has been made to meet this defect by a parish Celebration at 9 or 9.30. This is choral, sometimes sung by the congregation without a choir, and it has all the ceremonial which would have been used if the service had been at a later hour. The whole congregation communicates. It is in a real sense a parish Communion and much more akin to the service described by Justin Martyr, than either the Celebration with only a tiny group of communicants, or the choral Eucharist at which communion is forbidden or discouraged. In many

[1] P. 331.
[2] " Liturgy and Society," p. 210.

parishes this arrangement has been successfully adopted, but so far only by a minority of the churches which aim at making the Liturgy unmistakeably *the* chief service of the day.

There is another line of cleavage which tends to divide the manner of celebrating the Holy Communion into separate groups, though in most cases communicants can pass from one church to the other without any sense of inconsistency. There are the churches, by far the larger number, in which the Canon of the Prayer Book is strictly followed : there are others in which there are departures from it of minor or major importance. Liturgical correctness and devotion, it is contended, require the enrichment of our Canon as the supreme act of corporate worship, and to bring it more into line with the great Consecration Prayers of both the East and the West. Some advocate the use of the 1549 Liturgy of Edward VI : there are others who would like to borrow the Scotch Laudian Liturgy : there are others who desire in whole or in part the Canon of the Roman Mass, instead of our Prayer of Consecration. A few are not content only with asking for these changes, as they are perfectly entitled to do, but they have introduced them on their own authority and use them openly or secretly when they are celebrating, notwithstanding the solemn promise they repeatedly made " to use the form in the said book prescribed and none other, except so far as shall be ordered by lawful authority." Most of those however who ask for some revision or enrichment of the Canon are men thoroughly loyal to the Church of England, and keep strictly the promise they have given. They cannot be fairly described as " extreme " men. Their desire for a revision comes from their knowledge of liturgical principles and from the devotional needs of themselves and their people. In the 1928 Prayer Book an attempt was made to meet this wish. But there was strong opposition to the new Prayer of Consecration on the ground that it involved a serious departure from Western tradition. Comparatively few churches use it, and there is now no likelihood that it will ever be widely accepted. As this proposed Canon has been so severely criticised it is well to recall the statement of a distinguished continental liturgical student " if it should come into general and authorised use, the Church of England will possess one of the noblest of all evangelical liturgies."[1] The most practical immediate solution would

[1] Y. Brilioth, " Eucharistic Faith and Practice," p. 227.

have been the re-arrangement of our Canon without the change of any words, so that the Prayer of Consecration, the Prayer of Oblation and the Lord's Prayer follow one another without interruption. Archbishop Lang had been assured by leading Anglo-Catholics that this would be welcomed. So in 1942 this change was proposed by the bishops in the Upper Houses of Convocation for optional use. But unfortunately the Lower House of both Provinces rejected this slight revision on the ground " that the present time is not opportune for raising a question which might cause controversy in the Church." The bishops accepted this advice, but the archbishops, speaking for the Upper Houses, naturally replied : " If it is inopportune for the Convocations to take this matter into consideration, it is clearly inopportune for any parish priest to introduce variations into the Holy Communion on his own authority."

For the great majority of Anglicans, Matins and Evensong are still the chief services of the Sunday, and have by far the largest congregations. The Prayer Book services are substantially followed, though the Psalms are sometimes shortened, and in the second part, after the third collect, special prayers and intercessions are introduced. The older custom of combining Matins with the Litany and Ante-Communion has been widely abandoned. Evensong is often adapted to make it a popular evangelistic service. Music has an important place both at Morning and Evening Prayer. The standard of Church music has been improved, many of the more sentimental tunes have been abolished, choirs have become more conscious of their limitations and care is taken over the selection of both music and hymns, so that often even in small country churches the singing is both simple and good. These Offices, often unduly disparaged, are a noble contribution of penitence, praise, Bible reading and prayer. Rightly used they build up the spiritual life of the faithful, but much must always depend upon the reverence and care with which they are conducted by minister, choir and people.

If we may go back in imagination to our foreigner visiting England for the first time and including in his investigations a comprehensive tour of our churches and their services, he would probably carry away two main impressions of Anglican worship.

He would have been struck by the great variety of ritual and ceremonial. At times he would feel he was present at the

Roman Catholic services with which he was familiar on the Continent, at other times he would think the services closer to those of the Reformed Churches. In one church he would find the service conducted with the utmost simplicity, in another with rich and elaborate ceremonial. If he had been accustomed to the more orderly systems of Rome or Geneva he would have been bewildered and perplexed as to how within one communion such differences in worship could be possible. If however it is once admitted that strict uniformity in our Church is an impractical ideal, there is much to be said for the frank recognition within it of various types of worship. God has made His children very different from one another, He has deliberately avoided the dull monotony of uniformity in their appearance, temperament and disposition, is it therefore probable that He would wish them all to worship Him in exactly the same way ? He accepted the simple adoration of the shepherds and the rich offerings of the Magi. And does not human nature itself need to express itself naturally in different ways. One man is cold and logical, another warmhearted and emotional : one rational and critical, another impulsive and imaginative : one colour-blind to all beauty, while another has the poet's insight into all that is lovely. It is not possible that all these should express their devotion to God in one way. Spontaneity in worship would be crushed and devotion driven into narrow channels if uniformity was enforced. Where there is true love of God combined with reverence and humility, it is a minor matter as to how this love shows itself in worship. God who has made His children so different from one another will allow them to approach Him in prayer in the manner they find most natural. It is the glory of the Church of England that with all its many failures it has its door wide open to Christian men and women who wish to worship God in very different ways and thus enables them to make it their spiritual home.

And our foreigner would be impressed by the quiet and orderly reverence of our Anglican worship. There would be much he would dislike in it. He would find it hard to follow the long Psalms and Lessons. He would find our pews and fixed chairs cramp-giving after the moveable seats and open spaces of a continental church. He would consider the service cold and formal both on the part of the officiating minister and of the congregation compared to the freedom of movement and postures to which he had been accustomed at home. He would often miss the colour and sense of mystery, " the blessed mutter of the mass " and the taste of " good strong thick stupefying incense smoke." But he would feel and admire the reverence and quiet of the service. This at any rate was what struck most of all some Italian Roman Catholics who said to me that when they had the opportunity they came to our services " for they were so quiet." In the same way an educated Swiss Roman Catholic told me that he thought our services were " more reverent " than those of his own Church : and an Orthodox Bishop once told me he envied our reverence and the way in which the congregation takes part in the service. Some may miss from our worship the highest notes of adoration and emotion, but many others find in it a quiet and solemn reverence which is natural to their temperament and helps them to make their offering of prayer and praise. It strengthens their trust in God, bringing rest and comfort to their souls, and gives them a clearer vision of the Majesty, Holiness and Love of the most High.

Prayer Book Revision

But however much the regular Churchgoer may admire the Prayer Book services there is a growing conviction that some revision is necessary. It should have two aims, which are supplementary and not contradictory. First, greater simplicity is needed in many of our services. This is especially true of the Occasional Offices. The Forms for Baptism, Marriage and the Burial of the Dead are not simple and direct enough for those who only attend the services of the Church on these occasions. Simpler alternatives to Matins and Evensong should also be provided for use when the congregation is likely to consist largely of non-Churchgoers. The amateur services drawn up by local incumbents for special occasions sometimes secure simplicity at the cost of dignity and reverence, though too often, indeed, they are liturgical jungles through which both regular and occasional worshippers find it hard to make their way.

Secondly, enrichment of our services is necessary. In their desire for plainness the reformers lost much that is rich and splendid in the liturgies both of the Western and Eastern Churches. We should draw more freely on the treasure houses of devotion found elsewhere in the Catholic Church ; this would help to unite us with both the West and the East without any compromise of our distinctive position. This is especially to be desired in the Order of the Holy Communion, where it would be a great gain to include in the Canon thanksgiving for Our Lord's Resurrection and Ascension as well as for His Passion and Death, and a direct invocation of the Holy Spirit. More Collects, Epistles and Gospels are required for use on special occasions, though the 1928 Prayer Book has already done something to meet this need. Our public worship is also noticeably weak in its commemoration of the saints " who have been the chosen vessels of Thy grace and lights of the world in their several generations." The commemoration of the departed of all centuries with praise and thanksgiving would bring home the reality of Paradise and of the Communion of Saints.

Through ordered and regulated experiment the Church will gradually reach the form of worship which will best enable it to make its sacrifice of praise and prayer, and the worshipper to gain some clearer vision of God in His glory. But to leave such experiments at the complete discretion of the parish priest who is not necessarily a liturgist, will lead to hopeless confusion. The authorisation of such experiments must come from the diocesan bishops, but behind them there must be the con- currence of the Convocations. They should be asked to approve any proposed new forms of service. Only after these new forms of prayer have commended themselves by experience to the mass of Church people should formal sanction be sought for their inclusion in the official Prayer Book.

IV

THE CATHEDRALS AND CHURCHES

Through its cathedrals and ancient churches large numbers
each year come into contact with the Church of England.
No country is richer in ancient churches than our own.
While other Churches of Christendom can claim to possess
more cathedrals, it is doubtful if any of them have so many
of such age, size and splendour.

IV

THE CATHEDRALS AND CHURCHES
OF THE CHURCH OF ENGLAND

THROUGH its cathedrals and ancient churches large numbers each year come into contact with the Church of England. No country is richer in ancient churches than our own. While other Churches of Christendom can claim to possess more cathedrals, it is doubtful if any of them have so many of such age, size and splendour.

I. THE CATHEDRALS

Size is not necessary for a cathedral : what is essential is that it should possess the chair of the bishop. Many of our ancient cathedrals were originally small buildings, but the fact that they possessed the chair of the bishop gave them importance, and in succeeding centuries they were enlarged and enriched. The responsibility for their worship and work rested with a group of men attached to them who lived under rule and were called canons (from the Greek word for rule or regulation). They were either secular clergy, who lived in the world, or regulars—monks living under a rule stricter than that observed by the seculars. Until the Reformation the two systems existed side by side in England ; some cathedrals—Canterbury and Durham, for instance—were monastic : others—York and Lincoln among them—were secular. With the Reformation the monks were replaced by a Chapter of canons, with deans instead of abbots at their head : these are cathedrals of the " New Foundation." The cathedrals with secular canons retained their ancient statutes and belong to the " Old Foundation."

But whether the cathedral was governed by regulars or seculars, the connection of the bishop with it became very slight. He was always moving from place to place, his manors were often far away from the cathedral city, he was immersed in all kinds of business, and he had to spend much of his time at the King's Court on State affairs. The Dean and Chapter on the other hand, made the cathedral and its property their chief concern; they were the men on the spot and dealt with the daily problems of administration. They became a close corporation resenting any kind of outside interference, and in the course of time the bishop was regarded as one who was outside their life and whose rare interventions were treated as troublesome intrusions. The bishop thus came to have less authority over his own church—the cathedral—than over any other church in his diocese. He can use it for Synods, Visitations, Ordinations and Confirmations, and in the recently revised Statutes he is usually given the right to celebrate the Holy Communion and to preach on various occasions. He also has the important duty of formally Visiting the cathedral and of deciding disputes over the interpretation of the Statutes, as well as of seeing they are obeyed. In some of the modern cathedrals for a time the experiment was tried of combining the posts of bishop and dean. Theoretically this has certain advantages: there can be no dispute between bishop and dean, and the bishop—as dean—can control the worship and affairs of the church. In actual practice this has proved a failure. When Bishop of Southwark I was dean of its cathedral, but the pressure of work in the diocese made it impossible for me to attend sufficiently to the cathedral; its claims had to be sacrificed to those of the diocese. This plan has now been abolished, and the parish church cathedral has its provost, who—while rector or vicar of the parish—also acts as dean. As long as the diocesan bishop recognises and accepts the historical and traditional position of the Dean and Chapter, there is unlikely to be any friction, and the bishop can attend to his duties in the diocese, knowing that the cathedral is well looked after and that on special and other occasions when he wishes to worship in it his presence will be welcomed.

In our cathedrals we have indeed a great and splendid heritage. They are the noblest and most ancient buildings in the land, and moreover have been in continuous use for centuries. Most of the great castles are in ruins; the private dwelling houses of the Middle Ages have long vanished, but the cathedrals and churches still remain not as museum pieces, but as living centres of devotion. They give an impression of stability and permanence in an age of incessant change. The rate of change is so rapid that it is true to say that we are living through a revolution. Amidst great changes man looks for that which is permanent, and a reassuring sense of strength and stability is given to him by buildings which by their age, massiveness and beauty lead his thoughts upward to God.

For one of the purposes of a cathedral is to bear witness to the God to Whose glory it is consecrated—in the words of the Report of the Cathedrals Commission of 1924 : " The first supreme aim of a cathedral is, by its own beauty and by the religious services held within it, to give continuous witness to the things unseen and eternal, and to offer continuous and reverent worship to Almighty God." Each cathedral bears its witness in its own way. The Minster of York by its massiveness, its size, its towers, and its great interior spaces speaks of the Majesty of God : and the same is true of Durham and of Winchester—I never forget the thrill I felt when, as a boy of twelve or thirteen, I entered Winchester Cathedral for the first time and saw the great nave ; over forty years later I had the same impression of awe and wonder when I came up the nave for my enthronement as Bishop. My old Cathedral of Southwark, very much smaller, down by the riverside, almost hidden by warehouses and the railway viaduct, seems to witness to the condescension and love of God in coming to dwell among men. Lichfield and Salisbury with their spires pointing to heaven tell of the beauty of God.

Many of the cathedrals are histories in stone of Church and nation. This is especially true of Canterbury, York, Westminster, St. Paul's and Winchester. Canterbury is filled with memorials of the past—the chair of Augustine ; its crypt ; the transept of the Martyrdom ; the site of the shrine, the goal of so many pilgrims ; the Black Prince's Tomb—all recall the past. Westminster, though not a cathedral, proclaims aloud the history of the nation from the days of the Confessor. St. Paul's Cathedral is the Pantheon in which warriors and statesmen have their memorials and tombs. In cathedral after cathedral there are memorials of those who served both Church and nation. Tombs, brasses, gifts of various kinds, and even niches empty of the statues which once stood in them, and damaged sculpture and broken glass, speak of many centuries of history. In more recent years county regiments have chosen the cathedrals for their memorials in honour of those who died in the

Crimea, in India, in Africa or in the two World Wars. Sometimes, too, there is a Book of Remembrance with the names
of the fallen, and the pages day by day are turned over by a
soldier of the regiment which has given it.

A visitor coming for the first time into one of our greater
cathedrals may feel that the nave appears somewhat bare and
cold. In the Middle Ages it would have looked otherwise, for
it would have been broken up by numerous chapels and chantries : the chapels divided from each other by screens of iron
or wood. The great screen then, as now, shut off the choir
from the nave, but usually in front of it there were altars, and
set on the screen was the great crucifix with the images of
St. Mary and St. John. The high altar was long and narrow,
and originally had no reredos or screen as this would have
cut off the bishop and his attendants who sat behind the altar
facing west. Most of the cathedrals were rich with stained
glass windows, with numerous wall paintings and the gilding
of the screens and tombs. " If we try to picture to ourselves
the internal appearance of one of our cathedral churches as it
was during the century before the Reformation—the period at
which Church furniture reached its highest magnificence—we
must remember that wherever the eye rested the prospect was
broken by the screen-work of chapels. In every direction, too,
the eye was met by rich colour. Some of the effect of this
can be conceived at York, where the old stained glass remains
in all but a few windows, giving the church a subdued gor-
geousness of colour unequalled in any other English building
of similar size. When, however, the whole of the building,
the mouldings of the arches, the sculpture of capitals and span-
drels, screens, stalls, tombs and reredoses were covered with
painting and gilding, the effect, combined with the hues of
the stained glass, must have been dazzling."[1]

The cathedrals were the work of many hands. It is customary
to associate their building or enlargement with the bishop who
occupied the See at the time this took place. But in most cases
the names of their architects are unknown. They are the
offering of many who worked together for the glory of God.
There were the architects—possibly the master masons of those
days—who saw the cathedral before it took visible form :
there were the labourers who dug deep its foundations ; there

[1] " The Cathedral Churches of England," by A. Hamilton Thompson, p. 106.

were the masons who cut the stones, leaving on them their marks which can still be seen in ancient churches : there were the sculptors who carved, according to their own design, the heads of men and beasts, or the leaves and flowers in the capitals of the pillars : there were the artificers in wood and iron who wrought the stalls and screens : there were the glaziers who filled the windows with rich colour : and there were the women who embroidered the vestments, the banners and the hangings. And behind all these were the donors who gave liberally and freely so that the House of God might be exceeding magnifical.

Cathedrals were not in the Middle Ages built with large congregations in view. They were designed irrespective of the size of the congregation which might require them. They were for continuous worship conducted by the regulars or seculars of the cathedral. All through the day and often for part of the night there was an almost unbroken round of services, the corporate worship of a community of canons, vicars and choristers. Sometimes indeed part of the cathedral was used by a parish, but more frequently a church was built close by for the parishioners, as St. Michael-le-Belfrey within a few yards of the Minster at York. The nave was sometimes used for business and commerce. At Wells at the end of the thirteenth century the Vicars Choral left their stalls during the actual services to talk with and to purchase goods from lay folk in the nave. There were rare occasions when the cathedral was filled either for some special service, or to hear some sermon by a famous preacher, or if it possessed a noted shrine, by pilgrims who had come to pray at it. Usually, however, a chance visitor would have found the nave empty, but through the opening in the choir screen he would have seen the light of candles and lamps, and would have heard the murmur of a few voices offering the daily round of worship.

The Reformation and the Puritans' rebellion changed the interior appearance and character of the cathedrals. The shrines were destroyed, the sculptures defaced, the screens hacked to bits, the images of the saints broken, precious metal and stone were confiscated, and the glass windows shattered. It is impossible to estimate how much of value and beauty these great churches lost at the hands of the Reformers and Puritans. It is really amazing that so much survived their fanatical zeal.

It is said that William of Wykeham's Chantry was saved from the Puritan soldiery by one of their officers, an old Wykehamist, standing over it with drawn sword. Similarly it is supposed that the stained glass in York Minster was spared at the order of Lord Fairfax, the Commander of the victorious army and himself a Yorkshireman.

Then followed many years of neglect. Dr. Johnson, who claimed that he had visited all the cathedrals, said that they were mouldering by unregarded dilapidation. " It seems to be part of the despicable philosophy of the time to despise monuments of sacred magnificence."[1] Here and there the buildings were repaired when there seemed imminent danger to their fabric. Sometimes too, usually with unhappy results, attempts were made at internal decoration. But for long they gave an impression of neglect. In the early part of the nineteenth century a Government Commission enquired into the affairs of the cathedral bodies, and some of the worst financial scandals were removed. It was not, however, until the Oxford Movement made its influence felt that there came a real change over the life and work of the cathedrals. They were cleaned, restored and gradually brought into use as centres of worship. Dean Church's work at St. Paul's transformed the metropolitan cathedral from " a vast and dreary area abandoned to dust and damp and uselessness " into a home of worship and spiritual life. Everywhere else the same change took place. And not only were the old cathedrals restored and given new life, but new Cathedrals of Truro and Liverpool were built, and elsewhere parish churches were adapted as the cathedrals of new dioceses. Never in their long history have our cathedrals been used more fully for the service of God and man than they are to-day. Frequently in the year they are thronged by great congregations. They no longer stand apart from the dioceses; they are the Mother Churches in reality as well as in name. Different diocesan organisations come to them for their annual services. Representatives of the parishes visit them on pilgrimage. No longer are their doors opened only occasionally at the cost of a fee, but they are open to all who come to gaze or to pray. No longer is the public excluded from free access to the interesting parts of the building. I recall my boyhood when my small pocket money rarely allowed me to pass beyond the sanctuary

[1] " Works," IX, 20.

gates if a ticket had to be bought. Now the chapels have been carefully restored and made beautiful, and places for quiet prayer are set apart for those who have had sufficient sight-seeing.

The aims and uses of a Cathedral

First, a cathedral exists so that within it continuous and reverent worship may be offered to Almighty God. The building itself is a call to worship. Archbishop Benson used to quote Mr. J. L. Pearson, the architect, as saying " the question to ask oneself on entering a church was not ' Is this admirable, is it beautiful ? ' but ' Does it send you on your knees ? ' "[1] But unless within there is continuous worship, the building is a " National Monument " such as is often seen thus labelled on the Continent, or as a Frenchman once said to me : " A casket which has been robbed of the jewel it was intended to enshrine." In all our cathedrals there is now a weekly and often a daily celebration of the Holy Communion : and day by day the regular Offices are said or sung. They are once again homes of continuous prayer and praise.

Secondly, they are schools of Sacred Song. They should have a high standard of music which should be an example for the whole diocese. Dr. Iremonger, the Dean of Lichfield, looks forward to the day when our " ' Schools of Sacred Song ' will become not merely academies for the education of small boys, but also schools in which parish priests and organists will be able to sit at the feet of experts : from which there will radiate outwards through the diocese the knowledge and love of Church music : to which the most and least enlightened incumbents and choir masters alike can appeal for the solution of their problems and look for the technical guidance they sorely need."[2]

Thirdly, they are seats of sacred learning. Usually on the Chapter there is at least one scholar with the gift of teaching the clergy and the laity. Frequently there are lectures in the cathedral on Biblical and theological subjects to which all are invited. Often attached to the cathedral is a library containing

[1] " The Life of Edward White Benson " (abridged edition), p. 181.

[2] Sermon preached before the University of Oxford, 1943.

records and documents of great value to the scholar. In the cathedral library of Hereford there is a notable example of a collection of chained books. From cathedral Closes there come books of value and interest written by dean or canons. A striking list could be compiled of Biblical, theological, historical and devotional works which have been written by members of cathedral Chapters.

Fourthly, the cathedral is a treasury of Christian art. Our older cathedrals contain much that is precious in glass, craftsmanship, and in monuments. No other building in England has such a representative and full collection of stained glass as York Minster: and it would be difficult to find elsewhere such noble woodwork as the stalls of Winchester Cathedral. But modern art, as well as ancient, finds its place in them. Year by year they are enriched by the work of contemporary artists. To York Minster in the last few years there have been given a magnificent canopy for the font in the crypt, stalls made by a well-known Yorkshire craftsman, and screens of wrought iron. The choir of Winchester Cathedral has been made bright with cushions and kneelers designed and worked by a guild of Broderers. The retro-choir of Southwark Cathedral now has its four chapels divided by beautifully carved wooden screens. Liverpool Cathedral is full of examples of modern art, and the greatest care has been taken to see that only what is really good is admitted: from the locks on the doors to its reredos, font and memorials, everything is of the best workmanship.

In another direction there is a revival within the cathedrals of Christian art. In the Middle Ages the faith was taught in them by the performance of miracle plays. They were highly popular and drew great crowds. Recently under modern conditions religious drama has again found its place within our cathedrals. In Canterbury, Lichfield and elsewhere, dramatists have used their art for the presentation of Christian truth. T. S. Eliot's " Murder in the Cathedral " and Dorothy Sayers' " Just Vengeance " show how magnificently and reverently this can be done. No one who saw the *Persona Dei* bearing the Cross through the nave of Lichfield can doubt the unique suitability of our cathedrals for plays of this nature.

The Dean and Chapter

The increased opportunities given to cathedrals in our time causes the question sometimes to be asked as to whether the old method of placing their control in the hands of a Dean and Chapter is still satisfactory. A hundred years ago the dean and the canons had few demands made upon them; they lived apart from the life of the diocese, and spent their time in quiet seclusion, disturbed occasionally by their own quarrels or by the threat of some reform which might encroach on their privileges. Those days have long passed; much more is expected of the Chapters, and they on their side are anxious that their cathedrals should be a living influence in the diocese. The usefulness of many of the cathedrals is chiefly hampered by lack of funds, and for this no remedy can be found. There is, however, a suggested reform which has much to commend it. It is sometimes possible to find a Chapter consisting chiefly of elderly men who are past their work. Some of them, when much younger, were appointed not only as canons of the cathedral but for some special diocesan work, evangelistic or educational as the case might be : but ill-health and increasing years have made it impossible for them any longer to do it. Or again, there are some who were appointed solely for the sake of the cathedral, but who after years of faithful service have now settled into a groove, and are neither mentally nor physically equal to the new demands made upon them. They are capable of performing their statutory duties ; they are respected by all and loved by many, but they are " extinct volcanoes." The kindly phrase " the dear old canon " is almost as damning a description of amiable ineffectiveness as that of " the dear old bishop ! " There are obvious objections to the appointment of canons for a limited period of years : men would hesitate at accepting posts which might terminate at a time when their age would make it difficult for them to find work elsewhere : a man might reasonably decline a canonry at the age of fifty if he knew that at sixty he might be without work—and he would hesitate the more if he was married with a family. Yet unless some limitation is set on the term for which the appointment is made, there will always be the risk of the administrative Chapter consisting of men whose average

age is seventy, and who have lost their early vigour and fresh-ness. This danger would be removed if it became the rule that one, or possibly two, of the canonries should be held only for ten years. This would make it possible and easy to appoint men at a much younger age than at present. A man of ability at thirty-five or forty could accept a canonry knowing that within ten years he would still be young enough to move to responsible work elsewhere : his service at the cathedral would give him a period for study and writing, and he would do something to loosen the stiffening joints of an elderly chapter. It would be a gain to the cathedrals and to the diocese if always on the Chapter there was at least one of the canons under forty years of age.

II. PARISH CHURCHES

If the cathedrals call forth wonder and admiration, the parish churches evoke affection. For the few who are in frequent contact with the cathedrals there are millions who day by day see and love their parish church. It is hard to go very far in England without seeing the spires or towers of churches rising above the surrounding roofs or trees. They are found in great cities, almost hidden sometimes by blocks of buildings and warehouses ; in the centre of old market towns ; in small villages and in remote hamlets. They stand on windswept cliffs, or in the midst of dreary fenland looking over the marshes which surround them, or they are half concealed in lonely valleys and dales, or hidden in the folds of the Downs " little lost Down churches " praising " the Lord who made the hills." They are of all ages : some come from Anglo-Saxon days, though these are very small and few in number. There are massive Norman churches, some half underground as in the crypt at Lastingham : some with splendid threefold porches each richly carved and with massive pillars and capitals. There are churches of the later Middle Ages, with columns and arches of amazing grace and loveliness—Patrington, in South Holder-ness, is of these perhaps the most beautiful ; Archbishop Temple described it as " the most beautiful of all parish churches in England." There are the churches whose walls seemed to be built mainly as frames for great windows filled with coloured glass. There are churches of the English Renaissance, with wonderful wooden rails and screens. And there are the well-proportioned Georgian churches, whose merits we have lately begun to appreciate. They are churches of all sizes, some of them built only for the two or three of the small hamlet who gather together for worship, others are equal or even superior in size and majesty to many of the cathedrals : among the greater churches are those which once belonged to abbeys : Beverley Minster, Christchurch Priory, Hexham Abbey are notable among them. The ancient churches, whether large or small, give—like the cathedrals—a message of permanence and reassurance to our age of change. They speak of One Whose kingdom is everlasting, and against which neither the gates of death nor hell can prevail.

Within them many treasures can be found. They possess examples of native, and sometimes of local art from Anglo-Saxon days onwards—stones with Runic inscriptions and with crude carvings of men and animals ; simple fonts reputed to be Saxon, and others more massive and elaborate which have stood in the church since they were placed there by the Normans ; richly decorated wooden screens unequalled elsewhere ; canopies and stalls ; carved bench ends ; and splendid Jacobean altar rails and pulpits. On the walls can be seen paintings of Our Lord and the saints ; very often a gigantic St. Christopher bending under the weight of the small Child on his shoulders : and sometimes on the west wall, as at Chaldon in Surrey, the Doom with the redeemed welcomed into Paradise and the impenitent cast into hell. Here and there are pictures which once had their home in Italy, presented by some donor of later days. There are windows glowing with mediæval glass. There are effigies on the tombs, brasses set in the floor, and tablets on the wall which speak of those who once lived in the parish. There are chests of great age and strength : hatchments of more recent centuries : and in the vestry in the safe, which every church is supposed to possess, there may be splendid communion plate and registers dating back to the days of the Tudors. In the tower are bells, bearing inscriptions in memory of those who gave them, which have rung out in celebration of great national deliverances since the days of the Armada.

Within and without our parish churches are records in stone of the history of the village which they serve. Occasionally on the stonework outside the main entrance there can be seen deep lines or scratches traditionally supposed to have been made by the sharpening of arrows. There are doors with the marks of bullets fired at the church in civil war : and dials carved in the stone, by which the time for Mass was learnt. The successive enlargements of the church show how the hamlet grew into the populous village, and the galleries which deface it how the village church had to be adapted to the needs of the Church-goers of a town. In the churches, as in the cathedrals, sculpture and shattered glass witness to the stormy days through which Church and State have passed.

There are many parish churches which have been built quite recently. Of some of these the less said the better. They are tasteless imitations of Gothic churches ; for last century had some popular architects who apparently thought that pointed windows and arches, machine-produced sculpture, and marble fonts and pulpits would re-create a mediæval church. But the age of pretentious shams quickly passed and churches of beauty, dignity and originality soon succeeded them. Some followed one of the mediæval styles—I think of my old church at Portsea modelled after the churches of the Eastern counties, of great dignity, with wide spaces and lofty wooden roof, holding a congregation of two thousand. Very beautiful, too, are some of the modern churches in many of our towns, such as St. Agnes, Kennington (now alas, destroyed !) and St. Stephen's, Bourne-mouth. Later there was a return to the Byzantine style. And before the war many of our best architects struck out on original paths, building churches in which mass and line combined to give an impression of simple dignity and strength. And into these churches, as into their predecessors, good examples of contemporary art have been brought : paintings or carvings of beauty for the reredos ; stained glass windows sometimes as striking as those which survive in mediæval churches ; statues, carved screens, and font covers as carefully designed and worked as anything in the past.

The parish church has been for centuries the centre of the life of the village. In the Middle Ages it was the concert hall, the picture gallery, the theatre as well as the house of God to the people who lived round it. On Sundays and holidays it was crowded with the parishioners : it was their natural meeting place. There were no pews as now, the floor was strewn with rushes and reeds, the infirm or aged leaned against the pillars, or sat on the long stone seats by the walls. Until the fifteenth century there was rarely a pulpit; it was of stone and very small, standing isolated in front of the chancel. There were pictures and images to look at, and altars with lamps or candles burning; there was the low mutter of the Mass with the occasional response of the congregation, and the great moment when all whispering was hushed as the congregation adored the consecrated Host lifted on high by the priest. To-day many of the parishioners never enter the church, except on special occasions. In the great cities many are unaware of the church which is close to their homes, and are ignorant of its very name : when I first went to South London as its bishop I could only find my way with any certainty to the church by asking beforehand the name of the nearest public house ! But in the country village and town the position is very different. The villagers and townsmen know their church, they are conscious of its presence ; they are proud of any special characteristics it may possess ; they think of it as their church. They were baptized in it, and in time brought their children to its font : at its altar they and their parents were married : and its churchyard is full of the graves of their forefathers. On special occasions, on Harvest Festivals and on days of national Prayer and Thanksgiving, they turn to it for their worship. In the worst days of the raids some of the village churches were kept open all night so that the refugees from bombed cities might sleep under a roof. Day by day the parish church bears its witness to God. It is a witness to the unseen, and to a life which is eternal : every time its bells ring they give a summons to worship God : its services, its structure, its atmosphere speak of mysteries which science cannot fathom, and of a peace and trust which material civilisation cannot give. And its God's acre when well kept foreshadows rest after the storm of life.

Our parish churches are primarily intended for the worship of God : to this their archæological and architectural interest is subordinated. The parish priest is instructed in the Prayer Book to ring twice daily the church bell so that any who are free and willing to do so may join with him in saying Morning and Evening Prayer. Most of our churches to-day give to those who visit them the sense that they are used for regular worship. Many of them at their entrance have not only an account of their history and of their chief features of interest, but also the request that none should enter or leave without offering some prayer. It is much to be desired that our people would more frequently use their churches for meditation and private prayer, for within them they would find freedom from interruption and the silence which are often so difficult to secure elsewhere. Some compensation for the decline in attendance at public worship would be gained if in the week they were used more generally by Church people for their own prayers. But if this is to be so, there must be warmth in the winter— impossible in these days of fuel shortage—in the summer flowers which make the church attractive and friendly, and an atmosphere which welcomes and encourages the individual worshipper.

Destructive Agencies

Our cathedrals and churches have had to contend for their survival with the forces of nature : with the malice, and with the ignorance of man.

(1.) Age, storm, wind and rain have continuously assaulted them since they were built. Without incessant vigilance and care most of them would long ago have fallen into ruin. The wind would have loosened the roof, and the rain poured in, the damp would have soaked in through the walls, and the ivy, most pernicious of weeds, would have eaten its way into the stones which it concealed with its leaf. Until the war it was very rarely that a ruined church could be seen. Our churches seem so firmly built, that we forget that they have only been preserved through the continuous generosity and care of successive generations. Bishop Creighton used to say to his friends who were visiting a cathedral for the first time and wished to show to their guide some intelligent interest in it, " Ask him when the spire collapsed." For it is true that most of our cathedrals and ancient churches would have collapsed if from time to time the defective roof had not been repaired, the walls buttressed, and the stone-work of tower and walls renewed. A church neglected and deserted for sixty or seventy years becomes a ruin. The money spent on the repair and upkeep of the fabric of our churches exceeds by far their original cost.

(2) Many churches have suffered from the malice of man.
From the time when the Danish pirates landed and sacked
them to the years of the great war—when they were attacked
from the air—many have been destroyed or damaged by malicious
action. They have never suffered to the same extent as churches
on the Continent; we have been spared serious invasion since
1066, and our civil wars have never been so devastating as
those which swept across Europe. At the Reformation much
that was beautiful and precious in our churches was destroyed.
Nearly a hundred years later the work of destruction was carried
still further by the Puritans, and the churches left cold and
bare. In the world war many suffered from enemy action.
Among the cathedrals Coventry was destroyed, and St. Paul's,
Manchester and Exeter were damaged. The harm done to
Gothic churches was less than might have been expected, but
large numbers of the churches of the English Renaissance,
especially those built in London by Wren and his disciples,
suffered severely. One night in Southampton no less than six
modern churches were destroyed. Losses in Plymouth, Portsmouth, Bristol and Hull were severe. Here and there small
village churches were destroyed: the first in England to be
burnt by enemy action was the little mediæval church of Dibden
on Southampton Water. Many of these churches will be rebuilt or replaced, but the movement of population had made
some of those which had neither architectural nor historical
interest superfluous, and the violence of the enemy had only
hastened their fate.

(3) Greater damage has been wrought by the ignorance than
by the malice of man. Reformers and Puritans destroyed the
fittings and ornaments of churches, but left their fabric intact.
It was reserved for devout and generous Churchmen of the
nineteenth century to destroy the whole building, though
usually some of its memorials were preserved. In their eagerness to build larger and more modern churches, ancient churches
were pulled down and were replaced by Victorian Gothic. I
can think of church after church in the South of England,
strongly built but unattractive, where in the vestries can be
seen pictures of the Anglo-Saxon or Norman church which
they replaced. In Yorkshire the destruction was not so general:
there were fewer wealthy Churchmen to give to the work of
restoration. During this period of Church revival of the last

century more irreparable damage was done than by all the fanaticism of Reformer and Puritan. And within the churches which were " restored " uninstructed enthusiasm often worked havoc ; the old fonts and pulpits were evicted and marble monstrosities substituted, the mediæval paving torn up to make way for crudely coloured tiles with conventional designs ; the Jacobean altar table was removed to the vestry as inferior to a machine-made table ; while on a retable above the new altar was placed a row of brightly polished brass vases and candle-sticks : for the old reredos there was substituted an elaborate and fussy structure of stone, marble or alabaster. Old pews of oak were replaced by varnished deal. Carpets and hangings were introduced haphazard without any reference to their surroundings, or without attention to harmony in colour. The old frescoes were painted over. And too often the organ was moved from the west gallery to a position in the chancel where it blocked the view, and the newly-erected stalls overcrowded the choir.

It would be unjust to say that the destruction was universal. There were many churches which were restored or rebuilt with judgement and care. Nowhere within a comparatively small area do I know so many village churches either restored or built so beautifully in the last half century as those in the Yorkshire Wolds. And since the first outburst of uninstructed zeal the standard of Church building and restoration has been steadily raised. The greatest care is taken over the preserva-tion of old stone work and of the treatment of wall surface and flintwork both within and without the church. In every diocese there is now a committee for the protection of its churches and their treasures. To these committees applications concerning the repair of churches are submitted before per-mission to proceed is granted. The Central Council for the Care of Churches co-ordinates the work of the Diocesan Com-mittees and makes from time to time expert recommendations for their guidance. These committees have not only done much for the protection of the fabric, but they have saved many churches from unfortunate proposals for decoration and from the introduction of vulgar or incongruous ornaments. Not all incumbents, churchwardens and Church Councils have artistic taste, and even if they possess it it is sometimes difficult for them to resist a wealthy parishioner who wishes to give to the church some unsuitable memorial. These committees, though they have often caused local disappointment, have delivered churches from disastrous changes and unsuitable ornaments. Gradually many of the blunders of the nineteenth century are being undone, as opportunities arise for new and wiser restorations and substitutions. The abandonment of Victorian methods of Church furnishing is inevitably a lengthy process, but the improvement already is very remarkable. Care is taken to avoid restoration on the uniform principles which were at one time adopted by the State in France, and stamped many of the churches it had taken over as National Monuments into the same dreary pattern. " The safest guarantee for the future of our treasures is the broad artistic outlook which is now becoming generally accepted as a matter of course. . . . The productions not only of mediæval times, but of the Renaissance, early and late, are alike jealously guarded, and not only that but extreme care is usually taken not to destroy what is good and representative of the best in the Victorian period."[1]

*   *   *   *   *

There is still much to be done to make all our churches attractive shrines for both public and private worship. They must always be open—even though there is some risk of theft. The notice board and porch should be free from all unnecessary or obsolete notices. There should be in some conspicuous place a list of past vicars and an account of the history and architecture of the church. The building should be kept scrupulously clean, flowers or foliage in jars or vases should always be fresh. When there are too many pews or seats for the congregation, permission should be obtained to clear some of them away ; empty spaces add greatly to the dignity of a church. When the church is disfigured by unsuitable modern ornaments and hangings, tiles and carpets which would not be tolerated in the homes of educated people, application should be made to the proper authorities for their removal and replacement as soon as this can be done without giving offence to the donors. It is unreasonable to expect that succeeding generations should suffer indefinitely from the blunders of the past. In the course of time windows of poor glass might be removed. Above all, the parishioners themselves should be encouraged to use the

[1] " The Protection of our English Churches," Fourth Report, 1930, p. 2.

church on weekdays. Our ancient churches by their other-worldliness, by their beauty and their atmosphere can be made powerful instruments for the re-conversion of England. We must use their history, their architecture, their beauty, and their treasures to attract non-Churchgoers to them; and then the parish priest must see how best he can move their hearts and minds to the Lord and Owner of the House.

What I have written in the last paragraph was said much better three hundred years ago by George Herbert in "The Country Parson": "The Countrey Parson hath a speciall care of his Church, that all things there be decent, and befitting His Name by which it is called. Therefore, first he takes order, that all things be in good repair; as walls plaistered, windows glazed, floore paved, seats whole, firm, and uniform; especially that the Pulpit and Desk, and Communion Table, and Font, be as they ought, for those great duties that are performed in them. Secondly, that the Church be swept, and kept cleane without dust, or Cobwebs, and at great festivalls strawed, and stuck with boughs, and perfumed with incense. Thirdly, that there be fit, and proper texts of Scripture every where painted, and that all the painting be grave and reverend, not with light colours, or foolish anticks. Fourthly, That all the books appointed by Authority be there, and those not torne, or fouled, but whole; and clean, and well bound; and that there be a fitting, and sightly Communion cloth of fine linnen, with an handsome, and seemly Carpet of good and costly Stuffe, or Cloth, and all kept sweet and clean, in a strong and decent chest, with a Chalice, and Cover, and a Stoop, or Flagon: and a Bason for Almes and offerings; beside which he hath a Poor-mans box conveniently seated, to receive the charity of well-minded people, and to lay up treasure for the sick and needy."

V

THE BISHOP AND "THE BISHOPS"

It is true that on the Bench there are no longer to be found men like the giants of old, though if William Temple had lived he might have proved the greatest Archbishop the Church of England had ever possessed. I would, however, say that the standard of work, efficiency and pastoral zeal of the bishops is probably as high as it ever has been. Not all the bishops at any one time have ever been men of outstanding ability and devotion. We remember the leaders and forget the mediocrities. As a Bench we claim neither brilliance nor infallibility : but among us are good scholars ; capable administrators ; and faithful pastors. And in accordance with the gifts God has given us we are doing our utmost in difficult days for Church and nation.

V

THE BISHOP AND "THE BISHOPS"

IN the Preface to our Ordinal it is stated " that from the Apostles' time there have been these Orders of Ministers in Christ's Church : Bishops, Priests and Deacons " and " no man shall be accounted or taken to be a lawful Bishop, Priest or Deacon in the Church of England or suffered to execute any of the said functions, except he be called, tried, examined, and admitted thereunto, according to the form hereafter following, or hath had formerly Episcopal Consecration or Ordination." The Church of England is an episcopal Church and does not regard episcopacy merely as a convenient form of government, but also as the guarantee of continuity in apostolic teaching and ministration. Only those who have been duly consecrated by other bishops have the right to ordain to the priesthood and the diaconate, and only those who have been so ordained have the right to preach authoritatively the Word of God and to administer the Sacraments in the Church of England. It was for this reason that the utmost care was taken in Queen Elizabeth's reign to see that the new Archbishop was consecrated by those who themselves had been duly consecrated. It is one of the distinguishing marks of the Anglican Church, that with the exception of the Church of Sweden, it is the only reformed Church which has preserved the historic episcopate.

The Appointment of Bishops

While a bishop can only be consecrated by other bishops, his appointment can be made in very different ways. In the early years of the Church it was made by the clergy and laity of the diocese over which he was to preside ; there seems to have been general acclamation, rather than actual voting. Later on the appointment was made by the King, by the Pope, or by the Chapter of the Cathedral, and sometimes by all three acting together ; but the method did not affect the validity of the appointment, provided that afterwards the man who had been chosen was duly consecrated. Until he was consecrated, he had no spiritual authority—he could neither ordain nor confirm. His spiritual authority depended not upon his nomination, but upon his consecration. But Dom Gregory Dix rightly reminds us that " election by his own Church was as much a requirement, *sine qua non*, for the ' episcopate ' of a pre-Nicene bishop as his consecration by the hands of other bishops."[1]

Since the Reformation the Dean and Chapter of a Cathedral have been given by a licence from the King, commonly called the *congé d'élire*, the right to elect a new bishop when the see is vacant. But with the licence there is a letter containing the name chosen by the Crown and directing the Chapter to elect him. The name has been made public days or weeks beforehand, and the man selected has accepted the see and probably made all arrangements to move into it. The election by the Chapter is a foregone conclusion. If by any chance it should refuse to do so, its members would incur the penalties of *præmunire*, which include the confiscation of all property and imprisonment for an indefinite period. As the King acts on the advice of the Prime Minister, the appointment really rests with the latter, though Queen Victoria's letters show how powerful can be the influence of the Crown. In recent years great care has been taken by the Prime Minister in making these appointments, and almost invariably the Archbishop of Canterbury, and occasionally the Archbishop of York, has been consulted at some stage. Dr. Bell, in his " Life of Randall Davidson," by far the ablest and best-informed account of modern Church history of nearly half a century, thus describes the procedure : " The method which the Archbishop usually followed when a vacancy occurred was this. He would, without loss of time, speak or write to the Prime Minister about the particular bishopric. . . . If necessary the Archbishop would describe the general conditions of the diocese, or indicate the kind of bishop required at a particular juncture. As a rule, he would discuss both the diocese and the possible successors in conversation with the Prime Minister as well as in correspondence. And in all but quite exceptional cases, he would furnish the Prime Minister with some three or four names of people to be considered, and very rarely concentrating the whole of his strength on a single person. He would also make his own enquiries

[1] " The Apostolic Ministry." p. 296

from various sources as to names which might have been independently suggested to the Prime Minister, whether for his
own or the Prime Minister's guidance. . . . The two general
impressions left on the mind, after reading the extensive correspondence and memoranda concerning this quarter of a century
are, first, that though like other human beings they might not
succeed, Prime Minister and Archbishop both did their very
best to find the most suitable men for the Bench of Bishops :
and second, that Archbishop Davidson exercised a predominating
influence upon the character of that Bench."[1]   The Archbishop
always insisted on the Prime Minister's responsibility for these
nominations, but he wrote : " The Sovereign has always taken
a rather more independent position of personal ' say ' with
regard to ecclesiastical appointments than with regard to other
appointments."[2]

Even those who are most opposed to the present method
recognise that as long as the Church is established the Crown
must have a decisive voice in the choice of its bishops ; and
the Church should be grateful to successive Prime Ministers
for the trouble and care they have taken in the search for suitable
men.   Appointment by the Crown has some advantages ;   it
has done much to make the bishops representative of the
ordinary Churchman, while it has found places on the Bench
for men like Frederick Temple and Charles Gore who would
have had little or no chance of election if the choice had been
left to a purely clerical assembly.   It has avoided the wire-
pulling and canvassing, and the falling back on a third and weaker
nominee, in default of agreement over two stronger candidates,
a situation not infrequent when the clergy and laity have the right
of election.   But whatever merits belong to the present procedure
it is open to serious objection both in principle and in practice.

In principle it is impossible to defend the appointment of the
chief spiritual officers of the Church by a layman who may be
neither a Churchman nor even a Christian.   He may do his best,
but it is hard for him to have either the knowledge or the interest
of a man who is a member of the Church and has its welfare
naturally and deeply at heart.   Occupied with more engrossing
tasks, and with many demands on his time, he may take little
interest in the vacancy and give only casual consideration to the
names suggested for it.   There is also the danger that political

[1] Vol. II, p. 1337.   [2] Ibid., p. 1252.

factors may have undue weight. In the 18th century bishops were openly chosen so that by their votes in the House of Lords they might support the Whig Government. Dr. Bell mentions that some of Mr. Ramsay Macdonald's " colleagues in the Labour Party were at first perturbed because he did not appoint clergy who had served the Labour Party in their parishes."[1] With the tendency towards a Totalitarian State there will be the expectation that the Established Church ought to reflect and reproduce the opinions of the party in power and that it should be an agency for the promotion of the views which the State desires to impress upon its citizens.

Nor is all danger of unsuitable appointments removed by the fact that it is now the habit of the Prime Minister to consult the Archbishops. There is no guarantee that in the future the Archbishops will always be asked for advice, and that this will be taken. Archbishop Davidson used to say of Sir Henry Campbell Bannerman " that no one more constantly sought his advice and more seldom took it."[2] And even if in future the Archbishops' advice should always be asked and accepted it by no means follows that the results would always be satisfactory. The danger is not so much that the Archbishops will attempt to secure or to exclude the men of any one particular party— they will be most anxious to avoid this kind of partiality—but they are more likely to hesitate over recommending men who have the reputation of being " difficult " and who prefer to work as individuals rather than as members of a team. The very natural desire for harmony and agreement in Convocation and at Bishops' Meetings may sometimes exclude men who have gifts of leadership and initiative but who are inclined to plough lonely furrows of their own.

It is difficult to find a remedy short of Disestablishment. Most of the proposals which have been made to modify or temper the present system either only touch the fringe of the subject or are unlikely to be accepted. A Measure was introduced in the Church Assembly for the abolition of the penalties of *præmunire* which might fall on a Chapter which refused to elect the man nominated by the Crown. It is hard to believe either that a Chapter would refrain from doing its duty for fear of these penalties, or that they would be inflicted if the Chapter proved

[1] Vol. II, p. 1252.
[2] Ibid., p. 1239.

obdurate. The State would probably refuse to present the Chapter with the crown of martyrdom and would immediately make the appointment by Letters Patent. The well-intentioned proposal that a formal committee should be brought into existence to advise and help the Prime Minister or the Archbishop has found favour with neither. And it has been rightly pointed out that informal and confidential communication might easily be hindered by such a committee, unless its members knew how to keep their lips closed on subjects of special interest to so many. A leakage from the committee would raise hopes among individuals which might never be fulfilled ; and the known or suspected rejection of its advice might at the outset of his work prejudice a new bishop whose nomination it had neither recommended nor even discussed. The best safeguard is public opinion, which would criticise a series of unsuitable appointments and would probably resent the subordination of spiritual means to political ends. It must be remembered that the Prime Minister's choice is limited to those who have already been accepted and ordained by the Church, and that in the last resort the Chapter could refuse to elect and the Archbishops to consecrate. There are three minor reforms which would do something to ease the present position. The Archbishops should be consulted by right and not by courtesy before a nomination is made. The Dean and Chapter should on a vacancy be given an opportunity of expressing to the Crown their views of the special needs of the diocese. And before the nomination is made public the Dean and Chapter should be confidentially informed of the name proposed and asked if they wish to make any comments on it.

The Work and Office of a Bishop

(1.) The bishop is first and foremost the pastor of the flock committed to his care by the great Shepherd of the sheep. To be this he must both know and care for his sheep. The diocese is not to be to him a large administrative machine which he must control, but a fellowship of parishes, the clergy and laity of which he must do his utmost to shepherd.

He will exercise his work as pastor in the choice and ordination of fit men to take their place as the under shepherds of the Lord's flock. Bishop Thorold used to say that this was the most

G

responsible of all the duties resting upon a bishop. At one time there was considerable slackness both in the choice of candidates and in their actual ordination. The candidates were summoned to the palace a day or two before the Ordination and were accepted or rejected. That however they were not always accepted is clear by an indignant letter by the poet Keats on the Bishop of Lincoln of that day postponing the ordination of one of his friends " There is something so nauseous in self-willed yawning impudence in the shape of conscience—it sinks the Bishop of Lincoln into a smashed frog putrifying : that a rebel against common decency should escape the Pillory ! That a mitre should cover a man guilty of the most coxcombical, tyrannical and indolent impertinence ! "[1] Even to-day bishops receive vigorous remonstrances from the friends and the prospective incumbents of ordinands who have failed to pass the necessary examinations. But great care is almost invariably taken over the training and preparation of the candidates. The bishop is helped by Selection and Ordination Committees and by his Examining Chaplains, but the final decision rests upon him and it is he who must lay down the conditions for Ordination. The responsibility of Ordination is his alone and he can delegate it to no one else. In a large diocese where there are year by year many ordinands the bishop has a wonderful opportunity of exercising his pastoral care over the men he has ordained in the first and critical years of their ministry.

Only second to Ordination the bishop has in Confirmation a wide field for pastoral work. The importance of Confirmation has not always been recognised. In the Middle Ages the children were brought to the bishop whenever he happened to be in the neighbourhood so that he might lay his hands upon them. There could have been little if any preparation. When Wolsey at last visited his archbishopric we are told he confirmed children in St. Oswald's Abbey from eight o'clock of the morning until noon and then again from one to four. On the next day as he was riding towards York he confirmed another two hundred children who were waiting for him by the wayside. In the early part of the last century large Confirmations were held in the central churches of a diocese, often in the church itself there was much noise and confusion, and outside a holiday-making crowd of relatives and friends made uproar. When

[1] " The Letters of John Keats," edited by M. B. Forman, p. 59.

Bishop Wilberforce first came to the diocese of Winchester he had frequently to rebuke rowdiness and disturbance in the churches during the actual Confirmation. Now it is generally recognised how important the occasion of Confirmation should be. It is the completion of baptism, when the child renews the promises and vows which were then made in his name, and he receives the Gift of God to strengthen and help him on the threshold of youth. By his Confirmation he becomes a full member of the Church, entitled to receive Communion. The bishop has thus a great opportunity in speaking to these young members of his flock at a most critical stage in their lives. It is possibly the only occasion when most of them come into this direct personal contact with their bishop. Now in every diocese Confirmations are frequent and regular, and in almost every church one is arranged at set intervals.

Increasingly of recent years bishops have used the Institution of new incumbents as occasions for pastoral visits to parishes. An Institution at one time was commonly treated more as a legal formality than as a spiritual rite. When I was first ordained I knew old men who had been Instituted in a study, in the office of a legal secretary, or even in the waiting-room of a railway station. Sometimes the Institution now takes place privately in the bishop's chapel, while the Induction afterwards is performed publicly by the archdeacon. But when the bishop himself can take it in the parish church he can speak to the parishioners of the ideals which the new incumbent should always have before him, of the meaning of the service with its solemn declarations and oaths, of the responsibility of the cure of souls, of the duties of the parishioners, and sometimes of the special problems of that particular parish. Often the deed of Institution which is read for all to hear closes with the words "Receive your cure and ours," an excellent summary of the pastoral relationship of the bishop to the incumbent and the parish.

In addition to Confirmation and Institution there are the visits which the bishop pays to the parishes for preaching or for a private call on the incumbent. These go on week after week throughout the year. But happy indeed is the bishop if conditions allow him to walk through part of his diocese. Wearing his cassock, holding a pastoral staff, accompanied by his chaplain he visits parish after parish in the deanery. Usually there is an early morning celebration of the Holy Communion in the parish where he has slept the previous night and the rest of the day is spent in walking by lanes and footpaths to farms, hamlets and villages : talking to the woodcutters, ploughmen and others he may meet on the way, calling on some of the aged and sick to give them his blessing, paying brief visits to the village school, and holding open air services in the shade of a tree, near the war memorial, by the cross roads, or on the village green. Usually a number of the parishioners walk with him some of the way, and often farmers and cottagers come out to speak to him. The informality of a walk like this helps to break down reserve, enables the bishop both to know many people whom otherwise he would never have met and to penetrate to the more remote corners of his diocese. A few days spent in this way twice a year are some of the happiest pastoral experiences I have ever had.

The teaching ministry is an essential part of the pastoral duties of a bishop. Great prominence is given to this in the Archbishop's charge to him at the delivery of the Bible at his consecration " Give heed unto reading, exhortation and doctrine. Think upon the things contained in this Book." In primitive days it was widely recognised that the bishop should preach, and at the Eucharist described by Justin Martyr it is the President who gives the address. Many bishops have carried out this duty by the writing of learned books in defence of the Christian faith and in exposition of the Scriptures or the doctrine of the Church of England. The names of Lightfoot, Westcott, Gore, Headlam and Temple naturally rise to our minds when we think of the learned bishops, though Lightfoot and Westcott finished the more important of their books before they went to Durham. The pressure of a modern bishop's life does not give him much time either for deep thought or for writing. The majority of bishops to-day carry out their responsibility for exhortation by preaching, by pastoral letters and by occasional charges. Possibly episcopal utterances would carry more weight if they were less frequent, but " my people would have it so," and clergy and laity expect their bishop to exhort them without ceasing.

(2.) The bishop is also, as the name episcopal implies, the overseer of his diocese. The word diocese comes from the Greek "διοίκησις," which means administration, which in turn is derived from a word meaning " to keep house." It was originally employed to indicate large administrative districts over which a magistrate or judge had jurisdiction. At one time the Roman Empire was divided into twelve such districts or dioceses. Then the term had no ecclesiastical significance : but in the ninth century it was used for the areas presided over by a Metropolitan or Archbishop : when these were presently divided the name was transferred to the smaller district over which a bishop had jurisdiction.

If the bishop is to fulfil his duty as overseer two conditions are necessary. He must spend most of the year in his diocese and the diocese must not be of such vast size as to make impossible personal knowledge of its clergy and parishes. For many centuries a large number of the English bishops were absent for the greater part of the year from their sees and were occupied with political work. In the Middle Ages the bishops were often kept in close attendance on the King and his Court, they were his ministers and agents of state. Bishop Fox had never visited two of his dioceses, Exeter and Bath and Wells, it was as an old man of seventy that he came to Winchester to make his soul and to care for the souls whose bodies he pathetically admitted he had never seen. Wolsey never came to his diocese of Winchester and only went to York[1] when he was in disgrace. In the eighteenth century most of the bishops spent six months or more each year at their London houses, so as to be able to attend regularly the House of Lords. It was in the middle of the nineteenth century that a new conception of episcopal work arose. This was largely due to Bishop Samuel Wilberforce, who was successively Bishop of Oxford and of Winchester. He was himself a statesman bishop and took an active part in public affairs and in the debates of Parliament, but he regarded his duties in the diocese as of primary importance. One evening at Farnham Castle during the Ember Days previous to my Ordination to the Diaconate, Bishop Randall Davidson pointed out to me a portrait of Bishop Wilberforce with the remark " That is the man who did more than anyone else to change the whole conception of episcopal life and work, what bishops do to-day is largely the result of his example." His biographer says " the idea of Episcopacy with which Bishop Wilberforce set out, and which through life he consistently illustrated was

[1] He never reached the city of York, but was arrested a few miles south of it, at his house at Cawood.

essentially his own. According to him the bishop was to be as much the mainspring of all spiritual and religious energy in his diocese as a parochial clergyman is bound to be in his parish. It was the bishop's duty to supply not merely advice and counsel to his clergy, but also that momentum, which the sense of real supervision, however kindly and sympathising, always communicates to the mind and energy of the person supervised. It was his to care for the diocese as a whole, to learn for himself where needs existed, to take the necessary steps for supplying those needs, and to take care also that it was known he so acted, and that he was at all times not only accessible to all men, but also ready personally to investigate on the spot any case that was brought before him."[1] His example of ceaseless energy in travelling from place to place in his large diocese, seeing things for himself, encouraging and rebuking as the case might need, has been followed by many others. Bishop Thorold of Rochester and Winchester was a very different person, but his ideals of oversight were the same. When he came to Rochester he found it was a vast diocese, including South London, with no natural centre of unity " therefore the Bishop resolved himself to become its centre. Everything should revolve round him : everywhere his personal influence should be felt. To do this he must make himself a familiar figure throughout the cities and villages, by preaching, by speaking, by continual travelling, by willingly taking his part in all the important events, religious or secular, to which he might be invited."[2] Where in the past the visit of a bishop to a parish was an exceptional and rare event, now most bishops aim at visiting from time to time all their parishes. In this way they gain for themselves first-hand knowledge of their conditions, instead of relying solely on the reports of others.

Sometimes however the size of the diocese is so great that it is impossible for the most energetic of bishops to have personal knowledge of all its parishes. A diocese is too large when the bishop is unable to know his clergy and when the clergy are unable to meet together from time to time for prayer and counsel at some common centre. Many of the excessively large dioceses have been divided. In the enthusiasm for the creation of new dioceses mistakes were occasionally made and the new dioceses were sometimes so small that experience has shown they afford

[1] " Life of Bishop Wilberforce," Vol. I, p. 343.
[2] " Life of Bishop Thorold," p. 75.

insufficient scope for their bishop and unwisely limit the movement of the clergy. An unduly small diocese is an expensive
luxury for it needs all the machinery required by a diocese three
times its size. It must have its bishop with an endowment of
at least £3,000 a year, its dean or provost, its director of
Education, its archdeacon, its Sunday School organiser, its
missioner and various other paid organisers and secretaries!
It has numerous committees with a very limited number of
clergy and laity who can serve on them, and who loyally, if
reluctantly, hasten from one committee to another. The diocesan
machinery becomes top-heavy, and the clergy soon groan under
the thorough and conscientious oversight of a host of diocesan
officials. And while both dignitaries and inferior clergy are
loyal to their diocese the opinion is often heard from them that it
might have been wiser to have made its boundaries more extensive. And though the bishop through his more intimate
knowledge of his small diocese is alive both to the strength and
the weakness of his incumbents he finds that his opportunities
of rewarding the good worker, of changing the parish of the
man who has become tired and stale, and of giving another
chance to the failure, are most regrettably small. A diocese
of about 300 parishes ought not to be too large to prevent the
bishop knowing his clergy and leading laity, or to hinder the
clergy and laity from meeting conveniently together: and if
within the diocese there are both town and country parishes it
ought to be possible to secure the healthy circulation of the
clergy throughout it.

But whether the diocese is large or small the bishop is responsible for its oversight. He holds periodical visitations
either personally or through his chancellor. He has to make
inquiries about any clergyman who desires to officiate within
his diocese, and if the replies are satisfactory to grant him annual
permission or formal licence. He has to scrutinise the appointments which are made to benefices before he promises institution.
He has to spend much thought and time in finding men to fill
vacant parishes which belong to his official patronage: this is
one of the most difficult and responsible of his duties. He has
to preside at many meetings and committees. He has many
interviews with the clergy and the laity on special problems.
Above all he has a large correspondence which includes letters
of every sort and kind, some with requests for advice, a still

larger number offering advice, some complaining about incidents
in their parish, some giving information about parochial progress
or disappointments, some asking about prospective curates,
some with begging appeals, some enclosing forms to sign or
counter-sign. There are letters which are abusive, letters of
great length from cranks, letters which have come direct from
some mental institution, letters with bitter complaints about the
Church, its bishops and its clergy, and a fair number of anony-
mous letters which are promptly consigned to the waste-paper
basket. Day by day these letters pour in, especially when the
diocese is large and urban ; and the bishop never knows what
difficult and unexpected problem may come to him in the morning
post.

As the overseer the bishop must minister discipline. At his
Consecration he promised " to correct and punish such as be
unquiet and disobedient " within his diocese according as he
has been given authority by " God's Word and by the Ordinance of the Realm." He was exhorted by the Archbishop to
" Be so merciful that you be not remiss : so minister discipline
that you forget not mercy." Over the laity he has now little
disciplinary power, though he may order or approve of ex-
communication where the communicant is an " open and
notorious evil liver," or persists in " malice and hatred " towards
his neighbour. Over the clergy he has much more direct
authority, at their Ordination they promised that they would
reverently obey the Ordinary, following with a glad mind and
will his godly admonitions and submitting themselves to his
godly judgements. At their Ordination, licensing and institution
they confirmed this promise by the Oath of Canonical Obedience
when they swore that they would obey their bishop in all things
lawful and honest.

There are three classes of cases in which the bishop must
exercise discipline over his clergy. There are from time to
time men who have committed some grave moral offence.
When the criminal or divorce courts have already passed judgement, the bishop in certain cases can act at once upon this, formally depriving the offender of any ecclesiastical post he may
hold. Sometimes the bishop himself has to investigate serious
charges made against one of his clergy. If necessary he must
take action against him in his Court, and if found guilty he can
either censure him, deprive him of his work, or in very grave

cases, with the consent of the Archbishop of the Province, unfrock him. Usually the offender is penitent and ready to make amends for the wrong he has done, and so is prepared to accept judgement without any public hearing of his case. These moral offences cause more pain and anxiety to a bishop than any other problem. They mean scandal in the parish which it may take years to live down, and often great mental suffering and sometimes straitened circumstances for those who are nearest to the offending priest.

Next there are the cases of those who are negligent in the performance of their duties.[1] Of these there are usually a few in every diocese. Moral persuasion, admonition and censure are the chief means which the bishop can use for their discipline. Unfortunately this type of man is rarely ready to allow he is in the wrong. So the scandal will continue, and one negligent incumbent does harm far and wide to the good name of the Church. The bishop knows the facts, deplores them as strongly as any of the parishioners, but is powerless to take effective action.

Thirdly there are those who have offended against the doctrine of the Church and have broken its law of public worship. In the great majority of cases the bishop's regulations are accepted, however much it may cost the incumbent to give up some rite or ceremony to which he attaches importance. But there are groups of priests or individuals who refuse to accept the bishop's directions, they are conscientiously convinced that they are right in resisting him, they will not admit that his commands are in their special cases lawful and honest or that his admonitions are " godly," and in justification of their attitude they quote occasions in the past when the bishops made mistaken demands for the abandonment of practices now regarded as lawful. If the bishop appeals to the Courts he will find that the clergy in question refuse to recognise their authority, as they hold that even the Courts which are undoubtedly spiritual are bound by previous decisions of the Judicial Committee of the Privy Council. Under the guise of interpreting the law they fear that the State Court will change it. Without entering now into the merits of this position it is plain that judgements on spiritual matters cannot be enforced if large numbers of those most affected deny their moral validity. The Royal Commission

[1] *Vide*, p. 154.

on Ecclesiastical Discipline reported that " A court dealing with matters of conscience and religion must, above all other, rest on moral authority if its judgements are to be effective. As thousands of clergy with strong lay support refuse to recognise the jurisdiction of the Judicial Committee, its judgements cannot possibly be enforced."[1] Any attempt to enforce them would result in disobedience followed by imprisonment for contempt of court. Neither Church nor public opinion would tolerate the imprisonment of good and hard working men on account of their doctrinal views or practices in worship.

Various suggestions have been made for the reform of the Church Courts. One solution would be that all parties should agree to abide by the decisions of the strictly ecclesiastical courts without further appeal. But there is no sign that either party in an ecclesiastical suit would thus pledge themselves in advance. Numerous schemes for new Church Courts have been advocated, but there is very slight possibility that any of these would be accepted by Parliament. The legal profession is strongly represented in the Houses and its members find it hard to understand why the clergy should refuse to submit their cases to a Court which throughout the world is famous for its wisdom and impartiality. And even if a reformed Court of Appeal was set up, it would still have to administer laws made over 300 years ago, for it would be bound by an unrevised Prayer Book and Canons.

The bishop must therefore at present abandon all thought of prosecution. He must rely on his spiritual powers. He must reason with the offender and do his best to persuade him. The possibility that he may be misinterpreting in an arbitrary fashion the law of the Church can only be overcome if he associates with himself the great body of the clergy of his diocese. In a grave and difficult case where large principles are involved he should ask for the advice of the clergy in synod, giving the offender and his friends every chance of stating fully their side. If the bishop is supported by the synod, he should call upon the incumbent to obey him in accordance with his oath of Canonical Obedience. Then it will be plain to all that the bishop is expressing not his own personal opinion, but the mind of the Church. The incumbent must of course obey his conscience, and rather than act against it should resign. To retain his

[1] P. 67.

office and its emoluments while breaking the conditions under which they were granted to him cannot be justified by any standard of professional or personal honour. If there should be cases when an incumbent refuses either to obey or to resign, the bishop should then publicly censure him as a man who has deliberately broken his oath, and if he sees fit he can follow this up by inhibiting him from officiating outside his own parish. His defiance may continue, but it is far better that there should be occasional disobedience on the part of an individual rather than prosecution in Courts which the recalcitrant refuses to accept and which may give him unnecessary notoriety. His disobedience will be condemned by the corporate opinion of the clergy and laity of the diocese. In the long run the moral effect of this will be more powerful than any sentence inflicted by the Courts as at present constituted.

The Bishop and his Synod

In many English dioceses regular meetings of the Synod of the Clergy were held in the years between the two wars. In the Middle Ages the bishop used the synod as part of his visitation, but it does not appear to have been more than an occasional, and somewhat formal, gathering, in which he made known his regulations. In his " Reformatio " Cranmer intended that the bishop should hold a synod every year " to discuss all matters appertaining to the profit and well being of the people of God." But the first synod held in England for many centuries was that summoned by Bishop Phillpotts of Exeter in 1851. The revival of the synod as a means of church government has been approved by the Upper House of the Canterbury Convocation which, in 1922, resolved " that it is desirable that in this Province diocesan synods of clergy should be summoned by diocesan bishops for the purpose of mutual consultation on matters concerning faith, worship, morals, discipline and the pastoral office."

In overseas provinces of the Anglican Communion the synod is a regular and, sometimes, an essential part of the administrative machinery. But the term " synod " as used overseas often describes meetings not of the bishop and clergy only, but of the bishops, clergy and laity. They correspond much more to our diocesan conferences. The long establishment and the legal position of the diocesan conference in England has made it more difficult to revive the sacred synod, which would not include the laity.

The value of the synod is that it gives the bishop and the clergy opportunities of consulting together about their special spiritual and pastoral responsibilities. The bishop can speak directly and plainly to his clergy, and they can speak with equal frankness to him without the presence either of the laity or of the press. Such conference leads to the formation of a common mind on many matters which affect their work. In Southwark I had fairly frequent synods. They were held in the cathedral and attended by almost all the clergy. Controversial matters were discussed, especially during the time of Prayer Book revision. I found these meetings of great value. They helped me to know the mind of the clergy, while they valued the opportunity of expressing their views. I consulted them about various regulations before I issued them, and when they were published I was able to state that they came from the bishop "after consultation with the clergy." In the Winchester diocese it was more difficult to hold regular synods; I only summoned two, and I cannot pretend that there was much enthusiasm for them. Distances between the parishes made frequent meetings difficult. In York the difficulties are even greater, for the diocese covers a very large area, and many of the parishes are remote both from one another and from the centre, and during the war years the problem of providing hospitality for large numbers made it impossible to call together a synod.

Three conditions must be observed if these synods are to be of any value. First, it must be recognised that there is only one effective vote, and that is the vote of the diocesan bishop. This may seem to be a most undemocratic statement, but it is as well to be clear at the outset that the sacred synod consisting of the bishop and clergy meets only in an advisory capacity. It has no power to legislate or to administer. But this does not mean that the synod may not have great influence on diocesan decisions and opinion. The rulings of the bishop are strengthened when it is felt that they are not those of an autocratic prelate, but of a Father in God who has considered the advice of his family. On the other hand if the opinion of the synod is contrary to the course of action which he proposed, if he is wise he will think twice or thrice before he continues in the path he has mapped out. The general mind of the clergy, apart from the opinion of various groups in it, is usually sound and wise; but when all this has been said the bishop has the first and last word.

Secondly the discussion must be absolutely frank. The bishop must give dissentients and minorities every opportunity of expressing their point of view. No one should fear that he might be regarded as disloyal if his opinions prove to be unpopular. It ought to be possible for the most controversial subjects to be discussed freely between men of differing views. This is a safeguard against groups of clergy meeting solely with those whose views they share, and then imagining that they are representing the opinion of the whole Church.

And, most important of all, the synod should meet in an atmosphere of devotion. It should open with the Holy Communion. It is heartening to see men of different views kneeling side by side to receive the sacrament of unity. Every session should begin with the invocation of the Holy Spirit, and close with prayer and thanksgiving. It is a real gain if the synod can be held in the cathedral or some other church; this helps to give the right atmosphere.

As we pass out of the dislocation and unsettlement caused by the war it should be possible for synods gradually to become a regular part of the life of a diocese.

Central Claims

Unfortunately the bishop is unable to spend all his time in his diocese. He is consecrated to " the whole Church of God," and there are many demands on his time which come from outside his diocese. If he is one of the bishops who has a seat in the House of Lords, even if he does not regularly attend its sittings, twice a year he will have to spend a week in London so as to read prayers. Three times a year he must attend the Bishops' meetings at Lambeth. Three times a year there are the meetings of the Church Assembly. Twice a year there are the meetings of Convocation. There are also meetings of the Ecclesiastical Commissioners and of Queen Anne's Bounty which sometimes he must attend in the interests of his diocese. And, in addition, he is probably a member of various committees and sub-committees which seem to multiply every year. The time taken up by these central engagements is not so serious to those who live in or near London ; but for the bishop who lives in a distant diocese, the travelling increases the time during which he has to be absent. And, apart from these official engagements, there are societies, great and small, which expect some bishops to attend their annual meetings, and from time to time there are conferences at which some of the bishops feel bound to be present. There is no difficulty in refusing invitations to societies and conferences of an unofficial nature, but duty demands attendance at most of the more official meetings. The claims made by central work unavoidably interfere with the claims of the diocese ; there is a danger that they may become almost an intolerable burden. While the mediæval bishop was absent from his diocese through the claims of the Court, and the eighteenth-century bishop through the time he had to give to the House of Lords, the modern bishop is frequently called away by the demands of administration which is fast becoming over-centralised. He is in a state of perpetual tension between the demands of the centre and of his own diocese. The time has come when a halt should be called to the number of central meetings which a diocesan is expected to attend. But for the archbishops I see no hope of any reprieve !

The Archbishop of Canterbury

Among the archbishops and bishops of the Anglican Communion the Archbishop of Canterbury holds a special place. His cathedral is the Mother Church. He presides over the Lambeth Conference, and in Great Britain he takes precedence over any other subject. In the Middle Ages there were frequent disputes between the Archbishops of Canterbury and York. On one occasion there was bloodshed when their retainers disputed over the precedence to be granted to their respective masters, and the Archbishop of York sent a piteous letter to the Pope complaining that an official of Canterbury with " Satan and his satellites " had made a vicious attack upon him, and dashed the primatial cross to pieces. On another occasion there was an undignified scene when the Archbishop of Canterbury, arriving first, took the chair, and the Archbishop of York on his arrival, not to be outdone, seated himself upon his knees! Eventually the Pope decided that the Archbishop of Canterbury should have the title of " Primate of All England," while the Archbishop of York had that of " Primate of England." And while the former might carry his cross anywhere in England, the latter had this right confined to the north, and must make an offering of gold to the shrine of St. Thomas of Canterbury if he had his cross in the Southern Province. It is said that at some great service in Winchester Cathedral in connection with the College, the two Archbishops were present and had their crosses borne in front of them. As they approached the sanctuary, Benson, then Archbishop of Canterbury, whispered to the Archbishop of York : " Where is your golden offering ? " And the answer came back : " Where is your shrine ? "

The position of the Archbishop of Canterbury has greatly increased in importance since the Middle Ages. Not only did he inherit some of the privileges of his pre-Reformation predecessors who were Papal Legates, and retains the rights of conferring degrees, and of granting dispensations for pluralities ; but through living at Lambeth, the Archbishop is close at hand to be consulted by all who hold responsible positions in Church and State. With the increasing centralisation of the work of the Church he is in daily contact with those who are engaged in it. With the growth of the Anglican Communion, it is to the Archbishop of Canterbury that the overseas bishops turn naturally for advice on their many problems. The work at Lambeth is now incessant, but his staff has not grown with the ever-increasing duties of the Archbishop. He is now in the position of a Prime Minister who is also the head of a Ministry, but who is without a secretariat ; and whose work is continuous, without the intervals of relief from responsibility enjoyed by an ex-minister while he is in opposition. The Archbishop has not only to give the final decision on all manner of problems which come to him week by week, but he is also immersed in a mass of detailed administration involving the preparation of memoranda, many interviews, and heavy correspondence. It is necessary that the Archbishop should be given a staff more adequate to the claims made upon him. He should have experts close at hand whom he could consult at any time, and a sufficiently large staff of competent and experienced men to whom, with complete confidence, he could delegate some of the work which now he has to deal with personally. Unless this is done, successive Archbishops will break down under a strain which is fast becoming intolerable.

Bishops Suffragan

In one sense all diocesan bishops are suffragans, for they are summoned by the Archbishop of their Province to give their suffrages in Convocation. But the term is usually employed to describe bishops appointed under an Act of the Reign of Henry VIII to assist diocesans in their work. They are given a territorial title. They have all the spiritual powers of any other bishop, but they can exercise them only under a Commission granted by the bishop of the diocese. When a diocesan requires the help of a suffragan he sends, through the Archbishop of his Province to the Crown, two names as suitable persons to be appointed, and the first of the names is almost invariably selected.

It is impossible for any diocesan to speak too gratefully and warmly of the invaluable and unselfish assistance given to him by his suffragan or suffragans. The oversight and pastoral work of the larger dioceses would be quite impossible if much of the work and many of the responsibilities which would otherwise fall upon the diocesan were not delegated by him to his suffragan. The administrative responsibility and the central claims naturally fall less upon them, and they are able to devote all their time to the work of the diocese. Sometimes unfortunately financial and other reasons make it necessary to unite the work of the suffragan with that of the archdeacon ; but this does not always prove completely satisfactory, for it is difficult to combine the administrative duties of the archdeacon with the pastoral and spiritual charge of the bishop ; and conflicts between duty to the diocese and the cathedral also arise when the suffragan holds a residentiary canonry. Makeshift arrangements of this nature are bound to continue while suffragan and archdeacon are inadequately paid, as often is the case to-day. Recently in many dioceses attempts have been made to help the suffragans in their official expenses, which are sometimes heavy. The Church Assembly has also passed a Measure providing them with a pension on retirement—a reform long overdue.

When the office of suffragan bishop was first revived, it was assumed that he would always remain a suffragan, and for some time it was generally accepted that he would not be appointed to a diocese of his own. But for several years past many suffragans have been given diocesan bishoprics. Nine of the bishops on the bench to-day once held suffraganships; this is only right and reasonable, for among the suffragans are to be found not only some of the most hard working and pastorally minded amongst the bishops, but men of ability with outstanding gifts of leadership. With some advantage suffragans might be more frequently translated to other suffragan sees when there appears to be no likelihood of their being appointed to a diocese. After a period of ten or fifteen years in the same diocese some might welcome a change of work and scene.

" The Bishops "

The bishop receives almost invariably the greatest kindness and consideration from the members of his diocese. He is always received with courtesy, and usually with friendliness. He feels that he is the Father-in-God of his people, and he has reason to believe that though his utterances, actions and appointments are often criticised the clergy know that he has their welfare at heart. But if this is true of the bishop in his diocese, it is not true of him as a member of the college of bishops. He is not consecrated only as the bishop of a particular diocese, but of the Church of God. He therefore shares responsibility with his brother bishops for their decisions. He is a member of Convocation, of the Church Assembly and takes part in the private meetings of bishops. He is one of " the bishops," who are subjected to perpetual criticism. If they make a joint utterance they will be told from many sides that it is injudicious, mischievous, and ill-advised. If they are silent they are told that they are dumb while the clergy and laity are eagerly looking for leadership. If they speak or if they are silent the cry will go up that they have lost a great opportunity. Churchmen of different opinions find themselves sometimes united in deploring the " weakness " and " cowardice " of their leaders : they doubt their soundness in the faith, they are suspicious of their motives, and they condemn both their public acts and utterances. Reasonable criticism is always welcomed by sensible men ; the bishops do not ask to be exempt from this, often it has helped and informed them. But persistent criticism deteriorates into the habit of nagging, which is bad both for the critic and the criticised. It undermines confidence and weakens resolve, and those outside the Church are not attracted to join it when they find its own members are ready to attack and to abuse the leaders they are supposed to trust.

It is worth while examining this criticism in some detail to see if behind it there are causes which justify it and which might be removed. With the exception of one brief period, when the seven bishops were sent to the Tower by James II, the bishops have never been popular in England : nor for that matter do they appear to have been on the Continent. Dante places some bishops in Paradise, but many more in Hell and Purgatory. In mediæval England they were criticised for their pomp, their avarice, and for their repeated absence from their dioceses. Many of them spent most of their time as ministers of the King. It is thought that the Bishop of Winchester has the Channel Islands in his diocese because at one time as Chancellor of England he was responsible for the Fleet ! In the age of Wycliffe " we have the opinion of their contemporaries that worldliness was their characteristic and avarice their vice. They were not accused, even by those whom they persecuted, of atrocious crime or of sinful life. Respectability compassed them about. They were many of them hard working men, but they worked hard, not at the visitation of their dioceses and the supervision of their Spiritual Courts, but at the administration of the country and at the royal finance and diplomacy."[1]

In the eighteenth century the bishops were unpopular for the same reason. They were accused of state and great wealth and frequent absence from their dioceses. Like their mediæval dredecessors they were in London for a considerable part of the year on public business, but instead of holding responsible administrative posts as the King's officers, they were content with the humble duty of supporting by their vote the Government which had appointed them. In the much smaller House of Lords of that day the episcopal vote was of considerable importance, twice Walpole's Government was saved from defeat

[1] " England in the Age of Wycliffe," by G. M. Trevelyan, p. 106 (1920 impression).

by the votes of twenty-four bishops. There were notable exceptions both for learning and piety among the Georgian bishops, but the usual qualification for a bishopric was "political service or the support of powerful patrons in the Whig service."[1] Dr. Johnson's opinion of the bishops was characteristic of many. As a devout Churchman he paid great deference to them for their office; we read that his bow to an archbishop was "such a studied elaboration of homage, such an extension of limb, such a flexion of body, as have seldom or ever been equalled," but Boswell records his remark: "No man can now be made a bishop for his learning and piety; his only chance for promotion is his being connected with somebody who has parliamentary interest."

In the early part of the nineteenth century the bishops were criticised from many sides. The populace disliked them for their political views, their votes against Reform caused violent outcry and the burning of a bishop's palace. They were regarded as an instrument of class government. "Of the bishops eleven in 1815 were of noble birth; ten had been tutors or schoolmasters to a prince or a duke or a statesman."[2] They were attacked for their wealth which contrasted with the poverty of so many of the inferior clergy. "The impression left on the vulgar mind by the Church at the time of the first Reform Bill, was that prelates and pluralists drank port and hunted the fox, while poor curates worked and starved."[3] Devout Churchmen looked upon their bishops as worldly and unspiritual with no conception of the religious meaning of their high office. Later in the century their attitude towards the Oxford Movement brought on them attacks from two different sides. The majority of the bishops misunderstood its aims, and were fearful of its methods. Often they denounced and condemned where they should have supported and sympathised. Individual bishops sometimes acted with flagrant unfairness towards those they regarded as Romanists in their views and practice: they forbade what was really permitted, and even enjoined, by the Prayer Book: and ordered the disuse of ornaments and vestments, the legitimacy of which is now generally accepted. Much of the suspicion with which even now many of the Anglo-Catholics

[1] "The Whig Supremacy," by Basil Williams, p. 75.
[2] "The Age of the Chartists," by J. Hammond p. 219.
[3] "British History in the Nineteenth Century," by G. M. Trevelyan, p. 282.

regard the bishops as a body is an unhappy legacy from those days. On the other hand the laity who in their hearts dislike and fear Rome were greatly alarmed at the introduction of unfamiliar ceremonies and rites into their parish churches. Changes were frequently made in the accustomed order of the services without any previous explanation. The laity protested vehemently, and when the bishops refused to take action they denounced them for their failure to suppress acts which they regarded as illegal, and a movement which they felt was dangerous. It is forgotten sometimes by the Anglo-Catholics how often individual bishops withstood popular clamour and refused to forbid practices which they themselves disliked, but the legality of which they recognised. By so doing they earned from the laity a name for weakness and cowardice.

The bishops of later generations thus had an unfortunate reputation to live down. Their predecessors identified episcopacy with prelacy, and prelacy has never been popular in England. Some of the criticism directed against the bishops to-day is the result of ancient prejudice. Few if any now accuse them of laziness, political partizanship and avarice.

There are, however, five criticisms which are frequently heard. It is said that the bishops are so absorbed in administrative work that they are out of touch with their clergy : they lack unanimity in their pronouncements ; they give no leadership ; their incomes and houses are excessive ; and many of them are too old.

I have expressed above the opinion that there is a real danger that central and diocesan administration may encroach seriously upon the spiritual and pastoral duties of the bishop. It is, however, easy to exaggerate this. The valuable collection of essays recently issued under the title of " The Apostolic Ministry " gives the impression that since the beginning of the fourth century the bishop has deteriorated in a kind of Rake's Progress, from the simplicity of a liturgical and evangelistic minister, through wizardship, mediæval feudalism and eighteenth-century prelatism, into a " modern spiritual bureaucrat."[1] Possibly bishops themselves have given a mistaken idea of their work by complaining—as I admit I often do—of the amount of administration for which they must find time. But after all, when everything has been said, this usually occupies a com-

[1] P. 188.

paratively small proportion of the day. With the exception of the Church Assembly weeks, I can say without hesitation that month by month and year by year, by far the greater part of my time is occupied with spiritual and pastoral work : dealing with ordinands, institutions, confirmations, appointments to benefices and assistant curacies, interviews, visiting clergy and parishes, and the preparation and delivery of sermons and addresses. Compared with these duties, committees and money-raising take up little time. I believe this would be found to be the experience of the majority of the bishops. When a diocese has capable archdeacons and an efficient secretary to the Board of Finance the bishop is relieved of most of the administrative work.

The English diocesan bishops to-day are closer to their clergy than they have been for centuries. Neither in mediæval days, nor in the greater part of the period after the Reformation were the bishops in such personal relationship with them as they are now. I cannot recall any case in Trollope's novels where he describes a bishop visiting one of the parochial clergy. Now the bishop frequently visits the clergy and parishes of his diocese. Through synods, diocesan conferences, chapters and committees he consults the clergy and laity far more often than did his predecessors, even at the beginning of this century. The great majority of the bishops are to-day accessible to the clergy in a way they were not in the past, and they are ready to see and help them whenever they wish to consult them on some parochial or personal matter.

It is undeniable that there is occasional lack of unanimity among the bishops on certain questions of doctrine, worship and practical politics. This is inevitable if all Church parties are to be represented on the episcopal bench. A unanimous episcopal vote would be the result of the exclusion of all who held the views of a minority. As long as the Church of England is comprehensive there must be some variety of opinion among the bishops. The extent of this is often exaggerated. On all major issues on which the bishops lately have made pronouncements only a small minority among them have taken a different line.

Usually those who deplore lack of leadership are regretting that their own opinions have not been accepted by the bishops. The man who most energetically calls for leadership has already made up his mind as to the direction he wishes to go, and has no intention of taking any other route even if he is exhorted to do so by the whole bench of bishops. Occasionally when statesmen, politicians and others have failed to show the way out of some difficulty, irritation and disappointment express themselves in the demand that the bishops should say something. Archbishop Davidson used to comment that when people ask the Church to do something, it usually means they want the bishops to say something! But the bishops have no special qualifications to offer guidance on social and economic questions, if they attempt to do so it may soon be discovered that the blind are leading the blind. On religious and ethical problems the bishops have repeatedly given a lead. In the last quarter of a century they have summoned the nation to Repentance and Hope, to a Renewal of Religion, to the duty of missionary work, to home evangelisation : they have spoken plainly both collectively and individually on such great questions as disarmament, peace, worship, education, marriage, housing and unemployment. In our own days Archbishop William Temple stood out as a great religious and ethical leader. The pronouncements of the bishops have been often criticised, but the leadership is not less real because many dislike it and refuse to follow it.

Popular opinion both within and without the Church is more concerned with the large incomes and houses of the bishops. It is felt that they are inconsistent with the simplicity and poverty of many of the clergy ; and that the system of episcopal remuneration is extravagant as the money could be spent more profitably and usefully elsewhere. There is much to be said in support of these views, however unfairly they may be sometimes expressed. There are however two preliminary comments to be made on these criticisms. First there is to-day no extravagance or ostentation in the manner of life among the twentieth century diocesan bishops. Secondly, if their incomes are large, so are their expenses. Travelling, correspondence, secretarial help, necessary donations, hospitality to clergy and laity and, above all, the cost of a large house absorb most of the income when rates and taxes have been paid. Episcopal expenses are unavoidably greater than those of the clergy.

The heaviest expenditure which falls on a bishop is usually due to the large house in which he is expected to live. A bishop is bound to require a larger house than an incumbent, he must have an office in it for a secretary, for a mass of documents and correspondence, and possibly a room for a chaplain ; he should have a small chapel for many diocesan services, ordination retreats and occasional Confirmations : he must have sufficient rooms to be able to offer hospitality to those who come from some distance to see him and to those who have attended various meetings held in his house. At Southwark I had what my predecessors called an ideal bishop's house ; it was a modern house planned especially for a bishop, most conveniently arranged both for work and hospitality, not then expensive in upkeep, and in the centre of the diocese. At Winchester I had a charming Wren house, the surviving wing of a vast palace which was demolished in the eighteenth century, and a striking chapel which in its original form belonged to the old Norman Castle. But many bishops' houses are very large and most costly to maintain. My present house at Bishopthorpe is one of these. Rates, repairs, replacements and the indoor and out-door staff of servants and gardeners are a heavy and continuous drain on episcopal incomes. The increase in taxation and cost of living and the grave difficulty of obtaining domestic help will make it impossible for bishops to continue to live even in some of the smaller houses. But it is not so easy to dispose of them as is sometimes imagined. They have often the historical associations which would make many regret their loss to the Church ; their position close to the cathedral and their chapels would make it impossible to sell them without some restrictions on their use : and their size and arrangements would deter many purchasers. Nor will a Board of Finance always be ready to saddle itself with the upkeep of the palace as a house for diocesan purposes. And even if the house is sold it is very difficult at present to find alternative accommodation suitable for the bishop ; he must live somewhere, and in a house large enough for his special work.

Already in several dioceses the old palace has been given up for other uses and the bishop has moved to a smaller house. This is so in the cases of Newcastle, Salisbury, Ripon, Oxford : the great Castle at Farnham has been divided : other bishops are anxious to move and are only waiting until a suitable house elsewhere is available. Many of the new sees have comparatively small houses. This policy has been greatly helped by a measure of reform which deals with episcopal residences and incomes.

Under the Episcopal Residences and Incomes Measure of 1943 the Commissioners are able to take over both the official residence and income of a see on the application of the bishop. Part of the income is used for the upkeep of the house and grounds, or if they are sold, for the provision of alternative accommodation for the bishop, and for his official expenses, travelling, secretarial, chaplain and correspondence. The rest of the income is paid direct to the bishop ; out of this he pays income tax, rent to the Commissioners for the house, the wages of the indoor staff, hospitality (except the strictly official), subscriptions, donations, and personal expenses. In this way the income of the Archbishops of York has been dealt with : it removes misunderstanding over the size of the income, and it takes from the Archbishop incessant anxiety over the maintenance of a large rambling house on which a considerable sum of money has to be spent every year for necessary repairs. Other bishops have already taken advantage of this Measure. It is wrong that a man should either have to refuse a diocese because he has not the private means to meet the expenses of the house in which he is expected to live, or that he should be incessantly harassed by financial anxiety over the upkeep of a house far too large for his income.

It is highly probable that the increased cost of living and the impossibility of obtaining domestic help will lead within a comparatively short time to the abandonment of most of the old episcopal houses. There is little justification for retaining them when they can be used so rarely for hospitality. Some of them may be used for diocesan purposes or for retreat houses. When the building position becomes easier it is intended to divide Bishopthorpe : a suitable plan has been prepared, so that while the Archbishop lives in part of it, the greater part of it will be used for retreats and conferences. In these days of financial stringency it would not be right to spend large sums of Church money on the upkeep of episcopal residences which no longer serve the purposes for which they were originally intended. Notwithstanding the historical association and their charm, the time has come when many of them should be replaced by smaller houses and the nominal income of the bishop consequently reduced. This will not detract from the prestige of the bishop, for this should depend not upon his temporal circumstances, but on his spiritual office and personal character.

There is another criticism which is often heard, viz. that the bishops are as a body too old. The majority of the occupants of the Bench are usually well over sixty. There are occasionally men who are in possession of their full mental powers well into old age; but they should be more than counterbalanced by a much larger number of bishops who are comparatively young, or middle-aged. The older man has experience and wisdom, but he is inclined to be over-cautious, and he finds it difficult to enter into the outlook of those who belong to a much younger generation. An episcopal Bench which consisted largely of elderly men would tend to regard the administrative work of the Church as more important than the prophetic, and might be more kindly than vigorous, more fearful than courageous. Faced with new problems it would be perplexed and baffled, and would fall back on the watchwords and methods of a past generation. Some leavening of the bishops with younger men is of vital and immediate importance. Twenty years ago it was common for bishops to be appointed at a much younger age, sometimes in their early forties, but for some time past usually older men have been chosen to fill the vacancies; this has been the case in the State as well as in the Church and is partly due to the number of able men killed in the First World War.

Closely connected with this problem of the age of the bishops is the question as to whether there ought not to be a compulsory age of retirement. Stephen Gardiner told Pope Clement VII a " merry tale of the Bishop of Norwich's good heart, and being above fourscore years old, he would have a chamber devised near the ground, without any stairs, to lie in twenty years hence, when he knew well he should be somewhat feeble."[1] As far as I know there are no Anglican bishops of to-day who would look forward to retaining their sees well after the age of eighty! but there have been bishops who have delayed far too long their resignations, to the great damage of their dioceses and to the disadvantage of the whole Church. A hard and fast age for retirement would occasionally deprive the Church of men still capable of valuable work. Possibly, though it is very difficult to see in what way, some arrangement might be made for these exceptional individuals to be given a further spell of office. But some age limit should be fixed. No man is a safe and

[1] " Stephen Gardiner and the Tudor Reaction," by J. A. Mullen, p. 25.

impartial judge as to his own mental state. Others detect in him deterioration before he is himself conscious of it. Retention of bodily health does not necessarily mean that his mental powers are as strong as once they were. Physical health may even disguise from its possessor the approach of mental decay. Montaigne shrewdly remarked : " It is the body, which sometimes yieldeth first unto age : and other times the mind : and I have seene many, that have had their brains weakened before their stomache or legges. And forasmuch, as it is a disease, little or nothing sensible unto him that endureth it, and maketh no great shew, it is so much the more dangerous." The happier a man has been in his work the more reluctant he will be to lay it down. And the older he is the harder it is for him to remove from familiar surroundings. So when a compulsory age for retirement is fixed for the clergy a similar age should be laid down for the bishops. But until this has been decided upon those of us who are septuagenarians must be sternly on the watch against such decline in body or mind as might impair our powers of work : and as the human heart is very deceitful in judgements on itself we must be ready to listen to trusted friends should they tell us that the day has come when we shall best serve the Church by resignation.

But when all has been said in reply to current criticism on " the bishops," there still will be heard the complaint that they are not equal to their predecessors. They are compared unfavourably with great prelates of the past from Lanfranc and Anselm to Benson and Davidson. It is difficult for one of their number to estimate the justice of this verdict. It is true that on the Bench there are no longer to be found men like the giants of old, though if William Temple had lived he might have proved the greatest Archbishop the Church of England had ever possessed. I would, however, say that the standard of work, efficiency and pastoral zeal of the bishops is probably as high as it ever has been. Not all the bishops at any one time have ever been men of outstanding ability and devotion. We remember the leaders and forget the mediocrities. As a Bench we claim neither brilliance nor infallibility : but among us are good scholars ; capable administrators ; and faithful pastors. And in accordance with the gifts God has given us we are doing our utmost in difficult days for Church and nation.

VI

THE PAROCHIAL CLERGY

The work and influence of the Church of England depend more than anything else upon the character and efficiency of its parochial clergy. No appeals by the bishops will be effective unless the clergy are willing to act upon them. No spiritual or evangelistic movement will reach the great mass of the laity without their ready and active co-operation. In every parish they are the official leaders in religion. By their lives and examples the laity will judge the clergy. If the parochial clergy are lethargic, indolent and worldly the Church they represent suffers, if they have vision, holiness and zeal the Church grows strong in spiritual influence.

VI

THE PAROCHIAL CLERGY

THE work and influence of the Church of England depend more than anything else upon the character and efficiency of its parochial clergy. No appeals by the bishops will be effective unless the clergy are willing to act upon them. No spiritual or evangelistic movement will reach the great mass of the laity without their ready and active co-operation. In every parish they are the official leaders in religion. By their lives and examples the laity will judge the Church. The Episcopal Bench, Convocations, the Church Assembly, and the Ecclesiastical Commissioners are only names to the majority of the parishioners, but their parish priest lives amongst them, day by day they can observe him, and through his conduct and teaching they form their opinion of the Church. If the parochial clergy are lethargic, indolent and worldly the Church they represent suffers, if they have vision, holiness and zeal the Church grows strong in spiritual influence.

The Parish Priest in History

The influence of the parish priest has varied greatly in different periods. In the Middle Ages he was usually confined to the limits of his parish, though now and again through the visit of the rural dean or the still more dreaded visitation of the archdeacon he was reminded that he was an officer of an universal Church. His poverty was great, but it was mitigated by the fees he obtained from his parishioners, and by the receipt of the whole or a portion of the tithe. Contemporary records show that there were frequent quarrels between the priest and the people, not as to-day over questions of ceremonial and ritual, but over economic problems concerning the payments due to him either for a service rendered, or sanctioned by custom. The village priests were not much more educated than their parishioners. In 1281 Archbishop Peckham complained that " The ignorance of the priests casteth the people into the ditch of error : and the folly or unlearning of the clergy, who are bidden to instruct the faithful in the Catholic faith, sometimes tendeth rather to error than to sound doctrine." Mr. H. S. Bennett in his book on the English Manor 1150-1400 sums up by saying " we are forced to the conclusion that most of the ordinary parish clergy were inefficient, ill-educated, undistinguished men. It is unwise to indict a whole class, but it seems clear that much that was weakest in the mediæval religious system was primarily due to the ill-trained, ill-educated parish clergy."[1] Not all the clergy were illiterate or of the peasant class, among them were sons of the aristocracy who were training for posts in the Royal service or were qualifying for rich family benefices. It was probably against these that admonitions were addressed forbidding them to copy the fashionable laity of their day by walking about clad in a military rather than a clerical dress. Some wore red or blue dress instead of grey or black, with short swords instead of a girdle and a pair of beads, and their hair long instead of tonsured. In fact on one occasion at his visitation a bishop ordered the hair of his clergy to be cut short there and then![2] But these were exceptions : the greater part of the clergy were poor and illiterate, hardly to be distinguished from the peasants among whom they lived.

There was, however, an advantage in the clergy belonging to the class to which they ministered. They were able to understand and help them in a way almost impossible for a priest brought up in totally different surroundings. The author we have quoted above comments that the identity of interests between the priest of peasant stock and his flock is still a source of strength to the Roman Catholic Church " The ample priest with his soiled soutane and heavy boots, who clambers into the French autobus, and after greeting most of the passengers settles down in happy converse with them en route to their village, is the modern descendant of most mediæval parish priests. No one can view such a group without realising that there is some close relation between such people which the parson of the average English country parish, drawn as he is from a

[1] " Life on the English Manor," by H. S. Bennett, p. 325.
 Parish Priests in the Middle Ages," by E. L. Cutts, p. 167.

different social status and educated at the university and clergy school, will not easily achieve."[1]

There were no doubt various degrees of sanctity among such village priests. There were some who were avaricious, immoral and lazy. William Langland describes one of these in Parson Sloth, who says :

> I never visit the feeble nor the fettered men in prison
> I had rather hear ribaldry or a summer game of coblers.
> Or lies to laugh at and belie my neighbour
> Than all that the four evangelists have ever written.
> Vigils and fastening days slip unheeded.
> I lie abed in Lent with my leman beside me
> And when mattins and mass are over I go to my friars.

> I have been priest and parson for the past thirty winters
> Yet I know neither the scales nor the singing nor the
>   Saints Legends.
> I can find a hare afield or frighten him from his furrow
> Better than read *beatus vir* or *beati omnes*.

But against this we must set Chaucer's poor parson of a town who was rich in holy thought and work, and who staff in hand visited in rain and thunder the most distant of his parishioners. Probably the majority of the parish priests were neither as good as the one described by Chaucer, nor as bad as the one denounced by Piers Plowman. They were men with a somewhat higher standard than their parishioners, and rather more educated. They were the representatives of the unseen and the spiritual. By their ministry they brought their parishioners into contact with the invisible world and reminded them of the eternal consequences of all they did and said in this life.

With the Reformation there was distinct improvement in the social position of the clergy. The permission to marry took away a long-standing cause of scandal, while the abolition of many privileges removed some of the reasons for their unpopularity. In the sixteenth century their poverty was still great, and it was the more serious as a wife and children had to be maintained out of the miserably small income. Archbishop Whitgift stated that out of nine thousand benefices more

---

[1] " Life on the English Manor," p. 329.

than half had incomes of less than £10. Lord Macaulay's description of the clergy of the seventeenth century is almost too well known to quote—of the young Levite leaving the table before the sweets and returning to give thanks for a repast from the greater part of which he had been excluded—of the incumbent toiling on his glebe so that he could obtain daily bread. Here as elsewhere, when he is writing on ecclesiastical matters, Macaulay exaggerates and distorts. Not all the clergy were poor and of lowly origin; among the names of the incumbents of that period there are many of noble families. There is plenty of evidence to show that many were well educated. But it seems that the majority were both poor and with little learning. Even in the early part of the eighteenth century six thousand benefices had incomes of less than £50 per annum. Sycophancy and pluralism were the direct results of the poverty of the clergy. The half-starved parson sought and flattered the rich patron in the hope that he might find favour and preferment. He was ready to take charge of other benefices in addition to the one he already held if this would lift him out of the rut of dire want,[1] even if this meant that he had to delegate most of his duties to a poorly paid curate. Occasionally he had to be content to serve as domestic chaplain in the house of some nobleman or wealthy landowner.

Towards the middle of the eighteenth century the increasing value of the tithe attracted to holy orders many of the sons of the upper classes, and by the end of the century large numbers of the clergy were in their outlook and interests almost indistinguishable from the country gentlemen. They hunted, shot, entertained and lived as other members of their own class. They took their duty on Sundays, refrained from sexual immorality and gambling, and were charitable towards their poorer parishioners, but few seem to have had any strong sense of the greatness of their calling as ambassadors of Christ and shepherds of the flock of Christ. Goldsmith indeed gives an attractive picture of the Vicar of Wakefield in the days of adversity. We smile at and like Fielding's Parson Adams with all his absurdities, but against him we must set Thwackum with his coarse mind and bullying habits and his famous definition

---

[1] " The most prolific parent of place-hunting and pluralities has not been the wealth but the poverty of the benefices." " Bishoprick Papers," by H. H. Henson, D.D., p. 25.

of religion as "the Christian religion; and not only the Christian religion, but the Protestant religion; and not only the Protestant religion, but the Church of England": and Mr. Supple "the curate—a good natured worthy man: but chiefly remarkable for his great taciturnity at table, though his mouth was never shut at it." Nor at the beginning of the nineteenth century does Jane Austen give a very favourable picture of the clergy of her time: at the best they are respectable, decorous, wife-hunting men; at their worst [1] sheer figures of fun like Mr. Collins who announces that "having received ordination at Easter, I have been so fortunate as to be distinguished by the patronage of the Right Honourable Lady Catherine de Bourgh, widow of Sir Lewis de Bourgh, whose bounty and beneficence has preferred me to the valuable rectory of this parish, where it shall be my earnest endeavour to demean myself with grateful respect towards her Ladyship, and be ever ready to perform those rites and ceremonies which are instituted by the Church of England." During the first half of the century the clergy as a whole were good living, comfortable, self-complacent men, meeting as equals the country squires and magistrates, and though kindly to the poor and destitute had little or no sympathy with the daily hardships of their lot. They were content with things as they found them, violently prejudiced against all reform and deeply suspicious of any tendency to religious enthusiasm.

By the middle of the century the Evangelical and the Oxford Movements had led to great changes in the conception of clerical life and work. The parson became aware that he was a pastor and a priest: a pastor with the spiritual responsibility for the people committed to his care by his institution; a priest ordained to administer the Sacraments as well as to preach the Word of God; and the recipient at his Ordination of the gift of the Holy Ghost "for the office and work of a Priest in the Church of God." Anthony Trollope's novels give a picture of much higher standards of clerical life than we can find in the novelists of the eighteenth century: the vigorous and militant Archdeacon Grantley, the ascetic Mr. Arabin, the saintly Mr. Harding, the stern and hard-working Mr. Crawley, the gentle Mr. Quiverful, and the weak though attractive Mark Robarts "manly, tall and fair-haired, with square forehead,

[1] No! in her "Emma," Mr. Elton, Vicar of Highbury, is contemptible.

denoting intelligence rather than thought," have a larger place in his writings than the detestable Slope or the colourless Dr. Proudie. But even Trollope's age is one of rapid transition to a type of clergyman hitherto rare in the Church of England, in which high ideals of pastoral and priestly vocation are combined with vigour, hard work and efficiency.

The Position of the Clergy To-day

In actual numbers the clergy of to-day are insufficient to meet the demands made upon them. In 1930 in the provinces of Canterbury and York there were 16,745 in active work, irrespective of some 1,500 to 2,000 who had retired. In 1922 there were 17,162, in 1914 there were 18,180, and in 1905 there were 19,053. Thus in 1930 there were 2,308 fewer clergy than in 1905. The significance of this is only rightly measured when it is remembered that the population in this interval increased by over three million. The Report on the Staffing of the Parishes, from which the above figures are quoted, estimated in 1930 that for the next ten years an average of 630 ordinands per annum would be required to make up the existing deficiency, to replace losses, and to meet the growth of population. The average number of those annually ordained in this period was 559. The shortage of men is the more serious as their distribution is unsystematic and apparently unreasonable. They are often found in the largest numbers where the population is small, and relatively few in the great centres of population. In 1930 there were 1,139 parishes with a population of over five thousand in which there was no assistant curate. Since then the position has gravely deteriorated. During the war few were ordained, for though men in training for Ordination were exempt from National Service, the best and most vigorous among them postponed their ordination so as to share with their contemporaries the hardships and dangers of active service. Most of the theological colleges were closed. Large numbers of the younger clergy volunteered to serve as chaplains, and for many years had to be absent from their parishes. The result is that all our dioceses are understaffed. Instead of the 16,745 clergymen in active work in 1930, in 1946 there were only 15,500. Great town parishes which normally should be worked by several clergy have only the incumbent, who has to deal single-handed with work which once he had shared with several colleagues : and month after month benefices in the country have had to remain vacant with little hope of the appointment of a new vicar.

There has also been considerable loss in the social and political prestige and influence of the clergy. This is due to various causes : the State has taken over many secular duties and functions for which the clergy were once responsible. The Parish Vestry, of which the incumbent was chairman, has lost its old position. The Public Assistance Authority now gives the poor relief which was once dispensed by the clergy. The Church school has vanished from many parishes, and the incumbent has no longer an assured place in local education. Many charities once at the disposal of the incumbents and churchwardens are now in the hands of secular bodies. Clubs for recreation of men and boys are gradually being crowded out by State-provided community centres. And above all, a steady decline in the habit of Church-going has deprived the clergy of a large part of the field over which once a week for at least an hour they had undisputed authority. The pulpit is no longer a powerful channel for the propagation of religious or political views ; its place has been largely taken by the popular press and by broadcasting.

Nor must another cause be ignored. Traditionally in England the tenure of land has been a source of authority and influence. At one time the great landowners were the rulers of England. Their prestige has been vanishing with the poverty of the countryside, the break-up of great estates, and the rise of other classes. For centuries the clergy have been connected with the land. In the Middle Ages most of them were actively engaged in its cultivation. From Anglo-Saxon days they had been the owners of tithe. They possessed glebe which they either worked themselves or let out to others. They were thus interested in all questions connected with land and agriculture, and could talk easily and naturally with landowners, farmers and labourers. But now the tie with the land has almost gone, clerical tithe has been abolished, and most of the glebe has passed out of the hands of the individual incumbent. Very few of the clergy are magistrates, and the number who take part in rural administration is small.

Selection and Training of Ordinands

The loss of political and social influence is a very small matter if the clergy have gained in spiritual efficiency. There has been great and marked improvement in the training of candidates for ordination. Less than a century ago there was no special training—a degree, not necessarily in theology, was all that was usually required. The bishop's examination was frequently superficial and formal. A knowledge of Latin and Greek was almost a sufficient qualification for the cure of souls. Frequently the bishop left all arrangements for the ordination to his archdeacon and chaplains, who saw the candidates and decided who was to be accepted. Sometimes the bishop interviewed the men for the first time on the night before their ordination. Though most of the men ordained were of high moral character, many of them had little knowledge of the Bible, still less of theology, and had received no training in the devotional life. Practically all were from one social class. It was very rare for an ordinand to come from any but the professional or, sometimes, the commercial classes ; the cost of training at the universities was an insuperable obstacle to the sons of working men.

Great changes for the better have been made in this century. In the first place, poverty is no longer a fatal bar to ordination : Kelham and Mirfield led the way in opening the door to the priesthood to the boy whose parents could not afford to pay for his training. The Church owes them a great debt for the many good and faithful priests they have trained, who, but for the enterprise of these Communities, would never have been ordained. Since then, the Church and the various dioceses have raised large sums of money so that none who have a true vocation should be debarred from Holy Orders through the social or financial position of their parents. After the First World War a school, under the headship of Dr. Barry, the present Bishop of Southwell, was opened at Knutsford for the testing and preliminary preparation of promising candidates from the Forces. Recently the Archbishops have made an appeal for £600,000 for the training of men who were registered during the last war as possible ordinands. Over four thousand gave in their names, and some of them commenced their studies, and even sat for examinations, while they were prisoners of war.

As comparatively few men are now ordained from the Public Schools, it is more important than ever that the Church should cast very widely its net for ordinands. The majority of them now come from State-provided and secondary schools of various types; considerably over half of those who are preparing for ordination receive assistance by scholarship or grants towards the cost of their training at the universities. This is true not only of ordinands, but of the majority of those who in the universities are preparing for other work. It is a matter of thankfulness that the ministry of the Church of England is no longer the preserve of one class, but is once again open to all. Unhappily, the majority of ordinands do not come from the actual working class, but more frequently from the lower middle class; it is still exceptional to find among them the sons of the labourer, the artisan or the mechanic; the Anglican ministry will be regarded as a class ministry while it contains comparatively few from the homes of the working classes. It is difficult to over-estimate the gravity of the fact that the class which has proved itself capable, in the Cabinet, in Parliament and in local administration, of the highest gifts of government and leadership, should take such a small part in the ministry of the Church. Lately there has been some improvement, and among the Service candidates there are men who have worked on farms, in factories and in the mines.

In the second place there have been changes in the method of selection and training of ordinands. The bishops demanded a training which began at the university and ended in a theological college, or, as an alternative, a course of three years at some recognised theological college. But though this principle was generally accepted, the exceptions to it were more noticeable in some dioceses than its observance. Candidates had to sit for a central examination, commonly known as G.O.E. (General Ordination Examination), or its equivalent, unless excused by the bishop. In addition, most of the bishops had their own examination a few weeks before the ordination.

Since the war there have been further developments in the method of selecting suitable candidates. The old plan had two serious weaknesses: some dioceses demanded higher qualifications than others, with the result that they were avoided by the weaker men, who gravitated towards those in which it was thought that the kind-heartedness of the bishop would over-rule the decision of his examining chaplains. Another weakness arose from the fact that men occasionally were taken by theological colleges before they had been accepted by a bishop, and only after much time and money had been spent on their training was it discovered that no bishop was likely to ordain them. To remedy these difficulties it has been agreed by the bishops that before men under forty are accepted for training they should attend a selection centre, and that their acceptance should depend upon a favourable report from the examiners. These centres last five or six days; they are attended by twenty to thirty candidates at a time, and are conducted by specially chosen clerical and lay assessors, who make their reports after they have had interviews with the men and noticed how they mixed with one another. They decide whether they will recommend the candidates for further testing and training, and, if necessary, advise the course of training which should be followed. These centres have already proved to be a valuable method of selection, though, not unnaturally, they are criticised by the rejected and their friends. They will save unsuitable men from spending time and money on training which will only end in disappointment, and they will help to establish a generally accepted standard. From the men recommended by these centres the bishops will be able to choose their candidates. In all matters concerning the selection and training of ordinands, the bishops are advised by a Council with a somewhat cumbrous title—The Central Advisory Council for the Training of the Ministry—commonly known as CACTM. This Council also makes periodical inspections of the theological colleges, and the bishops only recognise those which it has approved.

Theological Colleges

These colleges have a very important part in the training of the future clergy. The men go to them at a critical and highly impressionable time in their lives, and the teaching and practice they learn at them will have a great influence on their ministry. They are often criticised and attacked as " party " colleges, and as turning out men with narrow ecclesiastical views. Most of the colleges have been founded in connection with one or other of the distinctive schools of thought in our Church. It is much to be desired that there were more of these colleges which were simply Church of England without any label attached. But all the colleges, whatever their churchmanship may be, have rendered two great services : they have given definite scriptural and theological teaching to many who would otherwise have been ignorant both of the Bible and doctrine, and they have trained them in the disciplined life of prayer and devotion. I would far rather have a party man who knew what he stood for, and followed an ordered life of prayer, than a man who was kindly, amiable, indefinite, of the " hang theology " type. As a matter of fact, in most of the colleges men are pruned of exotic views and practices, though there are always a few who will depart more deeply rooted in their opinions than when they were first admitted. Perhaps I may give my own experience : I went from Oxford to Cuddesdon. I did not particularly want to go to a theological college, for I had hoped to have spent a year at Oxford House, but Winnington-Ingram, then its head, urged me strongly to go to a theological college if I had to choose between the two. I never regretted his advice. In some ways I found Cuddesdon uncongenial after Oxford. I disliked its conservatism, for everything had to be done according to custom, and I was not interested in the ecclesiastical talk in which so many engaged ; its heartiness, with roars of laughter at trivial jokes often proved irritating. But I loved the beauty of the place, situated high on the hill, and the old parish church. I gradually came to appreciate its ordered life of worship, study and recreation. I began to learn more about the Bible, for I knew little of the Old Testament, though I could have argued more or less intelligently in defence of the Christian faith. On my first day I astonished the Principal by one of my answers to an elementary examination paper by showing that I thought the sojourn of the Hebrews in Egypt was the same as the Babylonian exile ! But, above all, at Cuddesdon I learned something about the life of devotion and gained habits of prayer and meditation which I have never entirely lost. Archbishop Lang had a lifelong devotion to Cuddesdon, and in a letter to his mother on his ordination spoke of it as " my own spiritual home, my true birthplace, the centre of the highest and deepest associations of my life."

We could not do without these colleges. It is impossible to exaggerate all that they have done for the devotional life of their students. Theology, when possible, should be learnt at the university, as the teaching staff of the college is often so overworked that it has no time to give more than rather elementary lectures in doctrine. This is the strong argument for the theological colleges being near a university. Pastoralia should be left to a competent vicar in the ordinand's first curacy. Often the syllabus of the college is overladen with secondary subjects of instruction. Enthusiasts urge the college to find space for the special matters which they regard as of paramount importance, from elocution to economics. There is no time to teach all these subjects within a few weeks. The main object of these colleges should be to train the students in the life of devotion and of worship; to this everything should be subordinated. When they are ordained they may quickly forget most of the lectures they have heard, but they will never forget entirely the habits of ordered prayer and meditation which they then acquired.

The Work of the Parish Clergy

The work of the parish clergy may be grouped under three heads—worship, teaching and pastoral; though it is obvious that pastoral duties include both worship and teaching.

(1) *Worship*. The parochial clergy are responsible, under the bishop, for public worship in their parishes and the administration of the Sacraments. The services of the Church of England are conducted to-day more frequently and more carefully than at any time since the Reformation. Until the middle of the last century the churches were usually closed throughout the week, and from Sunday night to Sunday morning no sound of prayer or praise was heard within them. This was certainly not the intention of the Reformers; the direction in the Prayer Book is most definite: " And the Curate that ministereth in every parish-church or chapel, being at home, and not being otherwise reasonably hindered, shall say the same (Morning and Evening Prayer) in the parish-church or chapel where he ministereth, and shall cause a bell to be tolled thereunto a convenient time before he begins, that the people may come

to hear God's Word, and to pray with him." In many churches the daily services are now said; even if no congregation assembles and the parish priest finds himself alone in the church, he says the service as an offering to the Most High on behalf of his people. One who had been for many years the rector of a small parish in Hampshire has written of his own experience in following the Prayer Book rule of saying daily the Offices of the Church: "Day by day, for nine years, each morning I walked across the fields from our lovely Queen Anne rectory to the lovely Norman church, unlocked it, rang the bell, and said Mattins. In the evening I rang the bell again, and said Evensong. For years it was a lonely worship: but gradually others joined me. I knew too that the men in the fields and the women in their homes liked to hear the bell, and to know that someone was praying for them. Strangers who came to see 'the most beautiful little church in Hampshire' realised that it was a house of prayer and not just an ecclesiastical museum. For me this routine meant habits of discipline."[1]

Very noticeable has been the increased frequency of celebrations of the Holy Communion. Three times a year gave place to a monthly celebration, and now there are very few churches in which there is not a weekly celebration. In most churches there is a weekday celebration in Lent and on Holy Days, and in many churches, especially in the towns, there is a daily celebration. In their anxiety to make the Holy Communion available to all their people some of the clergy have revived the ancient custom of reserving the consecrated Elements so that at any time they may be able to communicate the sick. Over this practice there has been much controversy. This has largely risen from the fear that the consecrated Elements may be made the focus of services and organised devotions which are neither primitive nor known in a great part of the Catholic Church, and which may obscure the fact that Communion was the primary purpose of the institution of the Lord's Supper. But the case for Reservation in our large parishes both for the sick and for those who are unavoidably hindered from coming to the ordinary celebration is very strong. Those who are most familiar with the conditions of urban parishes where the custom of frequent communion has been taught and encouraged

[1] "Pastor's Progress," by Arthur Hopkinson, p. 114.

are convinced that occasional or perpetual Reservation is necessary if the parish priest is to give Communion regularly to the sick and aged—the sudden calls are so rare, unless there is a hospital in the parish, that their possibility hardly adds any weight to a case sufficiently strong. The 1928 Prayer Book contained a rubric, which expresses the mind of our Church on this matter, authorising the bishop in connection with hospitals, or in any time of common sickness, or in the special circumstances of any particular parish to give licence to the priest " to reserve at the open Communion so much of the consecrated Bread and Wine as is needed for the purpose."

With increased frequency there has been greater care over the manner in which the services are conducted. There are still churches in which the minister is slovenly and inaudible, or repeats the words as if they had no meaning, or gabbles so as to give the impression he was speaking in an unknown tongue—but these are unhappy exceptions. In most of our parishes care and thought are taken by the clergy over the services they conduct, and when officiating they show they are mindful of the greatness and solemnity of their ministry. It is as the old monks would say the " *opus dei*," and for this work they know they must give their best.

(2) *Teaching*. At his Ordination the priest was reminded that he was called to " teach and premonish." He promised " to use both publick and private monitions and exhortations," and was given authority " to preach the Word of God." The teaching is as essential to the discharge of his responsibilities as the ministry of the Holy Sacraments. It has never been easy for a correct balance to be kept between preaching and worship. There have been times when the emphasis on preaching has almost excluded worship : while at other times preaching has been treated as of little importance compared to the ministry of the Sacraments. In a sound theology the preaching of the Word and the ministry of the Sacraments are always found together. In the Middle Ages both bishops and curates were frequently accused of failing to preach. One of the reasons for the early popularity of the friars was that they preached while the parish priest was dumb. Archbishop Peckham directed the clergy to preach four times a year and gave them an outline for their guidance. But the preacher did not always find a reverent and attentive congregation—the two old vices of

sleeping and talking were an irresistible temptation to the
mediæval sermon-goers.[1] To counteract this the preacher was
only too ready to spice his sermons with numerous anecdotes
and cheap witticisms. Readers of Dante will recall his denunciation of this practice :

> The preacher now provides himself with store
> Of jests and gibes : and so there be no lack
> Of laughter, while he vents them, his big cowl
> Extends, and he has won the meed he sought.
>
> (Paradiso XXIX)

After the Reformation the pulpits were carefully controlled by
the Government. Homilies were provided to be read in the
place of sermons. The failure of the Anglican clergy to preach
was one of the chief charges brought against them by the
Puritans. But gradually the sermon became an established part
of the Sunday service. Often it was of great length, and the
hour glass was turned over in the course of its delivery. No
service would have been regarded as complete without the
sermon. And though by the middle of the last century its
length had been considerably reduced, Anthony Trollope could
still write : " There is perhaps no greater hardship at present
inflicted on mankind in civilised and free countries than the
necessity of listening to sermons. No one but a preaching
clergyman has, in these realms, the power of compelling an
audience to sit silent and be tormented. No one but a preaching
clergyman can revel in platitudes, truisms and untruisms, and
yet receive, on his undisputed privilege, the same respectful
demeanour as though words of impassioned eloquence, or
persuasive logic, fell from his lips."

It would be impossible for anyone to-day to write the above
sentences. Preaching has fallen on evil days. The popular
press and, more recently, the wireless have proved themselves
powerful rivals to the sermon. No congregation would listen
more than once " silent and tormented " to a sermon lasting
for an hour. The modern congregation prefers a " sermon-
ette "—hateful term—of not more than ten minutes. It is impatient of rhetoric. But it is still a fact that a preacher who
has something to say and says it clearly and attractively will

[1] " Preaching in Mediæval England," by G. R. Owst," p. 175.

almost always have a good congregation. The parish priest is often, however, disheartened by a small gathering of the same people to whom he has preached time after time. He knows that he cannot compete either with the preacher on the wireless or with the Saturday religious articles in the daily paper. He is conscious, too, that his level of education is not so far above that of the congregation he is addressing that he can speak to it with a superior knowledge. As a result he sometimes wonders if it is worth while to take trouble over the sermon, and becomes content with an address which is either dogmatic without persuasiveness, or consists of the string of platitudes and truisms of which Trollope complains. A bishop so rarely has the benefit of hearing sermons, except the excellent Ordination sermons, that he should hesitate to pass judgement on the general state of preaching, but occasionally he listens to sermons on his holidays, and he often hears the opinions of the laity on the pulpit utterances of their clergy. Good sermons appear to be the exception, and it seems that preaching should be of a higher standard than it is at present. Whether he has a large or a small congregation, the preacher has an unrivalled opportunity of giving instruction Sunday by Sunday. His congregation expects neither an oration nor a sermon which might be an ethical leader on subjects of the day in a secular newspaper. It wants to hear about God and the Unseen ; about the Gospel ; about the mind of Christ applied to the problems of daily life. Where the preacher tries to meet these needs, he will find an attentive and grateful congregation. In town and village churches there are many of the clergy who do their utmost by their preaching to help and teach their people, but their sermons are not hasty productions thrown together at the last minute ; they are the outcome of thought, prayer, study and struggle. When a clergyman speaks contemptuously of preaching it means either that he is excusing his own laziness and incompetence, or he has never understood the meaning of the commission given to him at his Ordination.

Preaching is not the only way in which the teaching office of the Church is carried out. In Sunday School and Day School the parish priest instructs the children in the faith. In preparation for their Confirmation there is a great opportunity for continuous instruction over several weeks. At one time in many parishes there were large Bible Classes for men and women; these are not so common as they used to be, but lately the old class has been revived under the name of a Group or Cell in which there is both teaching and discussion under a leader who is probably one of the parish clergy.

(3) *Pastoral.* By the ministry of the Sacraments and by the Word of God the parish priest fulfils his pastoral ministry. He will not be content with public ministration; he will endeavour to build up the members of his flock one by one " unto that agreement in the faith and knowledge of God, and to that ripeness and perfectness of age in Christ, that there be no place left either for error in religion or for viciousness in life." To do this he must know individually his people, and help each in the spiritual life according to his or her special needs. In our Church we are wanting both in books and in teaching which will help the clergy in the work of edification. The Roman Church is far better supplied than our own in this respect. We have few books on moral theology, and the clergy are taught little about it; though Dr. Kirk, the Bishop of Oxford, has given much-needed help by his writings.

There are laity who go to the spiritual healer or to the psycho-analyst for help when really they should " open their grief to some discreet and learned minister of God's Word and by the ministry of God's Word receive the benefit of absolution, together with ghostly counsel and strength." There are a number of our clergy, who without any special training, have become experienced directors of souls. Many exercise their gifts in this way through the hearing of confessions, and at the same time giving advice and counsel. There are others who in less formal ways listen to the outpouring of an anxious soul. There are some who find help merely by speaking to one they can trust about their troubles, but they will only do this if they are perfectly certain that their confidence will be respected and that their disclosure will under no circumstances be revealed to any third person. Mr. Charles Morgan, in an Essay on " Singleness of Mind " which serves as a Preface to his play " The Flashing Stream," says that when he was at Oxford he asked the advice of an old man who was a country Vicar, the father of the friend with whom he was staying: " I asked that what I had to say should never be told again; he agreed, pledging his word, and I began to describe my difficulty to him. After a sentence he interrupted me, went to a corner of the room, and returned bearing a stole. ' I gave you my word,' he said, ' and have no reason to believe that I should not have kept it. But I am a talkative man; I am married. This '—he touched the stole—' makes secrecy absolute.' I have long forgotten his advice, but I recall to-day the pang of happiness, the sense of release, almost of redemption, which sprang from my encounter at a moment when the world seemed to be foundering under me, with a promise that could not be betrayed." There are innumerable parish clergymen who have not only given to their people complete confidence that no disclosure made to them will ever be repeated, but they have been able to give the spiritual guidance and help which above all things was needed. But this would be far more effective and general if the clergy had had earlier in their ministry special instruction on the cure of individual souls. Piety and good intentions without wisdom may easily result in harmful advice.

The true pastor does not discharge his responsibilities only by ministering to the members of his congregation or to those who seek him out in the church or the vicarage. By his institution he is given the spiritual care of all the people who reside within the geographical area of his parish. He must not wait until they send for him; he must go out seeking for them. There is a great tradition in the Anglican Church of pastoral visitation. The parish priest goes out among his people whether they come to church or not, and does his best to get to know them in their homes. When I was first ordained the curates of the Parish of Portsea were expected to visit four hours on five days of the week. We left the clergy house at two-thirty; if later in the afternoon by any ill chance we met the Vicar in the house most of us felt it necessary to explain why we were not in our districts! We returned at six or six-thirty, and then after high tea, we again went out until about ten, and during this time, unless we were at services, meetings or clubs, we were visiting those whom we should not find at home until the evening. This tradition of pastoral visitation had been in existence for many years before my Ordination, and at Portsea continued until the close of the First World War. In most well-worked parishes this visitation used to be regarded as essential. For obvious reasons it is no longer as common as once was the case. In large under-staffed parishes house-to-house visiting is now impossible. Elsewhere it is more difficult as the parishioners are not at home as frequently as they were twenty or thirty years ago; social customs in this respect have greatly changed. Some of the clergy claim that their responsibilities are confined to their own Church people; and some of them quite frankly have not the self-confidence to call at the houses of people they do not know. But whatever the reasons may be there has been a serious decline in the practice of parochial visitation. This has had most unfortunate results. The parish priest is often looked upon as the minister of a little group of pious or ecclesiastically minded people, out of touch with the interests and lives of ordinary men and women : and thus loses a great opportunity for evangelisation. Pastoral visitation is the normal evangelistic method of the Church of England. It is not a mere coincidence that in the parish in which a number of adults are presented for Confirmation, pastoral visitation is always given an important place. Well-arranged services and good sermons will not by themselves fill the vacant seats of a church; there is better hope of this if the parish priest carries the Gospel invitation to the people in their own homes.

I can think of large numbers of parish clergy devoted and capable. As a boy I can recall some of the incumbents of the country parishes near my home : most of them were true fathers of their people, though they would have disliked intensely the title "Father"; nearly all of them were elderly men, very moderate preachers who read sermons which were not always new; their services were of a very simple character, and except in Advent, Lent and Holy Days were held only on the Sundays : but they knew every man, woman and child in their parishes : they visited them diligently in sickness and bereavement : they were at home in the manor house, the farm house and the cottage. There were no parochial organisations with the exception of the day school and occasionally the night school, but most of the parishioners, with the exception of the Nonconformists and agricultural labourers, came to church at least once a Sunday. At Portsea I came into contact with some great parish priests—I will only mention those who are no longer with us. There was my first vicar, Cosmo Gordon Lang, a great preacher and teacher : I have never heard finer sermons than those he preached as Vicar of Portsea. On Sunday afternoons he lectured to five hundred men at a conference in the Institute : and in the week he took numerous Bible Classes. He was a born leader and made his influence felt throughout the town. He was succeeded by Bernard Wilson, one of the best parish priests I have ever known— no orator, but a clear teacher : a most capable organiser and financier, he would have made a fortune if he had been in business : and the most energetic and diligent of visitors—he would visit for hours at a stretch, often after a long day of meetings, setting off after supper to call on men in their homes : he spent infinite care and trouble over individuals, refusing to despair even of those who had disappointed him time after time. A man of considerable private means he gave the whole of his official income to the parish, and in addition he was always giving anonymously large sums of money to help both causes and individuals. Bluff and outspoken in manner, he was utterly unselfish ; and though he never suffered fools gladly, he had great patience in his dealings with all who were in real trouble. At the age of fifty he died from a stroke, due to sheer overwork. A very different man was Canon Blake, Vicar of what was then the fashionable church at Southsea : his outlook on life was tinged with melancholy, and his sermons were more lengthy and doctrinal than would be generally acceptable to-day, but he knew everyone in his great congregation ; he was a wise director of souls and though probably he never encouraged private confessions, large numbers came to him for spiritual advice. Father Dolling had left before my Ordination, but I had often met and heard him when I was a schoolboy at Portsmouth. He was a very different man to the three I have mentioned ; he would have been described as a " ritualist," but ritualism to him was only a means towards evangelisation : he was a missioner through and through, burning for the conversion of souls, bold in rebuke of the social sins of the times and fearless in his exposure of public immorality. His Clergy House had its doors always open to all.

When from Portsea I went to Southwark I found in that large diocese many outstanding parish priests. These were not confined to any one party ; many would have found it difficult to label themselves. Some were the incumbents of great town parishes with large organisations and good congregations : there were others who were content to work year after year in some obscure slum with only a handful attending their services. There was real heroism among many of these clergy ; complete self-forgetfulness as they devoted themselves to work which would have been heart-breaking to most, for the outward results were so small. Some of these men at all hours of day and night were in and out of the poorest streets and the most depressing tenement buildings. Often they had no lay workers, and every detail of parochial work fell on their shoulders. And while some toiled with grim and unflagging determination, there were others who flung themselves into their work with joy and hope.

Work in the diocese of Winchester is very different from that in a huge urban diocese. Most of its parishes are rural in nature. The tradition of great country parish priests like John Keble and Charles Kingsley is still carried on. In many of the parishes there are to be found true pastors whose courage never fails them under the difficult conditions which confront the country parson of to-day ; for his work is far more difficult than once was the case.

Now in the diocese of York I find the conditions of parochial work different from either Southwark or Winchester. The distances are much greater and many of the parishes, except those in the large cities, are in remote districts. The late autumn fogs, the long winter and the snow early in the year isolate them for considerable periods. The clergy consequently are more lonely and thrown more frequently on their own resources. Most of them both in town and country would compare favourably for devotion, pastoral zeal, hard work and practical ability with the clergy in any other part of the Anglican Communion.

Perhaps I may here recall a vicar who worked in a diocese with which I have had no connection. We had been fellow curates and close friends at Portsea, which he left for Australia to join a Bush Brotherhood. Two years before his death I stayed with him in his widely-scattered moorland parish. For miles round he knew everyone ; roadmen, woodcutters and labourers, he called them by their Christian names ; everywhere I could see they welcomed him as a friend : there was not a cottage we passed of which he could not tell me the history of all who lived in it. He told me he made a practice of saying his prayers for the people as he rode on horseback over his parish. It was a summer holiday month, and all day visitors were coming to the vicarage to ask about streams in which they could fish and the best cast to use, or where they could get ponies and safe rides for their children. His sermons were very short and simple, but his church was crowded and every detail of the service rendered most carefully. He excused himself to me for leaving for the church long before the service : " You see I like to be with the bell-ringers when they start, and then I pray for the people as they come into the church."

As I write I recall so many good parish priests : Dick Sheppard, Basil Jellicoe, Father Wainwright, Dom Clements, and so many others quite unknown beyond the borders of their parish. I think of a middle-aged curate who was known and loved throughout a London borough and given a civic funeral at his death ; of the vicar of a poor parish who frequently slept on the floor of his house so as to give his bed to homeless wayfarers ; of the " Abbot " of Beaulieu who shepherded and loved its people for over fifty years ; and in addition to those who have departed this life I have in mind many now living who, in great industrial parishes or in country villages, are giving year by year devoted service to their Lord and His flock. When the failures, the incompetent, the slack, and those who have lost their sense of vocation are criticised, we must not forget the far larger number who in town and country are quietly, faithfully and conscientiously showing themselves to be true Messengers, Watchmen and Stewards of the Lord.

Chaplains to the Forces

The war rapidly deprived most of our parishes of their younger men. The demand for chaplains was urgent and persistent. A few—a very few—conscientious objectors remained at home at their own desire. Others, wanting to join up, were ordered by their bishop to remain in parishes which were suffering, or likely to suffer, from severe raids. But most of the younger men, as well as many of those who were disqualified by age, were eager to minister spiritually to the men in the Fighting Forces. Some of the worse mistakes of the earlier war were avoided in the selection of men, for it was agreed that they should only be accepted as chaplains on the recommendation of their diocesan bishop. Some showed conspicuous gallantry : one, a fine swimmer, brought man after man, struggling in the water, in safety to the ship, and then, exhausted, was himself unable to reach his ship. Another in daylight, in full view of the Germans, took the burial service over some men who were lying in No Man's Land. Another crawled on the decks of his ship, under continuous dive-bombing, to give morphia to the bodies and spiritual help to the souls of the wounded and dying. There were other chaplains who volunteered to remain with their comrades as prisoners of war when they could have returned home. But, apart from acts of special distinction, the majority of the chaplains worked faithfully and quietly, sharing with officers and men their dangers and discomforts, and enduring with them the monotony of life behind the lines or at the home base waiting for the hour of invasion. On my various visits to the Forces overseas, commanding officers spoke to me in the warmest terms of the work of their chaplains ; they had nothing but praise for them : they showed keenness and initiative, holding their services under the most difficult conditions, adapting half-ruined buildings and barns as their churches, visiting the men at all times, and giving themselves completely to their work. In long interludes of quiet, and when the fighting was over, they made themselves responsible for various schools of moral leadership. And now, in occupied Germany, Church Houses for chaplains, officers and men have been opened. Among such a large body of men there were occasional failures and misfits, and at the chaplains' conferences there was sometimes a small minority, consisting of the weaker men, who raised time after time the question of their chances of preferment and work on their return to England. It was chiefly from this small minority that there came complaints in the press about the position of the chaplains in the Forces. But the chaplains as a whole worked devotedly and courageously, winning the trust and confidence of officers and men of all ranks.

" Disloyal Priests "

The charge is sometimes made that within the Church there is a considerable number of clergy who are disloyal to the teaching and practices of the Church of England. Often this only means that they do not happen to agree with the views of their critic. It would, however, be lacking in frankness to overlook the presence of a group of men who, in word and action, are disloyal to the Church which has ordained them, which pays their stipends and gives them their position. They are few in number compared with the great mass of the clergy, and are mainly found in two or three dioceses. The North is almost entirely free from them. They are not to be confused with the great majority of Anglo-Catholic clergy who are as loyal to the Church as any other of its clergy, and who dislike and repudiate men who would bring discredit on any movement with which they were associated. They are noisy, but with little influence : self-assertive without knowledge : and while lacking self-discipline themselves are hard and rigid in their dealings with others. Their influence is rapidly waning, for their churches are usually empty as they are suspected by the laity who find they cannot trust men who deride and disobey the Church which they are supposed to serve. Concerted disciplinary action would give them the notoriety which they seek. They will gradually disappear (possibly to Rome, if they do not shrink from its discipline), or the steady pressure of the opinion of loyal Catholics will bring them to a better mind.

The Marriage of the Clergy

Alone among the ancient Churches the Church of England allows its clergy complete freedom of choice as to whether they will remain single or marry. In the early Church many of its clergy were married, but usually these marriages took place before Ordination. By the end of the third century marriage after Ordination was forbidden to all above the sub-diaconate. The Eastern Church required that its parochial clergy should be married, but marriage before Ordination is the rule. It is said that the principals of some of the theological colleges help their students in the choice of a wife ! But it is the custom for bishops to be unmarried, as they are chosen from the monasteries. In the Ethiopian Church of Abyssinia the parish priest is allowed to marry once ; if his wife dies he must go into a monastery or engage in secular work. The Roman Church, on the other hand, has made celibacy compulsory for its bishops, priests and deacons. Under Archbishop Anselm this became a rigid rule in England. It was unpopular and difficult to enforce, and led in many parts of the Western Church to grave scandals or to recognised concubinage. At the Reformation Convocation repealed the canons forbidding marriage, and the Thirty-second Article of Religion states that it is lawful for bishops, priests and deacons " as for all other Christian men, to marry at their own discretion, as they shall judge the same to serve better to Godliness."

The arguments for compulsory celibacy are practical and disciplinary. It was an obstacle in the Middle Ages to the enrichment of great families at the cost of the Church : it made the clergy more mobile, without family attachments they can be transferred more easily and swiftly from place to place : financially it eased the burden on the Church for their support : and it was claimed that it enabled the clergy to concentrate entirely on their work, without the worries and cares which so easily beset the married man. Baron von Hügel frequently argued that the celibacy of the clergy is a striking witness to the supernatural and heroic virtue : " You cannot, to my mind, have the heroism as proclaimed, as central and as poignant, without the celibacy as you can with it."[1] There can be no doubt that a married priesthood has certain disadvantages and dangers. Young men are sometimes married soon after their Ordination ; if they had been clerks in some bank they might have been compelled to wait for some years. This practice has been on the increase in our own Church, with the result that men at the very outset of their work have to consider not where their services are most needed, but where the amenities are suitable for a young wife. As their stipends are small, time which ought to be spent in their districts is taken up with household duties. A large proportion of the men who pledged themselves at their Ordination to consider the claims of work

[1] " Letters." p. 328.

overseas, within two or three years find that they are now unable to do so as they have family responsibilities. Later when
a curate is offered a parish he may have to refuse it because his
wife dislikes the house, possibly for good reasons. Almost the
first offer of a parish I made as a Diocesan was refused by a
man suitable for it in every way on the ground that his wife
would not live in a house with a basement. If the clergyman
has married an unsuitable wife his work and influence may be
seriously hindered : if she is both strong-minded and tactless
she may do endless harm in the parish. Mrs. Proudies are not
to be found only among the wives of the higher clergy. Sometimes a patron is told of some curate or incumbent—" a good
man, but an impossible wife " ! There is a very strong case
in any Church for some of its clergy to dedicate themselves
voluntarily to life-long celibacy. Our Church would be much
the poorer if it did not find room for Religious Orders with
celibate priests. And the younger clergy, for the sake of their
work, should more frequently show the self-restraint practised
by their contemporaries in other professions, and refrain from
marriage during the first five or six years of their ordained life.
But it would be a mistake to attempt to lay down a hard and
fast rule ; individual cases are so different.

But the Church of England has gained far more than it has
lost by the marriage of its clergy. The married clergyman
often has sympathy and understanding in a higher degree than
his bachelor colleague. From his own experience he can
understand the anxieties and problems of family life. He has
to sacrifice many comforts and small luxuries which the unmarried can afford. His daily sacrifice and self-discipline for
the sake of his wife and children may easily be greater than
that of the celibate who has no expenses beyond his own. The
wives of the clergy have in many different ways supplemented
the work and influence of their husbands, often they have gained
trust and confidence where he would have failed. They have
been responsible in countless parishes for work which but for
them would never have been done. They have made thousands
of vicarages true examples of the happiness and beauty of the
Christian home : and have fashioned them into centres of
kindly and simple hospitality and friendship, so that the poorest
of the parishioners turn to them naturally in their hour of distress
and need. The parson's wife has to-day a long struggle to make

both ends meet and without domestic help the care of an unduly large house, but usually she is cheerful, friendly and hard working. To the wives of the clergy the Church owes much: among them are to be found some of the most devoted and unselfish of women, true saints of God: and from the vicarages of the married clergy there have gone sons and daughters to serve their country with distinction both at home and abroad.

Three Necessary Reforms

There are reforms in three directions which are necessary if the Church is to make the best use of its parochial clergy.

(1) *Patronage*. The existing system of patronage is far from satisfactory. Some of the worst scandals in connection with it are now rapidly coming to an end. The sale of the cure of souls will soon be an abuse of the past. The patron's unfettered discretion has been to some extent limited by the Benefices Measure of 1931, which gives the right of the Parochial Council to express its views on an impending appointment and which enables the bishop to refuse to accept the nomination of a man who is plainly unsuitable for that particular parish. But there is still a large element of luck, no other term is appropriate, as to when or where a man is appointed to a benefice. The bishop usually feels he must give the first consideration to the men who have already been working in his diocese, he knows their merits and limitations as well as the conditions of the parish in question: but there are numerous other patrons, the Crown, cathedral Chapters, colleges, party trusts, incumbents in virtue of their office, and private individuals. This mixed patronage has the advantage that it ensures that men of very different types and views will be appointed. As a rule great care is taken by patrons in selecting right men for the vacancies; but sometimes the patrons are ignorant of the conditions of the parish and know very few clergymen from whom they can make a choice. Incumbents and local trusts are the least satisfactory patrons; the former are inclined to appoint one of their curates, either as a reward for past services or as a happy opportunity of making a long desired change; the latter have a very limited area of choice and usually will nominate some clergyman who is the protégé of one of the trustees. The smaller party

trusts with rigid restrictions on certain matters of faith or ceremonial, accept men who have little other qualifications beyond that they can say correctly their particular shibboleth. The larger evangelical trusts take great care over appointments to their parishes. When the bishop has few benefices in his gift, the unbeneficed clergy of the diocese have to rely on other patrons. The pushful force themselves on their notice, while the best among the clergy will rarely make personal application for a benefice. " I see that my bishop has a letter from me at least once a month," a junior curate remarked to a friend : blissfully ignorant of the effect his repeated letters had on his longs-uffering Father-in-God. It is not always the most deserving who receive the most rapid preferment.

It is easy to see the defects of the present system, but not so easy to suggest a remedy. It would be a loss if all patronage was in the hands of the bishop or of a Diocesan Board, as it would tend to be exclusive, and appointments from outside the diocese would be rare. Selection by the parish would be disastrous, the Church Council would look for a Chrysostom " good with young people and with private means," and would end by choosing some mediocre preacher with no pastoral gifts. Probably the most hopeful policy would be to strengthen the Diocesan Board of Patronage so that it would be able to supplement the patronage in the hand of the bishop and to correct any party or personal bias which he might show in his appointments. As patrons find it increasingly difficult to fill the livings in their gift they will be the more ready to transfer them to the Board, which would eventually hold many benefices now owned by private individuals.

(2) *Clerical Incomes.* A more serious problem is the glaring inequality of the income attached to the different parishes. Sometimes the incomes are very small, more rarely they are excessive. The income is not decided by the importance of the parish, the amount of the work required, or the size of the population : it depends on historical or fortuitous circumstances which have no relation to the responsibilities of the incumbent. Various attempts have been made to remedy this : the Ecclesiastical Commissioners have steadily raised the incomes of the poorer parishes : the dioceses and parishes have co-operated to supplement them : at vacancies the surplus incomes of the wealthier parishes often have been redistributed among the poor parishes

in their locality : and through the union of benefices a living wage has been obtained. But the operation of the Tithe Act reduces by twenty per cent. the benefices which had depended chiefly on tithe and now the rising cost of living and increased income tax make the poverty of the clergy once again an acute problem. The discrepancy between different parishes cannot be defended on any moral or practical grounds. It is unjust that the incumbent of a comparatively small parish in delightful country surroundings should have an income of £600, while the incumbent of a difficult town parish with a large population should receive only £400 per annum. The difference in income between adjacent benefices is occasionally glaring, and a sense of unfairness is felt among the clergy and laity when they find that one parish in their deanery has a large income contrasted with the £400-£500 of the other parishes with populations quite as large. This variety in payment is also a serious obstacle to the free movement of clergy from parish to parish ; an incumbent, who with a wife and family, has enjoyed for some years an income of £600, naturally hesitates to change it for a parish with £500 though in other ways it may be more important and give greater opportunities than the parish he now holds.

Any attempt to reduce at once all parishes to fixed incomes plus allowances would meet with strong opposition. It is doubtful if Parliament would consent to this, while so much patronage remains in private hands. It would take away the incentive which parishes now have to raise the income of their incumbent. Nor would the dull uniformity of a hard and fast scheme appeal to our illogical English mind. But the incomes of the wealthier parishes should gradually be reduced by a percentage levy upon them, and what is far more important every effort should be made to raise the stipends of the poorly paid clergy, both beneficed and unbeneficed. Since the war their financial position has become most serious. It is impossible for many of the clergy to live on their present incomes : they are hopelessly inadequate. Much has already been done by the dioceses in this direction : but the rising cost of living has not yet been overtaken. Many of the clergy have a long struggle to keep free of debt, and financial anxieties hinder their work. Some of the additional income required should come from the surplus of the wealthier parishes, though this will really go a very little way : more through the union of parishes : considerable relief will also be gained through the sale of large parsonage houses, but this will not be possible until alternative accommodation be found. New money for augmenting the incomes of the clergy is urgently needed ; large sums of money will have to be raised immediately. Where it is impossible to secure the minimum income required, the bishop should be given power to refuse to institute, and the parish would be held in plurality with some neighbouring parish or would be ministered to in some other way. Sometimes this drastic action would bring home to parishes that they must be prepared to contribute to the support of their clergy, if they are to have an incumbent of their own. The conditions of the war, with the destruction of so many churches afford an unique opportunity for the redistribution of parishes and their incomes. The Re-organisation Measure will help in the bombed areas : but quicker and simpler procedure is required to enable parishes to be re-grouped in districts other than those which have suffered direct war damage.

(3) *The Limitation of the Parson's Freehold.* An incumbent when he has once been duly instituted and inducted can only be deprived for the gravest of reasons, and then only with considerable difficulty. He may persistently quarrel with all his parishioners, he may conduct the services carelessly and slovenly, he may only hold the minimum services which are required by Statute, he may neglect visiting both the sick and the whole, he may become eccentric or senile, almost incapable of doing his work, and yet it is practically impossible to remove him from his benefice. The parishioners may protest, his congregation may vanish, the archdeacon may visit, the bishop may remonstrate and censure, but the parson remains firmly entrenched in his freehold. Attempts to remedy this have been made ; the bishops are humiliated at their helplessness in face of the complaints of the parishioners ; the laity feel most deeply the scandal, but the Lower Houses of Convocation, fearful of placing the clergy at the mercy of an unfair bishop or of cantankerous parishioners, have not agreed on proposals which are likely to prove effective in ending this scandal. The clergy are naturally anxious to safeguard their freehold, for security of tenure helps to compensate for a small income and pension : and it has given them liberty of utterance and action. But as Dr. Henson writes : " It is difficult to believe that so gross an anomaly as

is implied in the parson's freehold will be able to sustain itself much longer against the waxing resentment provided by its practical inconvenience, and the ever-deepening repugnance of the Christian conscience."[1] A fixed age for retirement would do something to remedy this evil, though the lot of the retired parson must be made more favourable than it now is : a pension of £200-£250 a year is poor compensation for the loss of position, house and a much larger income. But it is morally indefensible that a man should continue indefinitely to hold his benefice and to enjoy its income while he is notoriously slack and in-efficient. This would not be tolerated in any other profession.

The recent Measures passed by the Assembly will probably prove too complicated to be of much value. If this should be the case another attempt will have to be made to frame some Measure by which all that is valuable in the freehold will be preserved, while it will no longer be a citadel in which the lazy and incompetent can take safe refuge. The Measure must however come from the clergy and be enacted with their complete good will. It is useless to attempt to impose upon them a limitation of their freehold which they felt was either unjust or a serious menace to their independence. Rather than create resentment among good men, it will be wiser to wait until they are convinced that for the honour of their calling resolute action must be taken to bring to an end the abuse of a privilege which causes scandal out of all proportion to the number of actual offenders.

To-day

Not for many generations have the parish clergy had to endure such difficulties as during the last few years. The war scattered their congregations, dispersed their workers, broke up or suspended many of their parochial organisations. Many, especi-ally in London and the great ports, saw their churches and large portions of their parishes destroyed by air raids. Amidst a general rise in taxation and the cost of living their stipends, often miserably inadequate, remained unchanged. In their large houses they had to manage as best they could without domestic help, their wives often suffering seriously in health through

---

[1] " The Church of England," by H. Hensley Henson, D.D., p. 174.

overwork. In addition there was spiritual and mental strain due to an age of rapid change and the swift passing of familiar landmarks. At a time when they were physically and often mentally exhausted they had to do their utmost to help their people in their sorrows and anxieties. No wonder that many of our clergy to-day are perplexed and disheartened and that as a result their work has suffered ; but it is a cause for both wonder and thankfulness that so many of them, notwithstanding all their problems and difficulties, have performed their duties so faithfully and have maintained such a high standard of life and work in their parishes.

VII

THE LAITY

The greatest need of the Church is not more laity, but better instructed laity. Nothing would strengthen the Church more than an increase in the number of its laity who are able to bear intelligent witness to their faith. No effort should be spared to build up in every parish a band of laymen and laywomen who are not only devoted to the Church, but who can give an intelligent reason for their membership.

VII

THE LAITY

THE great majority of the members of the Church consists of the laity. It is not however easy to define a layman of the Church of England, as the fact of Establishment confuses the position. In the Middle Ages there was no difficulty, every citizen belonged to the Church; but when new denominations came into existence the question arose as to how far their members could in their capacity as citizens still retain their status as laymen of the Established Church: the problem became even more complicated when large numbers had connection neither with the Church of England nor with any other Church, but nevertheless claimed the right to its ministrations. Some solution had to be found in deciding the franchise for election to the House of Laity as a constituent part of the Church Assembly. The choice was between a communicant or a baptismal qualification; in each case there would be a signed declaration of membership of the Church of England. Though there was strong support of the communicant basis, it was rejected on the ground that it might re-introduce the " tests " which had proved so harmful and that it would exclude many who regarded themselves as members of the Church of England. Eventually it was therefore decided that the qualification for admission to the Electoral Roll should be baptism combined with a declaration by those of eighteen years or upwards that they were members of the Church of England and did not belong to any religious body not in communion with it. On this franchise representatives are elected to the Parochial Church Councils, but these must be communicants of the Church of England; they in turn elect to the Ruri-decanal Conferences, which elect to the Diocesan Conference, which elects to the Church Assembly. A long and complicated process of indirect election, but its foundation is the register of those who declare themselves baptised members of the Church of England. A layman for electoral purposes is thus a man (or woman) of eighteen years or upwards who has been baptised, who declares that he is a member of the Church of England and does not belong to any Church not in communion with it. It is a very wide definition, but it excludes the unbaptised, those who might claim that citizenship is equivalent to Church membership, and all Free Churchmen and Roman Catholics. On the electoral rolls there are over three million names, but to discover the total lay membership of the Church of England there must be added the far larger number of those who have not enrolled themselves as electors, as well as those who are under eighteen years of age. The names on the electoral roll give a false impression of the number of those who claim to be the laity of the Church of England.

The Spiritual Rights of the Laity

The Roman Catholic Codex of Canon Law opens its section on the laity by a Canon declaring that the laity have " the right of receiving from the clergy, subject to ecclesiastical discipline, spiritual benefits and the most powerful aids necessary for salvation." The Church of England also provides spiritual benefits to its laity from the cradle to the grave.

Holy Baptism. As soon as possible after its birth the infant is to be brought to Baptism : according to the 1662 Prayer Book by the first or second Sunday after its birth : but the new rubric of the 1928 Book states the Baptism should not be deferred " longer than the fourth, or at furthest the fifth, Sunday unless upon a great and reasonable cause." The majority of children born in this country are baptised by the Church of England. There are however two reforms urgently required. The baptismal service should be made simpler for the sake of those who rarely attend Church and who are unfamiliar with its technical and theological terms. The 1928 Order is an improvement on 1662, but further changes are required if the meaning of Baptism is to be made plain to simple and uninstructed people. Far more important is the necessity of securing godparents who take seriously the promises made by them and who will do their utmost to see that the child is brought up in the Christian faith. At present many of the godparents are often non-practising Christians and it is improbable they will encourage the child to do what they themselves neglect. The whole subject is beset with difficulties, but there is growing feeling among the clergy that the present position is most unsatisfactory and that steps should be taken to remedy it. Indiscriminate baptism is a chief cause of the great difference between the numbers of those who are baptised and of those who are regular communicants.

The Catechism. The Church provides a Catechism to help in the religious training of the child. Modern educational theories are critical of this method of teaching. But whether the Catechism is learnt or not, there are Church Day Schools and Sunday Schools in which the child can be taught the faith of its parents. The Church Day Schools are rapidly declining in numbers, though some limited opportunities for denominational instruction are given either within or outside the State Schools. The numbers entering the Sunday Schools have also decreased, but the teaching and discipline in them have steadily improved. When I was first ordained there were large schools at Portsea in which children from seven to fourteen were taught without any attempt at grading according to age, and every afternoon there was held a Children's Service with well over a thousand children of all ages. It was only the firmness of the staff of curates and the devotion of a large body of teachers which saved these occasions from becoming bear gardens ! But within a few years most of our Sunday Schools were reformed : the children were graded and taught according to their age. Modern methods of instruction were introduced, and now in many dioceses there are experts ready to assist the teachers in the different parishes.

Confirmation. In the Church of England children are confirmed at an older age than either in the Roman Catholic or Eastern Churches. Though much criticised, fourteen is still the average age : it is argued that the child has then reached the age of decision, and that spiritual help is especially needed at a difficult time. There are many however who hold that the age should either be considerably younger or older. Careful enquiries at Visitations show that an equal number lapse whether the Confirmation is at twelve or fourteen. It seems unwise to lay down a hard and fast rule about age ; so much depends upon the child itself, on the conditions of its home, and on the preparation given. The Prayer Book assumes a younger age than that now usually accepted—" so soon as he can say the Creed, the Lord's Prayer and the ten Commandments." Far greater trouble is taken over preparation than used to be the case. Preparation at one time was brief and casual. Knowledge of the Catechism was regarded as sufficient. Nearly fifty years ago an old clergyman of eighty told me that he remembered an Archbishop of York after confirming several hundreds of children in the Minster calling out that he was willing to lay hands on any in the large congregation who had not yet been confirmed! Now Confirmation classes cover a considerable period, and those who do not seem to be ready are deferred until a later occasion. The position however is still far from satisfactory. A recent report on " Confirmation to-day " states that out of " every 100 children born, 67 are baptised, 34 attend Sunday School or Catechism, 26 are confirmed, and 9 make their Communion at Easter." There is clearly something wrong in our methods of preparation when so many of the confirmed fail to become regular communicants. In the report interesting suggestions are made that instead of the sequence of Confirmation and Holy Communion, there should be substituted either Confirmation, Communion and Ratification of Vows (separated from the laying on of hands), or that Communion should be at an earlier age, and Confirmation postponed until much later. But it is very doubtful if either of these suggestions will meet with general approval from the parochial clergy who have had first-hand experience of confirmation work. Most will agree with Dom Gregory Dix when he says : " that our established practice, whatever minor adjustments it may need, offers us an opportunity which is not at present open to either the Eastern or the Western Churches. It offers us the chance of retaining the Western practice of separating Baptism from Confirmation and retaining the ministration of the latter exclusively for the Apostolic minister, with all the significance that implies ; and at the same time restoring the fullness of the New Testament and primitive meaning of Confirmation, which the West has let slip and the East has largely obscured by retaining it only as a feature of *infant* Initiation. I would plead in favour of this that there is a great strength in an established and accepted practice, which cannot easily be compensated for by any changes, however desirable in themselves, for a long time to come."[1]

Holy Communion. After Confirmation the Church is ready to

[1] " The Theology of Confirmation in Relation to Baptism," p. 33.

THE LAITY

give the Holy Communion to its laity. Through the greater part of the Middle Ages lay communion was very rare. The laity were present each Sunday at the Eucharist, but as " spectators and listeners." " It is clear from a good many incidents in the lives of the saints that right down to the sixteenth century the mere fact of frequency was apt to arouse suspicion of extravagance or illuminism. It remained true, broadly speaking, of even later mediæval religion, that the priest as such was normally the only communicant."[1] When the Reformers insisted on the laity communicating " at the least three times in the year," they attempted to make a great advance on existing custom. For a long time however after the Reformation the laity only communicated on the three chief Festivals, and the Holy Communion was not celebrated usually more than once a month. With the Oxford Revival there came a remarkable change, and frequent Communion has become more general. To all its laity who have been baptised and confirmed, and who have faith and repentance the Church offers the Bread and Wine of Life, for the Church of England, unlike the Church of Rome, allows its laity to receive the chalice. In so doing it agrees with the primitive Church and the ancient Churches of the East, though, in the latter, Communion in both kinds is by the method of Intinction. It is possible that in the future Intinction may be permitted in some of our churches as it is already, for hygienic reasons, in some of the churches in the United States.

While repentance and faith, charity with all men, and the resolve to lead a new life are conditions of Communion, it is left open to each communicant to decide whether in preparation he will use the discipline of private confession and observe the ancient custom of fasting. With regard to fasting a rubric in the Revised Prayer Book expresses the mind of the Church of England : " It is an ancient and laudable custom of the Church to receive the Holy Sacrament fasting ; yet for the avoidance of all scruple it is here declared that such preparation may be used or not used according to every man's conscience in the sight of God."

Pastoral Counsel. The laity have also the right to go to their parish clergyman for advice in matters both spiritual and temporal. Some will therefore come to him burdened with the

[1] " The Shape of the Liturgy," by Gregory Dix, p. 598.

sense of sin, so that by the ministry of God's Holy Word they may receive the benefit of absolution ; others will turn to him for help and advice in saying their prayers and in resisting temptation ; others will look to him for help in solving intellectual and moral problems. By sympathetic advice, by prayer, and sometimes by the suggestion of suitable books to read, he will help the laity in their spiritual life. But, in addition to giving spiritual counsel, by a long-honoured tradition in the Church of England the laity often turn to the parish clergy for help in many of their daily problems, which may range from the witnessing of a signature to advice as to how best to deal with some difficult member of their own family. And often, though not so much in these days of social insurance as once was the case, the poorer of the laity turn to their parish priest for assistance in their bodily necessities. Izaak Walton's description of George Herbert is still applicable to many of our clergy : " Nor did he ever turn his face from any that he saw in want, but would relieve them : especially his poorer neighbours : to the meanest of whose homes he would go, and inform himself of their wants and relieve them cheerfully."

Marriage. The Church is ready with its blessing at the marriage of its members. It is here that the confusion is most evident due to the connection between Church and State. Many who are only nominal members of the Church expect to be married with its blessing, and appear to be totally unaware of the solemnity of the promises they must make that their union will be lifelong, to be broken only by death. So many difficulties and so much confusion arise that the solution may prove to be that marriage in the Registry should be the rule while the Church would subsequently give its blessing only to those who are genuinely its members and who accept its conditions. The Church makes its position clear by refusing to marry those who have a previous husband or wife still living, and by recommending that instruction on the meaning of Christian marriage should be given to all who wish the benefit of its blessing.

Visitation of the Sick. And when illness comes it is the duty of the parish priest to visit the sick man's house, bringing to him spiritual health and consolation. George Herbert in the " Country Parson " gives a description of the parson's duty in visiting the sick : " He followeth the Church's counsel, namely in persuading them to particular confession, labouring to make them understand the great use of this ancient and pious ordinance, and how necessary it is in some cases : he also urges them to do some pious charitable works, as a necessary evidence and fruit of their works, at that time especially : the participation of the Holy Sacrament, how comfortable and Sovereign a Medecine it is to all sinsick souls he plainly intimateth to the sick person." Often in these days the parish priest has to visit the sick in the hospital to which they have been removed instead of in their homes as in the past. At one time when almost any serious illness was more likely than now to prove fatal, the emphasis was naturally laid on preparation for death, but now more often the parish priest goes as a minister of spiritual healing. He believes that the church has a mission to the body as well as to the soul ; certainly body and mind are closely connected, and spiritual improvement will sometimes hasten physical recovery. As a sign of God's blessing he may lay his hand upon the patient, or anoint him with oil : but though to all who have penitence and faith there is certainty of spiritual benefit through these outward signs, they give no pledge of physical recovery. The actual words of the Visitation of the Sick are now rarely used, but the directions it contains still hold good. The minister must still move the sick person to penitence, forgiveness and amendment ; to make a special confession of his sins if he feels his conscience troubled in any weighty matter, and he should absolve him " if he humbly and heartily desire it." And if through infirmity he is unable to come to church, the Prayer Book provides that at his sick bed he should receive the Holy Communion. Often in these days the Communion is given by means of Reservation. If for some reason of extremity it is impossible for him to receive the Sacrament, the Prayer Book orders the curate to " instruct him that if he do truly repent him of his sins, and steadfastly believe that Jesus Christ hath suffered death upon the Cross for him : and shed His blood for his redemption, earnestly remembering the benefits he hath thereby, and giving Him hearty thanks therefore he doth eat and drink the Body and Blood of our Saviour Christ profitably to the soul's health, although he do not receive the Sacrament with his mouth."

Death. And finally when death comes the Church will lay to rest with its blessing, in its God's acre, the bodies of its children who have been called from this life, and it commends their souls in sure and certain hope of the life beyond the grave. And although in the 1662 Prayer Book there are no direct prayers for the dead, yet the custom is now general that prayers should be offered for them. They are prayed for not as dead, but as living in the unseen world. The ancient and Catholic practice of prayer for the dead finds expression in some of the prayers in the 1928 book, and in numerous manuals of Anglican devotion.

Thus, from the cradle to the grave, the Church stage by stage offers its blessing and its help to its children as they make their pilgrimage through life.

The Laity and the Government of the Church

The laity are given a place in the government and administration of the affairs of the Church. This is strictly limited : there are certain matters outside their province, for it is not within their competence to define the doctrine of the Church, to consecrate or ordain its ministers, or to administer the Sacraments (except Baptism in great emergency). But from the earliest days it appears that the laity were consulted on matters concerning the life and work of the Church, and that their assent by acclamation was usually expected. There are many opportunities of legislative and administrative work open to laymen and laywomen of the Church of England ; this is in striking contrast to the statement once made by a dignitary at the Vatican to Cardinal Manning : "What is the province of the laity ? To hunt, to shoot, to entertain ? These matters they understand, but to meddle with ecclesiastical matters they have no right at all."[1]

There are three directions in which the laity make their influence felt in the administration and work of the Church. First, they have a legal position in its government from the Parochial Church Council upwards. Every parish must now have a Church Electoral Roll on which there should be entered the names of lay members of the Church of England of eighteen years of age and upwards. This Roll should be regarded as of real importance. Only those whose names are on it are qualified for a vote in parochial matters, and if Parliament is doubtful about any Measure sent to it by the Church Assembly it will naturally desire to know how far it comes from a body which is really representative of the Church. To be of value these Rolls

[1] "Life of Cardinal Manning," by E. S. Purcell, Vol. II, p. 318.

need frequent revision. This should be as frequent and careful as the electoral rolls for a constituency. But they are often allowed to get out of date, and on them there may still be found the names of those who have long since moved elsewhere or who have died. There are numbers of church people who would be qualified to vote, but who have never taken the trouble to see that their names are on the Church Electoral Roll ; there are others who are afraid that their enrolment might commit them to subscriptions and responsibilities which they wish to avoid.

All those who are on the Roll are entitled to attend the annual Parochial Church Meeting. As a rule this meeting is very poorly attended, but it elects representatives to form the Parochial Church Council. Here an important difference should be noted —while the electors need not be communicants, only those who are communicants and of twenty-one years of age and upwards are eligible for election. The Church assemblies consist therefore only of those who are its communicant members. The primary duty of the Church Council is " to co-operate with the Incumbent in the initiation, conduct and development of church work both within the parish and outside." It takes over many duties which once belonged to the churchwardens and is the chief financial authority of the parish. When the benefice is vacant it has the right to make representations to the bishop and patron as to the type of incumbent it regards as most suitable for its parish, and under certain conditions it may appeal to the bishop against the nomination made by the patron. Many different opinions are expressed about the value of these councils ; some incumbents regard them as sheer waste of time or a dangerous encroachment on their authority ; there are others who have found them of great value ; many are still doubtful about their practical usefulness. This depends on the attitude adopted towards them both by the incumbent and the lay members. If the incumbent resents criticism and confines discussion to methods of raising funds or the arranging of a parish social, the council will soon become a register of his wishes, without initiative or any sense of responsibility. On the other hand, if its members only attend its meetings occasionally, or when they do come sit silent throughout them, and afterwards make their speeches to one another when the meeting has adjourned, they will soon discourage the incumbent from attempts at making the council a reality. But if the chairman sees and uses the possibilities of the council and does his utmost to educate it, and if on it there are members who are not afraid of speaking out their minds constructively as well as critically, it will become a powerful force for good in the parish.

The Church Councils or the parochial meetings elect to the Ruri-Decanal Conferences. These consist of the clergy and the elected lay representatives of the different parishes of the rural deanery. Though they have no legal authority they can elect to the diocesan conference. Their value consists in that they give an opportunity to the clergy and laity to meet and discuss together matters which concern not only their own parishes, but the whole of the deanery. In some deaneries these conferences have been useful in voicing the views of the church on local problems of morals and good government. Their importance will largely depend upon the vision and initiative of the rural dean.

The Diocesan Conference is of greater importance. This has now a legal place in the government of the church, and its constitution must be in accordance with the rules laid down by the Church Assembly. In many dioceses every parish sends a lay representative. At its meetings diocesan finance comes under review and reports of various committees are submitted to it for discussion and criticism. Often its meetings are occupied solely with business, but occasionally there are debates on matters of general interest to the Church. The Conference also appoints the members of its various committees and elects its lay representatives to the Church Assembly.

The Church Assembly is the climax of this somewhat complicated system of Church government. It consists of the three separate houses of bishops, clergy and laity, who on certain subjects vote separately. It does not supersede Convocation, nor does it assume any rights which belong to the Convocations alone, but it is " free to discuss any proposals concerning the Church of England and to make provision in respect thereof," and, as will be pointed out in a later chapter, it has also certain powers of legislation, subject to the two Houses of Parliament.

The Church thus has a lay electorate of its own, from the Parish to the Church Assembly. This is independent of the Parliamentary electorate. This system has been criticised, notably by Bishop Hensley Henson who looked upon it as

" sectarianising the National Church." But under the changed conditions of our time, when the citizens of the nation do not necessarily belong to the Church of England, or to any other Church, it is inevitable that the definitely Church electorate should consist of a minority. It is an advantage that the difference between the Church and the State should thus be made clear. The House of Commons represents the laymen of the nation, but not of the Church; the Church Assembly represents the laymen of the Church, but not of the nation. Archbishop Davidson in introducing the Prayer Book Measure in the House of Lords made this plain : " The House of Laity in the Church Assembly do not profess to represent the people of England, but they do profess to represent the Church of England : the people who care about these matters and go to Church, who want to use their Prayer Book, who care about the form that book should take, who understand the question, and who are the people really qualified to speak."[1] This structure of representative assemblies of the laity still needs to be filled in, so that each genuinely represents the majority of Church people of all classes. Their weakness, at present, is in the electoral rolls and in the lack of interest shown by many in the affairs of their Church and diocese. If, however, there should come to the Church some great shock, such as Disestablishment, the machinery is ready, and would not have to be improvised, to enable the Church to deal with its administrative and financial work.

Secondly, the laity have considerable influence in church work and life through holding the offices of churchwardens and sidesmen. It is hard to exaggerate the value of the work which has been done by many of them. Their keenness and devotion to their parish church sometimes surpasses those of the incumbent. It is *their* Church, for it belongs to the town or village where they have their home. Some of them know every stone of the church. There are wardens who have learned everything they can about its history. Year after year in all weathers they have been regular in attendance at its worship. They look after its seating, its fabric, its heating; they see it is clean and kept in good repair; church council or no church council, to all intents and purposes most of them control its finances; incumbents and assistant curates come and go, but the churchwardens remain : " I have seen six vicars," said one of these

---

[1] " Randall Davidson," by George Bell, Vol. II, p. 1245.

wardens to a new vicar " and I hope very much that I may yet see a seventh ! " Sometimes, indeed, their devotion to their church is so great that when old age and infirmities have crept on, they find it almost impossible to surrender the office they have held for so long, and neither incumbent nor church council dare suggest to a faithful servant that the time for his resignation has come. They dislike innovations, and are suspicious of departures from accustomed ways, so they give to their church and parish a valuable element of stability and continuity.

There are a considerable number of parishes in lay patronage. Through their appointments to them the laity have a direct influence upon the clergy. Where the patron is resident in or near the parish and takes an active interest in all its affairs he will probably make as good an appointment as a bishop or a board of patronage. I have known many lay patrons who have taken infinite trouble over the appointments they have had to make, making full enquiries about possible men, interviewing them, sometimes even privately visiting the church in which the clergyman recommended to them is officiating, and forming their opinion both of his preaching and of the manner in which he conducts divine worship. There are however patrons who make their choice on grounds largely irrelevant—one patron told me : " I always ask a man how long he preaches ; if he says fifteen minutes I have done with him ; if he says ten I shall probably appoint him ! " On another occasion the lay patron of a country benefice told me that he always looked first for a good cricketer ! But usually the exercise of lay patronage is careful and conscientious. Difficulties are more likely to arise if the patron has no interest in the parish ; then to save himself trouble he is tempted to appoint with little enquiry one of the many applicants who write to him. On the balance however the Church has gained rather than lost by lay patronage ; the lay patron usually looks for men who are likely to be " good mixers " and will take an interest in the everyday life of their parishioners, rather than men who are eloquent in the pulpit and correct in the conduct of worship. They have their ideals as to the kind of man they want for their parish priest, and these are usually healthy and sensible. They may not always express them, but they really want a man who will first and foremost be the pastor of his flock.

The Duties of the Laity

Privileges carry with them corresponding duties, and the laity in response to what the Church offers them should worship, witness, serve and give. Their first duty is worship. At one time this was generally recognised ; Sunday by Sunday the faithful laity took part in the worship of their parish church. Charles Morgan in one of the most charming of his essays in " Reflections in a Mirror," describes the regular ritual of Churchgoing in his childhood : " the fields, the bells, the angle of the sun, of other figures approaching down the convergent lands of the hill opposite. In the Churchyard, if the five-minute bell had not yet begun, there was a pause for neighbourly conversation, and it was possible to wander among the graves and read again an inscription which long ago had been learned by heart. Inside the church itself was a mingling of daylight and lamplight ; a pattern of glass which would presently darken, a low gleam of stone and wood." The description brings back my childhood of nearly seventy years ago, when in the morning the " quality " came to church, occupying the front pews ; the farmers and small tradespeople sat just behind them ; and the Sunday School away at the back. In the evening these places, with the exception of the front pews, were taken by the servants and the villagers ; at the last stroke of the bell a crowd of lads clattered in and rather noisily filled the back seats. In the country almost everyone came to one or other of the two services, some indeed came to both. Usually those who did not appear felt it necessary to make some excuse. Jane Austen's mother always had a severe headache shortly before the hour of Morning Prayer, though usually it disappeared in time for the midday meal. No doubt there was much that was conventional in this regular Churchgoing, social custom favoured it then as much as now it discourages it, and in the poorer parts of the great cities it has never been a regular habit. The laity of to-day should recognise that it is part of their duty to God and His Church to be regular at public worship. It should be treated as an obligation which should over-rule disinclination.

The laity should not be merely passive witnesses of worship. As far as possible they should take an active part in the offering of prayer and praise. In the Liturgy of early days the whole congregation took some part. " In the early Church the deliberate effort was made to divide up the functions of worship among as many people as possible. The bishop was, when possible, the celebrant, and was surrounded by his priests who (at least at Rome) con-celebrated with him ; the deacons, headed by the archdeacon, and the sub-deacons had their share in the reading of the lessons and the ceremonial of the altar : chanters and choir, acolytes and doorkeepers all had their place ; the people too had their share in the action, in the offering of the gifts and the kiss of peace and the communion."[1] The bishops, priests and deacons had their special functions to perform, but the laity also had something to do, and not only to watch and hear. They took their part in the great intercession ; they made their offerings—the oblations—and they received the consecrated bread and wine. Between the New Testament days and the fourth century the Eucharist was fundamentally regarded as something done, rather than said, and this was done not by the clergy alone, but by the clergy and laity together, each order performing its special function. The layman received the Spirit for his liturgy by confirmation, the cleric for his special function by ordination.[2] Unfortunately in our Order of Communion, the laity have no opportunity of joining in the intercessions except by the " Amen." But they respond with the Kyries, repeat together the Creed, make their special offerings in the collection, and join in the Sanctus, the Lord's Prayer and the Gloria. In recent years much has been done to give the laity an active part, as in primitive days, in the celebration of the Liturgy. There are lay servers who help to prepare the altar, to light and extinguish the candles, to hand the offertory to the priest, to bring to him the oblations of bread and wine, and sometimes lead in saying the Confession. Occasionally, too, the Epistle is read by a layman, and recently the necessity of the priest receiving help in administering to large numbers of communicants has resulted in Convocation approving of the bishops granting permission in certain cases for a layman to administer the chalice. The more the laity can be found an active place in the liturgy, the nearer we approach to the early conception of it as an offering of the whole Church.

[1] " Liturgy and Society," by A. G. Hebert, p. 75.
[2] " The Shape of the Liturgy," by Gregory Dix, Chap. II.

The same principle is seen elsewhere in the worship of the Church. The laity are given opportunities of assisting in it. Some are now licensed to take the greater part of Mattins and Evensong in the absence of the priest, or to help him when present. There are others who, Sunday by Sunday, not only take the service, but preach the sermon. In many parishes it is usual for a layman to read the Lessons; and in almost every church laymen, and sometimes laywomen, are found in the choir leading the people in prayer and praise.

Worship that does not show its fruits in life and conduct is worse than useless; so it is the duty of the laity to witness to the reality of their faith by the holiness of their lives. The Church of England is a school of saints, and has had a great company of laymen and laywomen who have borne their witness to their Master by their character and work. Saintship in the Church of England is usually of the quiet, restrained and practical type, rarely expressing itself in the ascetism or vehement fervour characteristic of South Europe or of the East. Nicholas Ferrar, John Evelyn, Izaak Walton, Robert Nelson, William Wilberforce, Lord Shaftesbury, Roundell Palmer (Lord Selborne), W. E. Gladstone, the late Lord Halifax are typical of English lay Churchmanship. In our own day there have been tens of thousands among the laity of all classes who have borne quiet, consistent witness. I think of so many known to me personally—of a wealthy stockbroker who led a strictly disciplined life in secret, and who anonymously gave away large sums of money; of a woman of property who used her wealth to live among and to nurse back to health convalescents from the poorer parts of London; of a layman who gave his time and money to work among some of the roughest lads of a great city; of a retired general of wonderful charm and generosity who not only gave hours of his time in raising money for church extension, but who until the day of his death was the friend of rich and poor in the parishes in which he lived. In Moscow I saw under an eikon of Heaven an inscription—a chance survival from the days of anti-Christian propaganda—drawing attention to the fact that though it showed kings, priests, warriors and nobles among the redeemed, there were no mechanics, artisans, or poor and needy folk. But all who have lived in working-class parishes can recall the names of many of such who have witnessed to Christ. Here again I think of some I have known—of the young man who by his quiet courage and steadfastness brought to Confirmation half a dozen of his comrades in the workshop who had once joined in mocking him : of a woman on the old age pension who by her gentle love and unselfishness opened to the clergy the doors of half the houses in a street from which religion had seemed to be banished : of a man who year by year suffered persecution in a blasphemous shop and by his own courage heartened those who were weaker : and of scores of others whose lives were more effective than most sermons. It was not that most of these men and women of different social position spoke frequently about their religion ; it was just what they were and did in their daily life which had most influence on those who came into contact with them. To them there may be applied the description which was given by Sir Claud Schuster of a mountaineering friend : " He was the only man of my acquaintance," he wrote, " who deliberately and perseveringly modelled his life on what he conceived to be the principles of the Gospel. He never said so, nor did he ever in my hearing allude to any matter of religion. It was by what he said about other things, and by what he did not say : and by what he did and by what he did not : and by the way in which he spoke and acted and refrained that you could guess the mainspring of his life."[1]

It is also the duty of the laity to render active service in the building up and the extension of the Church. Our Church has a great army of keen workers. In one sense all honest and useful work is Christian work. But here the term " Church worker " is applied to those who make themselves responsible for some definite Church work, from that of a choir boy to that of a licensed lay reader : theologians, lay readers, organists, servers, clerks and vergers, bellringers, choir boys and choir men, day and Sunday school teachers, district visitors, helpers in clubs and youth organisations, moral and social welfare workers, journalists, artists and craftsmen all help to make up a great army of Church workers probably unsurpassed by any other Church in Christendom. The work they undertake is so varied that it is impossible to enumerate all its forms. This development of lay work both among men and women has been one of the most encouraging features in the life of our Church in the last half century. Often personal service is given through great organisations such as the Mothers' Union, the Church of England Men's Society, the

[1] " Men, Women and Mountains."

Girls' Friendly Society, the Church Lads' Brigade. Special mention must be made of the Church Army, which for town and country parishes provides lay evangelists; but in addition to this it has its evangelistic teams and mission vans, its labour homes, its hostels, its huts and recreation rooms for the men in the Services, and it even has its own housing programme. Though a clergyman is at its head, it is essentially a laymen's movement showing remarkable initiative and enterprise.

The laity must also give to the support of the Church according to their means. In the past wealthy laymen have given munificently to the Church : they built great churches and schools, and made rich contributions to Church funds. Their gifts, combined with the endowments of the Church, gave the impression that it was immensely wealthy and that its resources were sufficient for all its needs. Whatever may have been once the case, this is no longer true. The necessary expenditure on Church work has gone up with the general rise in the cost of living, while those who once were the chief financial supporters of the Church have become poor through heavy taxation. Some, too, who at one time would have given to the Church now prefer to support hospitals and advanced education. The Church has therefore to rely on a large number of small subscriptions instead of a few substantial gifts. This is a much sounder position, though it creates new problems. Many of the laity find it difficult to realise the changed conditions of to-day, and though they have to pay more for wages, furniture and entertainment, they do not always appreciate how large have been the increases in the payment of living agents and in the running expense of the buildings and organisations of the Church. In many parishes the Free Will Offering and the Duplex Schemes have been adopted with marked success. Under these schemes the laity whether they come to church or not on any particular Sunday pay regularly a stated amount towards its upkeep. Often a definite proportion of their contribution is spent on missionary work. This is far more satisfactory than dependence on the Sunday collections, when a series of wet Sundays may bring the parochial finances to a bankrupt condition. A vigorous campaign is required to bring home to the laity the gravity of the present position. Unless they give in proportion to the rise both of their own incomes and to the rise in Church expenses it is inevitable that much valuable work will have to be abandoned and all hope of Church extension suspended. The Prayer Book in one of the rubrics at the end of the Order of Communion reminds the laity of their duty to support the clergy : " And yearly at Easter every parishioner shall reckon with the Parson, Vicar, or Curate or his or their deputy, and pay to them or him all Ecclesiastical Duties accustomably due then and at that time to be paid."

Three Groups of Laity

The laity of the Church of England can be grouped into three classes. The first consists of those who are instructed and convinced Churchmen and Churchwomen. They are devoted to their Church, prepared to work for it and to give to it to the utmost of their ability. Some of these are to be found in every parish. No trouble is too great, no sacrifice is too severe ; they are ready at all times to do their utmost for the Church of which they are thankful to be members. They are attracted neither by Rome nor by Nonconformity, but will live and die in the Church of their Baptism.

Next there are the laity who make their Communion occasionally, attend church fairly frequently, and are ready to make their contribution—on a moderate scale—to the funds of the Church. They cannot be described as enthusiastic Church members. They are critical of the way in which the Church is managed, and especially of the way in which their own clergyman preaches and conducts the services. If the Church is attacked they will come to its defence, but they are vague about its faith, and sit loose to its discipline. They dislike changes— what was good enough for their fathers is good enough for them. They look on the Church as a national agency for teaching sound morals, though they are uncomfortable about its attitude towards the marriage of the divorced. They are afraid of being thought narrow, and wish that on certain matters the Church was more broad-minded. They shrink from definite statements about the supernatural, and prefer vagueness to precision in matters of doctrine. But as baptized, confirmed, and occasional communicants, they would claim without hesitation to be regarded as among the laity of the Church of England. This is not a group with rigid boundaries ; many pass from it into the ranks of those who are convinced and zealous in their Churchmanship. And with more intensive teaching on the faith and worship of the Church, many more would change a passive and traditional assent into enthusiastic and whole-hearted allegiance.

There is a third group : those who call themselves " C. of E.," who claim the benefits of the Church on rare occasions in their lives, but who never attend its services, except on some special day of prayer and praise. They know nothing of its doctrine, worship or discipline ; but they would be indignant at any attempt to un-Church them. They expect their children to be baptised by its ministers ; they would wish to be married with its rites, and as a matter of course they assume that at death they will be buried with the Prayer Book Service in consecrated ground. It would be wrong to despise this large group. Those who belong to it have never committed themselves to hostility against the Church ; most of them faintly and uncertainly are pre-disposed in its favour. They take the position of Burge in Bernard Shaw's " Back to Methuselah " when he says : " The Church is all right essentially. Get rid of the establish-ment : get rid of the bishops : get rid of the candlesticks : get rid of the Thirty-Nine Articles ; and the Church of England is just as good as any other Church : and I don't care who hears me say so ! " In this group the Church has a large field for evangelisation. Possibly it could best be reached through discussion classes and meetings, such as those which were held as " Padre's Hours " in the army during the war. Leadership Courses, which were so successfully inaugurated by the R.A.F. for men who wished to know the meaning of Christian leader-ship, might well be adapted to civilian life. Many who would hesitate at committing themselves to Church-going might find a half-way house towards it through attendance at these dis-cussion groups or courses.

The greatest need of the Church is not more laity, but better instructed laity. Nothing would strengthen the Church more than an increase in the number of its laity who are able to bear intelligent witness to their faith. No effort should be spared to build up in every parish a band of laymen and laywomen who are not only devoted to the Church, but who can give an intelligent reason for their membership.

VIII

THE CHURCH AND STATE

*The Church should frankly face the dangers of its position.
At the moment Parliament has no desire to exercise active
control over the Church or gratuitously to interfere in its
concerns. But within a few years a neutral attitude may
have changed into hostility, and the Church will find it is then
useless to ask for reform or for greater freedom. It should
not acquiesce any longer in a relationship with the State
which might suddenly prove to be inconsistent in practice
as well as in principle with religious freedom. Churchmen
are so accustomed to the existing relationship between
Church and State that they fail to see how strange and
anomalous it appears to other Churches especially those
which attach importance to religious freedom.*

VIII

THE CHURCH AND STATE

SEVERE criticism has been lately directed against the existence of national churches. This is vigorously expressed by Professor Arnold Toynbee, in his great work " A Study of History." He writes that in Protestant countries the œcumenical Catholic Church has been replaced " by a plurality of parochial ' churches,' each of which is borne upon the establishment of some particular parochial sovereign state, is subject *de facto* to the sovereign power in the state to which it belongs, and is confined in its membership to such Christians as happen to live within this particular state's frontier. In the freest flight of imagination it would be difficult to conceive of a sharper contradiction of the essence of Christianity—and the essence of all the other historic ' higher religions ' as well—than is embodied in this monstrous product of the impact of Parochialism upon the Western Christian Church in the Modern Age of our Western history."[1]

All Christians would agree with Dr. Toynbee that a national Church might become so parochial that it contradicted " the essence of Christianity," but it does not necessarily follow either that the Roman Catholic Church transcends all national boundaries or that a national Church suffers from the defects so vividly described in the above passage. Two wars have proved that the Roman Catholic citizen is as nationalist and patriotic as the Anglican, the Greek Orthodox or the Protestant. German, Austrian, Polish and Italian Roman Catholics have supported their nation as ardently as the Dutch Calvinist, the German Lutheran, or the American Baptist : Cardinal Hinsley and his co-religionists did not allow their religion to prevent them from serving their country as patriotically as Anglicans. Nor is the Papacy itself free from the taint of nationalism. Professor Toynbee deplores " that at a time when to all appearances the Parochial Sovereign State has become

[1] Vol. IV, p. 222.

the chief obstacle to human welfare and, indeed, the arch-enemy of the human race, the Pope should have ranged himself, even if only formally on the side of this pernicious institutional anachronism by reassuming his own title to parochial sovereignty."[1] While before Italy joined in the war the Pope made a series of remarkable pronouncements which most Christians welcomed, there was a noticeable change in tone when his own country became one of the belligerents. There was then no denunciation of the unjustified attack on Abyssinia, nor of the cruelties committed on its people by the invaders. Even more significant was the silence of His Holiness in face of the appalling atrocities perpetrated against the Poles, the Czechs, the Russians and the Jews. General pronouncements were still made, but there was no clear and uncompromising denunciation of the Nazi arch-criminals. The silence was only broken when there seemed some fear that Rome itself might suffer at the hands of the allies, and the outspokenness which was absent when Abyssinia, Warsaw and London were bombed resounded when the Holy City seemed to be in danger. National sympathies once again were of greater weight than œcumenical claims.

On the other hand, a National Church need neither be so circumscribed nor State controlled as might be gathered from Professor Toynbee's statement. The Church of England is in close communication and friendly relationship with Churches both reformed and unreformed in different parts of the world, and its members can make their communion freely in Churches belonging to the Anglican Communion both in the East and West. And while State control is a great danger to a national Church, the Church of England as we shall see later has in practice freedom which is hardly equalled by any other Church or sect : the Church of Scotland, though established, has complete spiritual freedom ; and many of the Continental Churches have offered vigorous resistance to illegitimate claims on the part of the State.

The Idea of a National Church

The central idea of a National Church is that it should manage its ecclesiastical affairs without external interference : it is the

[1] Ibid., p. 221.

result of the demand for freedom from foreign dictation. " The root idea of the National Church in England is simply this— that England can manage its own ecclesiastical affairs without interference from outside, because experience had shown that that interference was a hindrance and not a help."[1] All through the Middle Ages there had been frequent conflict between the nation, represented by the Sovereign or the Parliament, and the Papacy. The Church of England was in full communion with the rest of Western Christendom, with minor exceptions and additions it obeyed the same Canon Law, and it recognised the spiritual authority of the Pope. But there was frequent irritation and friction caused by the claims of the Pope to inter- fere with the domestic arrangements of the Church. He de- manded sees and benefices to which he could appoint Italian and French ecclesiastics ; he exacted large sums in taxation, which sometimes went into the coffers of kingdoms at war with England ; and he encouraged appeals to Rome from the national courts. The climax came in Henry VIII's reign when the Pope refused, for political reasons, to give to the King of England the annulment requested and summoned him to plead his suit before his court at Rome. This was only the last of a long series of troubles between the English State and the Papacy. The Reformation in England was first political and administrative in character ; changes in doctrine and wor- ship followed later. The ideal of the Papacy as the source of spiritual authority above all nations was noble and inspiring, but in actual practice the Papacy had become a highly centralised bureaucracy, slow and cumbrous in its movements, exacting and grasping in its demands for money, and pursuing a policy as worldly and realistic as that of any other European state. The King's repudiation of Papal authority was thus in harmony with the growing sense of national sentiment, and it was en- dorsed by the Convocations in 1534 when they declared that the Roman Pontiff has no " greater jurisdiction bestowed on him by God in the Holy Scriptures in this realm of England than any other foreign bishop."

A National Church, therefore, exercises the right to arrange its rites and ceremonies and to order its discipline in the manner most in accordance with the customs and outlook of the nation. This is asserted in the Thirty-fourth Article : " Every particular

[1] " The Church and the Nation," by Mandell Creighton, p. 212.

or National Church hath authority to ordain, change and abolish
ceremonies, or rites of the Church ordained only by man's
authority, so that all things be done to edifying." This does not
refer to doctrine or to the nature of the ministry. Truth remains
always the same, and the doctrine of the Church of England
is the doctrine of the Catholic Church. There is no claim made
by the Church of England to ordain, change or abolish the
Scriptures, the Creeds, the Sacraments or the historic ministry.
These are the common possessions of the whole Catholic Church.
But rites and ceremonies appropriate in one part of the Church
may only invite amusement and astonishment elsewhere:
" what is supremely edifying in Honolulu may be grotesque
in London."[1] A nation has its own special modes of expression,
its traditions and its customs : these, when possible, should be
used and sanctified by the Church in its worship. In the early
Church no attempt was made to impose an iron and rigid uniformity on all the Christian congregations ; there was freedom
and elasticity. Pope Gregory instructs Augustine not to force
upon the newly-converted English all the Roman customs, but
to make choice of anything he has found in the Roman, or the
Gallican, or any other Church, which may be more acceptable
to Almighty God, and sedulously to teach it to the Church of
the English. " Choose from every Church those things that
are pious, religious, and upright, and when you have, as it
were, made them up into one body, let the minds of the English
be accustomed thereto."[2] The Church of England has asserted
its right to order its own rites and ceremonies as may best help
its people to worship God. It has freely borrowed them from
many Churches and centuries, as well as making its own contribution to the worship of the Church Universal.

Originally the National Church was the nation on its religious
side. Its faith and worship were the faith and worship of the
whole nation. In the Middle Ages it was unthinkable that in
the same nation there should be more than one form of religion.
The existence of different and competing bodies of Christians
all tolerated by the State was then inconceivable. There was
one Church and one Nation. The Church and State naturally
grew together. There is no special moment in English history
of which it can be said that the Church was established when

[1] E. J. Bicknell, " The Thirty-Nine Articles," p. 377.
Bede's " Ecclesiastical History," p. 39. " Everyman " edition

previously it had no connection with the State. The controversies between the Church and the State were between different sets of officials within the nation, representing respectively ecclesiastical and secular interests. After the Reformation the theory survived for a time that there was complete unity between Church and State—every citizen was naturally a Churchman. Richard Hooker expressed this when he wrote : " There is not any man of the Church of England but the same man is also a member of the Commonwealth : nor any man a member of the Commonwealth which is not also of the Church of England." The ideal was that the whole nation should belong to the same Church, hold the same faith, and worship with the same prayers and in the same manner. In Church and Nation thus constituted, the Convocations were the assemblies of the clergy, and the two Houses of Parliament the assemblies of the laity. There was a clear distinction of function ; the Christian Prince, that is the individual Sovereign or the State, representing a Christian nation " rule all estates and degrees committed to their charge by God, whether they be Ecclesiastical or Temporal, and restrain with the civil sword the stubborn and evil doers " ; [1] but the Temporal power made no claim to minister God's Word and Sacraments ; this was exclusively the work of those who by ordination had been set apart for it.

But the theory of the complete union of Church and Nation speedily broke down, though strenuous attempts were made to maintain it by penalising those who did not conform to the national Church. Harsh laws were enacted against both the Roman Catholic and Protestant minorities. After a long struggle the principle of toleration was accepted, to the great and lasting benefit of religion. Disabilities which penalised those who were not members of the Established Church were gradually removed, until complete religious freedom was gained. But external unity has vanished, for in addition to the Church of England there are other Churches which have their own organisations, worship and doctrines. And with the coming of toleration, Parliament is no longer exclusively Anglican in its membership. In both Houses there are many who do not belong to the Church of England, and there are some who have no religious belief. At any time both the Government and the House of Commons may contain only a minority of

[1] Article XXXVII.

Churchmen. This is the case at present. From these changes it follows that neither the Church of England exclusively represents the religion of the nation, nor is the House of Commons an assembly of the laity of the Church. The position, therefore, has been profoundly changed since the days when the Church and State were regarded as identical, and when the Church was undisputedly the Church of the nation. Under the different conditions of to-day the question is bound to be asked if the Church of England can be still rightly regarded as the National Church?

The National Church of England

(1) The Church of England has been associated in the closest way with the birth, growth and development of the British nation. It introduced civilisation to the Anglo-Saxon peoples : it gave them through its own unity the conception of a united kingdom : it brought the island kingdom into contact with the religion and culture of the continent : it gave the English people their first literature and their noblest buildings : it sheltered its earliest Parliament in the Chapter House of its Abbey at Westminster : it softened the fierceness and cruelties of mediæval life : it provided great schools and colleges : through the translation of the Bible it brought the noblest literature of mankind to the homes of rich and poor, and helped to form the English tongue : it fashioned prayers which have been used by millions in all parts of the world : its sons and daughters have been foremost for over a thousand years in serving the nation in every department of public life : it has helped in the creation of the national ideals of duty, responsibility and service. Our cathedrals and ancient churches are standing witnesses to the interweaving of the fortunes of the Church and the Nation for over ten centuries. The cathedral I know best is the history in stone of the Church and the Nation. On the choir screens at Winchester there rest six mediæval mortuary chests containing the remains of Anglo-Saxon kings, three of them belonging to the seventh century. Among the bones of the eleven persons in these chests are those of Cynegils, first Christian king of the West Saxons ; Egbert, the grandfather of Alfred the Great and crowned " King of all England " ;

and the Danish King Cnut. Here, too, are the bones of Queen Emma, described in a now destroyed Latin inscription as " The Wife and Mother of Kings." These remains, more than any other relics in Great Britain, carry us back to the earliest day of our nation's history. On the floor of the choir is the reputed tomb of Rufus, slain in the New Forest and brought to Winchester in the cart of a charcoal burner. Close by in the South partition wall of the choir screen is the leaden coffin of the second son of the Conqueror, also killed in the Forest by the goring of a stag. In the nave are the chantries of William de Edyngton, Lord Chancellor to Edward III and first Prelate of the Garter, and of William of Wykeham, the great Chancellor and the Founder of Winchester College and New College. Elsewhere are the chantries of four famous bishop statesmen— Cardinal Beaufort, William Waynflete, Richard Fox, Stephen Gardiner—all Chancellors of England. The eastern part of the Lady Chapel is a thank-offering for the birth of Prince Arthur, the eldest son of Henry VII, christened in the cathedral. In Bishop Gardiner's chantry there is preserved a chair in which it is believed that Queen Mary sat at her marriage with Philip of Spain. The shattered glass in the Great West window is a memorial of the days when the Puritans brought destruction into the cathedral. The two large volumes, a Bible and a Prayer Book on the altar, were Charles II's gifts to the cathedral. In the nave are Rolls of Honour with the names of officers and men of Hampshire regiments who, in the last war, had made the great sacrifice. Stained glass windows commemorate the Jubilee of George V and the Coronation of the present King and Queen. Almost at every turn there can be found memorials of those who have left their mark on the national life—ecclesiastics, warriors, educationalists, philanthropists and writers. The story of the Church and Nation unrolls before our eyes as we walk through the cathedral. What is true of Winchester is as true of Canterbury, York, Westminster Abbey, and when we come to modern history, of St. Paul's. In a less degree it is the same with every cathedral and ancient church throughout the land, they speak through tombs, memorials, inscriptions, gifts, and even through the damage wrought in troubled days, of the long unbroken partnership of Church and State in the history of the English people.

(2) Numerically, also, the Church of England still has some

right to be regarded as the National Church. Proportionately to the growth of population, its membership is smaller than in the past. The electoral rolls contain about three and a half million names : the communicants on Easter Day are fewer, just under two and a quarter million : but these figures do not include children, nor the very large number of adults who regard themselves as " C. of E.," though only very occasionally attendants at its services. In the Army it is estimated that about 70 per cent. of the men would describe themselves as Church of England, though their membership is often only nominal. But these loosely attached members bring their children to be baptized in the church, are married by its clergy according to its rites, and would wish their dead to be buried in consecrated ground with the Anglican service said over their bodies. It has been said, though I am unable to vouch for the accuracy of the statement, " that there are seven chances to three that every Englishman is baptized by the Church, three chances to two that he is married by it, and nine to one that he will be buried by it."[1]

(3) We are on firmer ground when we claim that the Church of England far more fully than any other religious body makes spiritual provision for the people of the nation. The whole country is mapped out into parishes, in each of which there is one or more of the clergy ready to conduct divine service and to give religious help to their parishioners. The parish church is intended for all who care to come to worship within it, its bell rings to call all to prayer and praise, its doors are open so that all may enter who care to do so. There is no hamlet however small and remote, no farmhouse however isolated on the moors or in the mountain valleys, for which there is not a clergyman who has the responsibility of the spiritual charge of those who live within them. There is no slum in the dreariest areas of a dock town for which there is not a clergyman charged with the duty of ministering spiritually to those who live in its wretched houses. When new housing estates are built and tens of thousands are moved to them from the more densely crowded districts, the Church makes provision for their spiritual needs. During the thirteen years I was Bishop of Southwark new houses were built in South London

[1] Quoted by Dr. C. M. Ady in her most informative book, " The English Church," p. 197.

and its suburbs for nearly a quarter of a million people, for them twenty-five new churches and halls were built as centres of spiritual and social life. This has been true in diocese after diocese : in London, Chelmsford, Coventry, Sheffield and elsewhere the Church has formed new parishes, built the churches and halls, and provided the clergy for the spiritual needs of the multitudes which so suddenly poured into the houses which now cover land where only a few years before corn was grown and cattle grazed. Coleridge regarded the widespread parochial system of the Church of England as its outstanding merit : " That to every parish throughout the kingdom there is transplanted a germ of civilisation : that in the remotest villages there is a nucleus, round which the capabilities of the place may crystallise and brighten : a model sufficiently superior to excite, yet sufficiently near to encourage and facilitate imitation ; this unobtrusive, continuous agency of a Protestant Church Establishment, this it is which the patriot and the philanthropist, who would fain unite the love of peace with the faith in the progressive amelioration of mankind, cannot estimate at too high a price." The claim that the Church of England has made this provision throughout the country is not intended to ignore all that has been done by other Churches, with smaller financial resources—they too have built their churches and sent their ministers to the new housing areas.

(4) The Church of England still in many ways represents the religious aspect of the nation. This is most notably seen at the Coronation, when amidst all the splendour of pageantry and colour two figures dominate the scene—the King, representing the State, and the Archbishop the Church. It is the Archbishop who presents the King to the people for their acclamation ; it is he who anoints the King, who hands the Sword to him, who delivers to him the Orb with the cross shining on it, who places in his hand the Sceptre, and receiving the Crown from the altar sets it on the King's head. All through the service the Archbishop blessing and exhorting the King is also hallowing the State. And throughout the rite the King is seeking the help of God for his great office, now kneeling previous to the anointing while the Holy Spirit is invoked, afterwards for the Archbishop's blessing, later to make his oblation, and finally to receive the Holy Communion. No service could be designed to bring out more

magnificently the meaning of a Christian State. The Church, hallowing the King, calls upon the State to remember that it is the servant of the spiritual order, and that all its power and glory are a trust from God to be used for His purposes. This is most clearly brought out by the exhortation at the delivery of the Sword of State which is solemnly brought from the altar and placed in the King's right hand : " With this sword do justice, stop the growth of iniquity, protect the holy Church of God, help and defend widows and orphans, restore the things that are gone to decay, maintain the things that are restored, punish and reform what is amiss, and confirm what is in good order : that doing these things you may be glorious in virtue : and so faithfully serve our Lord Jesus in this life, that you may reign for ever with him in the life to come."

There are other occasions of national importance when the Church leads the nation Godwards. It is responsible for the forms of prayer which are used at times of rejoicing or crisis. It is significant that on these occasions the people naturally flock to the cathedrals or the parish churches. A church half empty for most of the year is often filled on the Armistice Days or on Remembrance Sunday. The Jubilee and the death of the late King, the Coronation of George VI, the outbreak of war, the days of national intercession and of thanksgiving for victory, filled the churches to overflowing. It is easy to over-rate the significance of these special occasions, but they show that in an emergency the people of the land naturally turn to the old parish church and expect the clergy of the National Church to lead them in their intercessions or praise. It is, however, a happy feature of these special services that so often the minister and people of other denominations are ready to join with their Anglican brethren in an act of united worship. Nor is it only when the nation is deeply moved on some great occasion that the Church expresses in worship its penitence, joy or intercession as the case may be ; for on many other occasions of parochial or local importance, such as the opening of a civic building, or the dedication of a war memorial, the clergy of the National Church are asked to hallow the event with prayer. Regularly by prayers at the daily sessions of Parliament, at the opening of the Assizes, and by providing Chaplains for the Forces of the Crown, as well as for many public institutions, the Church is able to witness to the need of the sanctification of the daily life of politics, business and work in which God so often is forgotten.

(5) The bishops have their seats in the House of Lords. The two archbishops, the occupants of the three sees of London, Durham, Winchester and twenty-one other bishops according to the seniority of their consecration to English dioceses, are summoned to the meetings of Parliament. The votes of the bishops have not always been such as to commend the Church to the nation. In recent years the growing demands of their dioceses have made it impossible for the majority of them to attend the House of Lords. Only on rare and exceptional occasions are the episcopal benches filled. But on days when some question of national importance is debated, nearly always one of the archbishops or bishops is present to express the views not only of the Church but of all Christians on the religious and moral issues involved. Frequently they have taken the initiative in opening a debate on some international or domestic question where there seems necessity for the expression of the Christian conscience. From the episcopal bench speeches have been made on the treatment of the Jews by the Nazis : on the danger of starvation in Europe : on dispossessed persons : on German prisoners of war : and on domestic subjects such as housing, education, nutrition, conditions of labour. Whatever may have been the case in the past, in the last quarter of a century the bishops now use their position in the House of Lords for the application of Christian principles to political and social problems.

Spiritual Independence

When the Church was freed at the Reformation from the danger of Papal interference, it was exposed increasingly to the dangers of control by the State. Powers exercised in the past by the Pope were taken over by the Crown. The Royal Supremacy was recognised by the Church. It was first exercised by the sovereign personally, but with the development of constitutional govenment it is now exercised only on the advice of the Government of the day. The control by the State over the Church is considerable ; the Crown appoints bishops, deans and to many benefices : the consent of Parliament is necessary for changes in statement of doctrine or in forms of worship, and for any change in the legal, constitutional and administrative fabric of the Church which is at the present time regulated by Statute law. The Church Courts are controlled in their procedure and practice by numerous Acts of Parliament, and there is an appeal from them to the Judicial Committee of Privy Council. No new Canon can be passed or promulgated without the royal licence or approval.

The result of the possession of these powers of control by the State over the Church led both statesmen and churchmen in the seventeenth and eighteenth centuries to look upon the Church as a department of State. Politicians assumed that this was so, and churchmen rarely raised their voices in protest. Its bishops were the nominees of the party in power, its Convocations were silenced, legislation concerning it was carried without its advice or consent, and its pulpits were tuned in accordance with the will of the Government. Neither the State nor the people regarded the Divine Society as anything but an organisation controlled and administered by the State for the conduct of divine worship in accordance with the Acts of Uniformity. And to their shame the great majority of Churchmen were content for many years to accept this position. But in the second half of the nineteenth century the Church became conscious again of its nature as the Body through which Christ works. It recognised it had a supernatural life and call. The spiritual forces it had always possessed, but which for long had been dormant, awakened to vigorous life. As the Church was filled with new ideals and endeavoured to realise them it became aware not only of abuses and scandals in its organisation, but also of the need for new methods of work and fuller outlets for its worship.

Soon, however, the Church discovered that in many directions it was powerless to remove scandals which gravely injured its work and that it was unable to amend its organisation to meet modern demands. Before there could be any legal change in its worship, or in its legal, constitutional and administrative machinery, the assent of Parliament was necessary. But Parliament had comparatively little interest in ecclesiastical problems, and there was no time to spare for them in an overcrowded session. In the years 1880-1913, out of 217 Church Bills introduced into the House of Commons, 162 were never discussed

at all, and only 33 were passed. Churchmen collected large
sums of money for new dioceses, but the Bill authorising their
creation was blocked year after year by a small group of members
who objected to the Church. The position was intolerable.
In 1919, however, after an educational campaign conducted
by the Life and Liberty Movement, Parliament gave special
powers for Church legislation to the Church Assembly. This
Assembly had not been created by Parliament, but by the
Representative Church Council and approved by the Convocations : it consisted of the members of the two Upper and
the two Lower Houses of Convocation of the Provinces of
Canterbury and York, and of laymen elected by the diocesan
laity. Measures passed by this Assembly are presented to
Parliament and receive the Royal Assent if a resolution asking
for this is passed by each of the two Houses.

The Assembly has justified many of the hopes of those who
created it. It is a large gathering representing all the English
dioceses. It is businesslike in its procedure, and considering
the comparatively short periods it meets it has transacted a large
amount of work. Its chief defects are to be found in the age
of its members ; most are over fifty, and the almost complete
absence of representatives of the working classes. This is inevitable while its members are unpaid for loss of time, and
only partly for their expenses. Its debates on important occasions rise to a high level ; some of its members are both
eloquent and persuasive. The Assembly appreciates both ora-
tory and humour, and will listen to any speaker who really
knows his subject even if he is halting in his utterance. Like
all large deliberative assemblies it is the happy hunting ground
of the bore, and it suffers more or less patiently from a few
speakers who feel it necessary to express their views on every
possible occasion. But on the whole the speeches are practical
and to the point, and made by those who have personal knowledge of their subject. On general subjects the House is inclined to pass rather easily and quickly far-reaching resolutions
which should demand much more thought and consideration.
It has been most successful in its legislative work. Over sixty
Measures have received the Royal Assent, most of them concerned with various administrative and financial problems.

But success did not attend the efforts of the Assembly on
the most important subject it has had before it. For many

years the Convocations had been engaged in the revision of the Prayer Book. The proposed revision was accepted after long debates by the Church Assembly; but although there were large majorities in favour of it in all three Houses, the Measure was rejected in the House of Commons by thirty-three votes. Some slight modifications were made in the revision to remove misunderstandings which appeared to have influenced some of those who had voted against it in the House of Commons, and the Measure was again approved by the Assembly, sent up again to Parliament, and was rejected by forty-six votes.

The House of Commons was within its constitutional rights in rejecting in a few hours the work of many anxious years. Nonconformist members and members from constituencies which would not have been affected by the Revised Book were only exercising their full legal rights in throwing out a Measure which was approved by the majority of the English Members of Parliament. But whatever were the reasons behind the votes of the majority, the rejection of the Measures made it plain that the Church does not possess full spiritual freedom to determine its worship or over the manner of administering its Sacraments.

The bishops, in view of the moral authority behind the Book, accepted it as the standard which they would use in administering their dioceses in matters of worship. The Archbishop, on behalf of the entire episcopate, made in the Assembly the formal declaration : " It is a fundamental principle that the Church—that is the Bishops, together with the Clergy and Laity—must in the last resort, when its mind has been fully ascertained, retain its inalienable right, in loyalty to Our Lord and Saviour Jesus Christ, to formulate its Faith in Him, and to arrange the expression of that Holy Faith in its form of worship." The bishops have taken the new Book as a useful guide in deciding what to allow and what to forbid, and with the exception of the new Order of Communion, its services and prayers have been largely adopted in the parishes. The opponents of the Book, satisfied that it is not legalised, have made no attempt to interfere seriously with this policy : though from time to time resolutions of protest have been carried by various party societies. But grateful as the Church should be for this temporary acceptance of an anomalous position, the hard fact remains that it cannot legally determine its worship without reference to Parliament, and that Parliament is prepared to use its veto on changes desired by the spiritual and constitutional assemblies of the Church.

A Commission, therefore, was appointed in 1930 by the Archbishops to enquire into the present relations of Church and State, and to report if any legal and constitutional changes are required. In due course the Commission made a number of important recommendations ; these included a somewhat cumbrous scheme for ecclesiastical legislation which would enable the Royal Assent to be given without debate in either House of Parliament, proposals for the reform of the existing Diocesan and Provincial Courts and a new Court of Final Appeal, for a synodical Declaration to ease the conscientious difficulties caused by a rigid interpretation of the Declaration of Assent and for some changes of minor importance regarding the appointment of bishops. These proposals merited careful consideration, especially those which dealt with legislative procedure. But unhappily, by some strange error of judgment, the Commission placed in the forefront of its proposals the request that the Archbishops by " summoning a Round Table Conference or otherwise," should seek to secure agreement on permissible deviation from the Order of Holy Communion and on the use and limits of Reservation. This was a fatal proposal : at once it raised again the old controversies : it gave opportunities for those who were opposed to the other recommendations to obstruct progress by refusing this preliminary agreement, and it aroused suspicion as to the purpose of all the other proposals. This preliminary condition for agreement on the Order of Communion and Reservation doomed from the outset the Report to failure. Various meetings and conversations were held ; but there was no likelihood of substantial progress or agreement when further proceedings were interrupted by the outbreak of war.

It is very uncertain if Parliament will ever agree to legislation which will take from it its veto on proposed changes in the Prayer Book. Nor does there seem much hope that it will agree to the revision of Church Courts as proposed by the Commission : it is even doubtful if its very modest proposals affecting the appointment of bishops will be accepted. These facts must be considered in relation to the tendency towards Totalitarianism in the State. The State increasingly exercises control over every department of the life of the community. It is not likely that the Church will escape from this movement. State control is more likely to be intensified rather than eased over the Church. Through the appointment of bishops, deans and through the patronage of many benefices, it would be possible for the State to control the Church for its own purposes. It would be no longer, as in the past, the laity of the Church expressing in the Commons their views ; it would be a Parliament detached from and uninterested in religion manipulating the Church for political ends. A Church so controlled would be unable to develop freely its spiritual life, to organise its worship, express its faith, and to bear its witness against political injustice and social wrong.

The Church should frankly face the dangers of its position. At the moment Parliament has no desire to exercise active control over the Church or gratuitously to interfere in its concerns. But within a few years a neutral attitude may have changed into hostility, and the Church will find it is then useless to ask for reform or for greater freedom. It should not acquiesce any longer in a relationship with the State which might suddenly prove to be inconsistent in practice as well as in principle with religious freedom. Churchmen are so accustomed to the existing relationship between Church and State that they fail to see how strange and anomalous it appears to other Churches especially those which attach importance to religious freedom. For long Free Churchmen have viewed our position with surprise and dislike. But members of the ancient Orthodox Churches are also perplexed. I can give two examples of this. When in 1943 I visited Moscow I discussed with the Patriarch and other leading ecclesiastics the freedom possessed by our respective Churches. They found it difficult to understand how a Church could be really free when its bishops were appointed by the Crown. I did my best to explain how great was the freedom we actually enjoyed, but I fear that my explanation did not satisfy them, for they kept returning to the point that the Crown in appointing to vacant sees is advised by the leader of a political party who need not be a Christian. A year later I met the Orthodox Synod at Athens ; for local reasons its members were then especially interested in the subject of ecclesiastical Courts and asked me about our practice. They did not conceal their surprise and perplexity when I told them that not only did laymen preside over our Courts, but that the final appeal from them on matters of doctrine and worship was to a Court of lay judges appointed by the Crown. Sooner or later by a vote in Parliament, by a decision in the Courts, or by some conflict over a moral problem, it will be brought home to all that the spiritual freedom we now undoubtedly enjoy is on sufferance, and is really inconsistent with the strictly legal relationship between Church and State. The Church is drifting towards disaster if it allows year after year to pass without making a determined and sustained attempt to readjust a position inherited from ages when the Church and the Nation were one, but which now in a time of rapid change has become fraught with danger.

Through its constitutional assemblies the Church should agree on the reforms required to reconcile freedom with establishment. Agreement on a policy is an essential condition of success. Unanimity is impossible to expect, there will always be vociferous minorities who will claim that they speak for the whole Church. It should however be possible after full discussion to secure large majorities in the Convocations, the Church Assembly, and the Diocesan Conferences for four major reforms. First for some machinery by which the Crown could assent to proposed changes in worship without reference to Parliament. Secondly for the establishment of Courts which are really spiritual, and from which an appeal to the Civil Courts for " redress " would be made only when the ecclesiastical Courts had failed to observe the rules under which they act. Thirdly the Church should be given at some point the right to be consulted in the appointment of its chief officers. Fourthly the Convocations should receive license to frame and enact new Canons. Reform on lines such as these would vindicate the freedom of the Church and would still retain its connection with the State.

If however the Church cannot agree to these reforms, or if Parliament after due consideration refuses to accept them, then Disestablishment and Disendowment will be unavoidable. In theory the two can be separated, but it is inconceivable to any with some knowledge of public affairs that the State would give the Church freedom of Disestablishment and yet allow it to retain all its endowments. If spiritual freedom can be gained in no other way it will be necessary to pay the heavy price of disendowment. But the Church must have genuine freedom and retain its cathedrals and ancient churches. It is sometimes assumed too easily that Disestablishment carries with it spiritual freedom, but if its property is bound up by narrow trusts the Church would find that it has less liberty than it possesses at present.

But there is an important reservation to be added to the above. I for one do not yet feel able to ask for Disestablishment, though I am prepared to accept it without opposition if the State demands it. If the State makes it plain that it considers the divergence of the Church from the nation on matters of faith, of worship, of morals, (and I think especially of the marriage laws) is so serious that its connection with the Church is an anachronism, then the Church should without further demur confer with the State how best its wishes on this matter can be carried out with the greatest smoothness and fairness. But Churchmen should not take the initiative in demanding Disestablishment unless circumstances make this inevitable; there are so many more vital matters which should be occupying our thoughts and time. Disestablishment and Disendowment would divert the energies of Churchmen for many years from pastoral and evangelistic work into problems of reorganisation : and the poorest parishes would suffer the most severely through the loss of the Church's endowments. And most serious of all Disestablishment, at a time when paganism is fiercely attacking Christianity in every land, would be regarded however illegitimately as the national repudiation of religion. The reasons which should make Churchmen hesitate at asking the State for spiritual freedom at the cost of Disestablishment are admirably expressed by Mr. T. S. Eliot—who is in favour on principle of an established Church—"We must pause to reflect that a Church, once disestablished, cannot easily be re-established, and that the very act of disestablishment separates it more definitely and irrevocably from the life of the nation than if it had never been established."[1]

However much we may desire a more complete spiritual freedom we must not underestimate the amount of freedom which our Church now possesses. It has complete and unfettered freedom in the vital matters of the choice of ordinands, it can accept or reject them without any kind of State interference.

[1] " The Idea of a Christian Society," p. 49.

It has in practice greater freedom in its worship and in its preaching than any other Church in Christendom. Its laity are bound by few rules : its clergy to all intents and purposes are free from the control of the laity and the State, and only subject to the mildest control of the bishop to whom they have sworn canonical obedience. Never in the whole of my ministry have I felt hindered in its exercise by the fact that I belong to an established Church, while I have been conscious of greater opportunities given to me both at home and overseas as one of the representatives of the national Church. While therefore we must be jealous for the spiritual independence of the Church, and prepared to make the greatest sacrifices to secure it, we must not allow this to lead us into exaggerated statements about the interference of the State in spiritual matters, nor must we forget the large amount of liberty which in actual practice both the Church and its individual members already possess. If we either ask for Disestablishment or accept it, it will be because our freedom is endangered, as it easily may be in the future, for without freedom the Church cannot fulfil its spiritual commission to the nation.

IX

THE CHURCH AND PEOPLE

In the future, as in the past, the chief contribution which the Church can make to the people is spiritual. In century after century it has given to the men and women of this land its message about God and His purpose for man; it has ministered to them its sacraments; it has taught them the Word of God; it has brought to them the certain hope of another and better life than this; it has encouraged the dying and comforted the mourner. In the days of darkness, which may soon come, when the people find that their civilisation is built on shifting sand, the need of God may once again be felt. It is then that the Church will be able to give to the people its special message and to offer them the spiritual help which it has at its disposal. It is not through its political or social witness, but through its Gospel and spiritual resources it will be able to give the best and truest service to the nation.

IX

THE CHURCH AND PEOPLE

THE relationship between the Church and the people has not always been happy. At one time it was usual for sentimentalists to draw ideal pictures of life in the Middle Ages. Its chivalry and amusements were dwelt on, its hunger, dirt, squalor and cruelty were ignored. The Church was pictured as the protector of the poor and downtrodden, with the unhappy and oppressed turning to it with loving trust and gratitude. That the Church set forth splendid and true ideals of an all embracing Christian Order will be readily admitted. But the gulf between the ideal and its realisation was perhaps greater in the Middle Ages than at any other period of history, the very splendour of the ideal made this almost inevitable. The writer who attempts to draw a picture of life in the Middle Ages by relying exclusively on the Encyclicals of popes, the Pastorals of bishops, and on Canon law will easily be misled as to the actual facts. The Church was accepted as a natural part of life itself, but its clergy and its administrative system were often unpopular with the nation as a whole. Though there were noble exceptions among them the higher ecclesiastics showed little consideration for the lot of the poor. The monasteries were generally disliked, for the monks were hard landlords, though perhaps not so hard as the lay landlord : it has been said that a tenant of the monks might be five per cent. better off than if he had been under a secular landowner. The popular hatred of bishops and priors was shown in the Peasant Rising of 1381 when the Archbishop and many priors were murdered by the mob, and a demand was made for the abolition and disendowment of the hierarchy. The parish clergy were themselves impoverished by the monasteries which, by gifts and bequests, had become the proprietors of large numbers of parochial benefices. They took two-thirds of the tithe and appointed a priest (a vicarius) to take charge of the parish. The parishioners resented the payment of the tithe to a distant monastery which used the greater part of it to increase its wealth, setting aside only a small portion for doles to the hungry who came to its great doorway clamouring for help. The payment of tithe was exacted strictly and caused much bitterness and friction—it was a tenth in kind of all the produce " theoretically at least down to the very pot herbs of their gardens. Moreover the law was pitiless to the peasant. Tithes of wood were held to include even the down of his geese : the very grass he cut by the roadside was to pay its due toll."[1] In addition to this there was the heriot or mortuary, by which on a peasant's death the landlord had the right to take his best beast and the priest his second best, while in the town the bed was often taken in payment of this death due. With these taxes—for the tithe would be equivalent to two shillings in the pound—and the exactions at death, it is hardly to be expected that the Church would be popular. The clergy were also disliked by the peasantry as their competitors in farming; often their advantages they regarded as unfair. In our day we know of the criticisms which have been directed against the Church as an owner of tithe and of mining royalties, and the relief which has been felt by many Churchmen at their abolition as sources of ecclesiastical revenue, even though this has meant serious financial loss. It must not however be assumed that the Church was everywhere unpopular in the Middle Ages. The cult of Thomas Becket, the honour paid to St. Hugh of Lincoln, and Chaucer's ideal picture of the parish priest prove that among all grades of ecclesiastics there were men who were loved, and even at the worst the priest had a special place in mediæval life. " His sacred calling gave him an authority and a special place which were generally unchallenged. . . . The priest consoled, advised, admonished, encouraged : he was with them at the great moments of life and death, and for good or ill he was emphatically the parson—that is *the person* of the village. Hence we may well regard him as a focus of all those forces making for good in the parish, and a constant warrior against evil and superstition."[2]

After the Restoration and during the anti-Roman resistance to James II the Church had brief periods of national popularity. It had shared with the Royalists persecution under the Commonwealth, so its unpopularity in the reigns of the first two Stuarts

[1] G. G. Coulton, " Ten Medieval Studies," p. 124.
[2] H. S. Bennett, " Life on the English Manor."

was forgotten. In reaction from the rigidity of the Puritan régime the people rejoiced at the restoration of the old Church services and feasts. Later when the seven bishops were sent to the Tower they were regarded as the representatives of national opposition to despotic rule and to the attempt to re-establish Roman Catholicism. But the enthusiasm for the Church died away, and under the Hanoverians the nation became increasingly Erastian. By the end of the eighteenth century it was, as it never had been before, the Church of one class. A French historian thus described the position " Nearly all the bishops belonged to aristocratic families, whigs or tories, following the party in power. As for the lower clergy, they were chosen sometimes by the King, sometimes by the local squire. Out of eleven thousand benefices, five thousand seven hundred are at the disposition of " patrons." Naturally they appoint men of their own class, often their own family ; sons, nephews, cousins. . . . These are the ' gentlemen ' who have the tastes, the faults, and sometimes the virtues of their class. The pastor who hunts does not shock anyone. Often he is a magistrate and sits on the bench with his uncle and cousins. So the religious armament of the country underlines and reinforces its political armament. In both the landowners form the principal element. The Church of England finds itself associated with the local power of the governing classes, but it loses all contact with the people."[1]

Never has the Church of England been so unpopular as it was during the first quarter of the nineteenth century. It is no exaggeration to say that it was regarded with hatred by the working classes. Not only were its bishops and clergy drawn from the class which was oppressing them, but the Church as an institution had condoned the oppressors and had been silent when it ought with flaming indignation to have raised its voice in defence of the poor. It had allowed the peasant to be robbed of his rights in the common holdings and lands, and it had failed to protect the workers in the new manufacturing towns from oppressively long hours and miserably inadequate wages. It had done nothing through its bishops to protest against the savage and unjust sentences passed on the unhappy men who in Hampshire, Wiltshire and Dorset had taken part in the peasant rising of 1830. Here and there were individual clergymen who

[1] André Maurois, " Histoire d'Angleterre," p. 597.

at the risk of prosecution by the Government lifted their voices against those who oppressed the poorer members of their flock. There were also many who showed personal kindness and consideration to the hungry and penniless, even Cobbett describes with appreciation Bishop Sumner's treatment of a band of sturdy beggars he met about a mile from his castle at Farnham "They stopped his carriage, and asked for some money, which he gave them. But he did not prosecute them : he had not a man of them called to account for his conduct, but the next day set twenty-four labourers to constant work, opened his Castle to the distressed of all ages, and supplied all with food and other necessaries who stood in need of them. This was becoming a Christian teacher." Instances like these stand out against the general apathy of Churchmen to the wrongs of the poor. But the silence of the bishops was in striking contrast to the bold utterances of Bishop Latimer who three hundred years previously before the King and his Court thundered against the high placed oppressors and spoilers of the small landowners and tenants. After all these centuries it is impossible to read some of these vigorous, homely outspoken sermons without being thrilled by their passion and conviction. But in the early part of the last century no Latimer made his voice heard in the House of Lords. It is impossible for any Churchman to read the records of these days, of the people dispossessed of their holdings, of women and children worked to death in factory and mine, of the men underpaid and exploited without a sense of utter shame and humiliation at the silence of the Church. It is, however, right to remember that as years before a layman of the Church, William Wilberforce, had fought successfully for the abolition of slavery, so another layman, Lord Shaftesbury, led the agitation for the improvement of the conditions in factories at home.

Nor can it be truthfully pleaded in extenuation of the Church's neglect of the physical welfare of the people that it was concentrating all its attention on the salvation of their souls. Even Wilberforce argued that the poor have the advantage over the rich as they have the peace that religion brings without the temptations that assail the worldly ! Paley maintained that in most respects the poor were as fortunate as the rich : "The peasant, whenever he goes abroad, finds a feast, whereas the epicure must be sumptuously entertained to escape disgust."

Hannah More in her tracts reminded the poor that their sufferings here were as nothing compared to the glory which awaited the faithful Christian in the next world. Most of the churches were treated as the resort of the well-to-do : pew rents put the poor man at a disadvantage, at the best a place would be found for him at the back of the church behind the cushioned pews reserved for the rich. The pew rent system encouraged then as now the prosperous but is a fatal deterrent to the poor. In the country, where pew rents were unknown, the squire and his family lounged in comfort in their square pew, shut off from the view of the congregation by curtains, the farmers and small tenants came next with less honourable seats, and at the back of the church narrow seats and hard boards were reserved for the labourers and their families. No wonder that the Chartists made it a practice to march in procession to churches and occupy their seats before their tenants arrived. Later Churchmen however attacked the system of pew rents as un-Christian in principle, while architects pointed out the disfigurement pews often caused to the building. In many of the great towns there were no churches or clergy for the growing populations. The existing churches in Manchester, Leeds and in other industrial cities were quite inadequate. The people in the poorest and most crowded districts were uncared for and unshepherded by the Church of the Nation. In the Nonconformist chapels which were rapidly springing up they often found the spiritual homes which the Anglican Church at this most critical time had failed to provide.

The Recovery of the Church

At one time, therefore, it looked as if the Church of England had been hopelessly alienated from the working classes. Their leaders and the rank and file regarded it with hostility and scorn. If it survived the gathering storms it would do so as the Church of a small and exclusive class. Disestablishment and disendowment seemed inevitable. But within less than a century hostility to it largely disappeared and the Church came into closer and more sympathetic contact with the people than at any time since the Reformation. This remarkable change was due to three causes.

(1) The Church no longer was associated with one political party. A Conservative Government could no longer rely on the bishops supporting them at a critical division. The bishops were more concerned with work in their dioceses than with debates in the House of Lords. The clergy though still mainly conservative in their outlook and votes, educational controversies, and the fear of Disestablishment had much to do with this, felt it unbecoming to throw themselves into the party fight and to exhort their flock to vote true blue and thus to support Church and State.

(2) In the Church itself there was increasing sympathy with the working class movement. This was largely due to the influence of a group of Broad Churchmen in the middle of the Nineteenth Century. When the first hopes of the Chartists were disappointed and their movement appeared to be on the verge of complete collapse Charles Kingsley, Frederick Denison Maurice and J. M. Ludlow appealed to Christians to arouse themselves against the glaring social evils of their times. Their mantle fell on a series of successors foremost among whom were Bishops Westcott and Gore, and Canon Scott Holland. Societies were formed to educate Churchmen in their social duties, the Guild of St. Matthew and the Christian Social Union, the League of the Kingdom of God, and the Industrial Christian Fellowship. These have helped to bridge the gulf which once separated the Church from the great mass of working men and have aroused the social conscience of Churchpeople.

Expressions of the deep concern of the Church over the disabilities under which so many of the poorer members of the community suffer have been given repeatedly by the official assemblies of the Church. The Lambeth Conference at different times has declared that " the Church can pronounce certain conditions of labour to be intolerable " : that " property is a trust held for the benefit of the community," " Members of the Church are bound to take an active part, by public action and by personal service, in removing those abuses which depress and impoverish human life. In company with other citizens and organisations they should work for reform, and particularly for such measures as will secure the better care of children, including real opportunity for an adequate education, protection of the workers against unemployment, and the provision of

healthy homes."¹   The Lambeth Conference represents the whole
Anglican Communion, but the Convocations have been equally
outspoken.   In 1918 the Lower House of Canterbury passed a
resolution sympathising " with the demands of Labour for
a minimum wage, for State provision against unemployment,
for housing reform, and for the recognition of the status of the
workers in the industries in which they are engaged."   Three
years later the Upper House reaffirmed the Lambeth Conference
resolution that a fundamental change in the spirit and working
of our economic life is required.

At one time the bishops used their votes in the House of
Lords against social reforms.   A melancholy list of deplorable
votes is easily compiled from the records of the sessions of the
House of Lords early in the nineteenth century.   But these
unhappy days have long gone.   Those who attack the bishops
for their votes in the Lords are half a century out of date with
their facts.   In 1907 a Cabinet Minister smarting under the
sense of personal failure and disappointment made a violent
attack on the bishops : " I cannot recall a single great cause
they ever advocated.   I cannot recall a single victory they ever
won : hardly a word they ever said in the cause of humanity."
Archbishop Davidson took up the challenge by pointing out
that for twelve years in the House of Lords he had steadily
advocated and supported a large number of social reforms.
To this the Minister could only reply that he was " sick of
controversy and very much overworked." ! ²   In the twentieth
century bishops in the Lords have repeatedly spoken for and
urged the cause of social reform.

Many of the clergy have thrown themselves into the movement
for social and industrial reform.   In the urban areas they have
taken an active part in demanding improved social conditions,
some have joined the Labour Party and appeared on its platforms,
others have been elected as Borough or Rural Councillors and
have worked for better housing.   It was a clergyman of the
Church of England, Canon Barnett, of whom M. Clemenceau
once said : " I have met but three really great men in England,
and one was a little pale clergyman in Whitechapel."   He was
the founder of Toynbee Hall, the first of many Settlements which
became centres of social and welfare work and formed a common

¹ Lambeth Conferences 1897, 1908, 1920.
² Bell, " Randall Davidson," Vol. I, p. 541.

meeting place for university men, public school boys and the members of the artizan classes. A few foolish people spoke of winning the working classes to the Church by showing it was interested in social problems, but no ulterior motive of this kind prompted most of those who took part in these attempts to improve the conditions of the poor. The motive which inspired them was anger at long tolerated injustice and a passionate desire to secure for the great mass of their fellow countrymen opportunities for a fuller life.

(3) But even more powerful as a factor in bringing about the change of attitude towards the Church was the extension of its pastoral work throughout the great towns. Reform followed reform. The scandal of non-residence was abolished. Very large parishes were divided, or were worked by a staff from a clergy house. Mission churches were built for the poorest districts when it was thought that their population would not come to the parish church. In most churches pew rents were abolished, and in the new churches all seats were free and open. A new type of clergy appeared who spent hours in visiting from door to door, and making themselves known to the poorest of their parishioners. Often they were aided by a band of sisters, deaconesses and layworkers who all took their part in bringing the influence of the Church to every house. No longer was it possible to accuse the Church of being distant from the people and indifferent to their needs when day by day its ministers could be seen in every street. Men who themselves had no intention of joining the Church and who often labelled themselves as agnostics were prepared when they criticised it as an institution to make an exception for the clergymen who knew their children by their christian names, who shepherded their boys into their clubs, and who were ready to " look in " on them in the evening for a talk.

The Social Work of the Church

The old jibe that the Church cares only for the souls of men and neglects their bodies has lost its sting. But sometimes in these days when the State has taken over so many activities which were once the province of the Church it is forgotten how much has been done in the past by the Church both in the country and town for the social well-being of the people. Two illustrations drawn from personal experience will make this clear.

My childhood was spent in a small country village of which my father was Vicar. He belonged to the older school of clergy, he had been at Oxford when Newman was preaching at St. Mary's, and half his ministry had been spent as a chaplain in India. He had no experience of parochial organisations, nor was he a systematic visitor : he knew however all the people of the parish, talking to the men at their garden gates, in their allotments or in the fields, and faithfully visiting them in sickness. My mother was a most diligent visitor, she was in and out of every cottage in wet and fine. Though the village had a station of its own and was within three miles of Aldershot, sixty years ago it was very isolated. Most of the people were agricultural labourers, working on one of three large farms. The roads were muddy and narrow, and in the winter if people went out at night they usually carried lanterns. There were no motor-cars, no wireless, no cinemas, no village dances. Parish Councils and Old Age Pensions were still in the future. The village inn was the one place to which in the evenings the men went for warmth and society. The church and the school were the only public buildings, though later a village hall was built. In those days everything centred round the Vicarage. Twice a week my father gave religious teaching in the small school. My mother as well as looking after a large family, made herself responsible for work among the women and girls, superintended the Sunday School, and twice a week in the winter evenings taught at a night school, where a dozen or so young men and youths learnt to read and write. Sometimes penny readings were organised, at which Dickens and Thackeray and other well-known writers were read. There was a small library in the schoolroom from which books for a halfpenny could be borrowed. Lectures on foreign countries, and more rarely on historical subjects, were occasionally given, illustrated by a magic lantern, which was usually worked rather erratically, the slide frequently appearing upside down to the audible delight of the junior section of the meeting. For the women there was the Mothers' Meeting, later the Mothers' Union started by Mrs. Sumner then the wife of a curate in the neighbouring town of Farnham, and a sewing party in which garments were made for the cold weather : occasionally there were classes on nursing and first aid. All relief and charity, with the exception of Poor Law Relief and the dreaded " House," were administered from the Vicarage. Help in money and in kind was given from the sick and poor fund which consisted of offerings in church and the contributions of Churchfolk. As a small boy I can remember in a very severe epidemic of diphtheria mothers and elder sisters coming regularly to the Vicarage for nourishments and delicacies which could not be made in the stricken homes, for there was no thought then of moving sick children to an isolation hospital. There were coal and clothing clubs into which members paid weekly and when the time for withdrawal came the amount over was almost doubled by the subscriptions which had been collected. There were also special gifts of bread and money made at Christmas from some mysterious charity to those who were very poor or who had large families —and some of the families were very large indeed. Nor was recreation forgotten, two or three village concerts were organised, they are easy to caricature now and no doubt they were in many ways absurd, but at the time they gave equal pleasure both to performers and the audience. Sometimes there was a play, with much heart burnings as to who should take the leading part. There were annual " treats " or " outings " when the schoolchildren had sports and a tea, and when the choir were taken by train for a long and exciting day in London or at the seaside. More important still there was the cricket ground provided also by the Church and matches were played which increased the intense dislike and contempt felt for neighbouring villages. The climax of all was the Harvest Festival, the day to which the village looked forward for months and discussed and criticised for months after it was over. It opened with a Service on a week-day afternoon, the church decorated with gigantic vegetables of every kind, and as the farmers gave their men the afternoon off the whole village crowded the church. After church the congregation went to the Vicarage garden where under a large marquee was a flower and vegetable show, all the morning experts had been judging and great was the excitement to know who had won the prizes. My father would announce the names of those who had won prizes for the best gardens, he himself was a keen gardener, and encouraged in this way his parishioners to make their little gardens as bright and beautiful as possible. Presently the garden emptied and the people poured across the road into a magnificent old barn, now, alas, pulled down, in which the harvest supper was held. There were masses of food and gargantuan appetites, after supper followed speeches and songs, later in the evening when much beer had been drunk there was a little anxiety as to the nature of these, but usually they were old English songs with a rollicking chorus roared out by all. And at the end when " God save the Queen " was sung there was still an element of excitement, for the village Radical always chose this moment to testify to the strength of his convictions by putting on his cap and remaining seated, until with perfect good temper it was removed and he was pulled to his legs by his staunchly Conservative neighbours.

We were by no means a unique or an exceptionally well worked parish : of every rural parish near us it would have been true to say that practically all its education, charity and recreation were provided by the Church. The incumbent who failed to take the lead in these was condemned by the public opinion both of his parishioners and by the neighbouring clergy. It all seems very superficial and inadequate in these days when charity is scorned as patronage, and when the poorest have opportunities of education and amusement undreamt of half a century ago. But *then* it meant much to the people. When there was no one else to do so it was the Church which cared for the bodily welfare and recreation as well as for the souls of the countryman. If the Church had not done this village life would have been even more monotonous and dreary than it was. This must not be forgotten when we hear of the neglect of the non-resident rector of previous generations, or of the failure of the Church in the past to care for the poor.

When nearly fifty years ago I was ordained as a deacon to Portsea Parish Church I saw the Church at its best in a large working class parish of over 40,000 people. The Parish Church and its worship were of course the centre of work and influence. On Sundays it had very large congregations, queues waiting for the doors to open. Its five district churches were also well attended. But quite apart from the worship of the church there were two features which stood out. First the large number of Church organisations for the education, recreation and relief of the people of the parish. On Sunday afternoon all through the winter months there were Conferences for men, these had been started by Mr. Lang, afterwards Archbishop of Canterbury, who at the time of my Ordination was Vicar of Portsea. They were attended by over 500 men, mostly engaged in the Dock-yard. Addresses were given by the Vicar on historical and literary as well as on religious subjects and after the address half an hour was devoted to free and open discussion. The educational value of these Conferences was great, and it was recognised that nowhere else in Portsmouth did men of strongly opposed views have such an opportunity of expressing their opinions. For recreation there was a whole network of clubs for boys and girls of different ages : these were organised by the Church and held in Church halls : the clubs had their foot-ball and cricket teams, and in the poorest district there was a good gymnasium and institute. There was much poverty in parts of the parish, especially in seasons of unemployment. The Church had its relief committee which made grants to those in distress, provided convalescent treatment for those who had been ill, often making itself responsible for the expense of sending the invalid for two or three weeks rest in the country. There were labour homes for men and women out of work and who wanted temporary employment after they had been discharged from prison. There was a crèche in which mothers when they were at work could leave their babies.

Even more impressive than the many organisations which kept the Church in contact with the lives of the working people was the fact that the great majority of the parish helpers were themselves members of the working classes. There were a very few district visitors from Southsea, and a still smaller number who took classes and guilds of various kinds, but most of the helpers were artizans, mechanics, dockyard men and ex-service men. They constituted the bulk of the leaders in the Sunday Schools, they were the members of the Church Councils, by direct gifts or through sales of work they raised the funds required for the work of the Church. They were the churchwardens, the sidesmen, the choirmen and the bell ringers. This was not a case of the Church approaching the people as an outside organisation, but they themselves maintained and carried on its work. And what was true of Portsea was true also of innumerable other parishes in every part of England. There was no hostility to the Church on the part of the people, for the people knew that it was theirs and its work largely depended on them. And in parishes of this nature if the Church was attacked and criticised for denominational or political reasons the people themselves were the first to defend it.

Education

In no direction has the Church made a greater contribution to the welfare of the people than through education. In the Middle Ages it was the Church alone which provided it: it founded schools for poor students and colleges for those who wished a higher education to enable them to serve Church and State. The Reformation did not result immediately in more general education. Edward VI's grammar schools gave him an undeserved reputation for zeal in the cause of education, for the schools which bore his name were founded at the cost of older and larger educational establishments. But after the Restoration, Charity Schools were started in which the children were taught reading, writing and the elements of arithmetic: the motives behind the promoters of these schools were more practical than educational, they wished to give the children the power of reading the Bible for themselves, and to make them more efficient servants and workers. The State left the education of the poor to the Church, and the Church regarded it as a national duty. Early in the nineteenth century the National Society was founded " for the education of the Poor in the Principles of the Established Church throughout England and Wales." This was the beginning of a movement by which Churchmen built schools in every parish. Often they were small and dark buildings, more picturesque outside than convenient within, the teachers were frequently untrained and their methods would cause the present-day educationist to cry out in dismay, but the majority of the children who received any kind of education had it given to them in these schools. In 1870 an Education Act established Board Schools, and ten years later attendance at school was made compulsory : in the past the Church had had as its rival British Schools in which Nonconformist teaching was given, these had always been few in number compared with those which were supported by the National Society, but now a much more formidable rival had entered the field. The new School Boards had power to build schools and to control the education given in them, and the teaching in them was to be under the Cowper-Temple clause which provided that " no catechism or religious formula which is distinctive of any particular denomination shall be taught in the school " : this met the wishes of the Nonconformists, but not of Churchpeople or of Roman Catholics who by their rates and taxes were compelled to support schools in which it was illegal to teach their children the faith of their parents. This was a cause of long continued strife which seriously hindered educational reform.

For a time Church Schools continued to flourish side by side with the new schools. But the advantages given by the State to the Board Schools were too great. The Church could not afford to erect the spacious buildings required by modern educational ideals, and the number of the children taught in its schools gradually diminished both absolutely and relatively to the increase in population. There were in England and Wales in 1938, 10,100 Council schools and 9,100 Church schools. The pupils in Council schools numbered three and a half million, in Church schools one and a quarter million. Since 1902 the Church had lost 2,620 schools and one hundred were closed or surrendered every year. Under the recent Elementary Education organisation schemes large numbers of the older children have been moved from the Church schools to the Senior Council schools. So serious has this been that many have questioned whether it is worth while the Church continuing to retain schools which soon will be attended almost exclusively by the younger children. But on this a Committee appointed in the Diocese of Winchester reported " It is a well accepted principle of religious education that the early years of a child's life are of primary importance. There seems little doubt that through the pre-adolescent years children are more sensitive to spiritual influences and more receptive than during the adolescent years. Excellent religious instruction is given in most of the Council schools : but the link with the Church in the case of the Church schools, and the fact that the clergy are in close personal contact both with the teachers and the children, provide an atmosphere, and prompt loyalties, which seem to us of great value."

The whole future of Church schools has become most uncertain. The cost of alteration and maintenance of the buildings grows greater, the demands of the Authorities increase; parents contrast the humble accommodation of the Church school with the palatial buildings erected by the Local Educational Authority, and are usually indifferent as to the special type of religious education given to their children; many of the laity regard Church schools as an unnecessary financial burden, while the clergy doubt their value under changed conditions. Now a new national education policy is about to be put in operation: very large numbers of the Church schools will be condemned as superfluous, and others will have to be rebuilt almost entirely to meet unprecedented requirements. The sums necessary for the preservation of the Church schools will run into millions of pounds. It is very doubtful if the Church will be able to raise the money required. Unavoidably most of the schools will be taken over by the Local Authority, and Churchmen then will have to use fully the opportunities for religious teaching which will be afforded. Agreed syllabuses will give some foundation for Christian teaching, and on it the faith and worship of the Church must be built. If it can be assured that definite Christian teaching will be carefully and universally given in the schools, then Churchmen may feel that their own schools have done their work for the nation. In future they should concentrate both on the building and upkeep of first-rate Training Colleges which will supply a succession of fully-qualified Christian teachers, and on using to the full the facilities for religious teaching and worship given by the new Act. No care and trouble can be too great to see that there is a sufficient number of clergy and laity who are thoroughly trained for work which is vital for the future of Christianity in our country.

The Future

While the Church is no longer regarded with the hostility that was shown to it early in the nineteenth century, its influence is considerably less than it was sixty years ago. Congregations are smaller, it is harder to obtain workers, finance becomes increasingly difficult, and the influence of the Church on national and civic affairs is relatively slight. There are ominous signs also of a definite anti-Christian tendency in some of the great cities. The position is regarded with much anxiety, and some of the clergy and laity are inclined to be defeatist, predicting that within the next fifty years the Church will be a negligible force in the life of the people.

Those who adopt this attitude under-rate the present strength of the Church, and its capacity for adapting itself to new conditions. It still covers the land with its churches and organisations : and it still provides for every parish or group of small parishes a man whose one duty is to build up the Kingdom of God. The total number of those who attend church on Sunday is still large, and among them are men and women who are loyal and whole-hearted members of the Church. Its wide-flung parochial organisations still can supply in an emergency the help that is most required. In the war there were many remarkable instances of this. In the confusion and distress that followed some of the air raids, when the machinery of the local authorities broke down under the strain, on many occasions the parochial clergy took charge of the situation, opening the parish halls, providing temporary shelter for the homeless, arranging for their removal to the country, and generally encouraging them by their example. There are many parishes in which the clergy for weeks on end, night by night, regularly visited the shelters, and were recognised and welcomed by crowds who never attended their churches but who knew that they lived in their midst and shared their dangers. The same has been true of many of the parishes outside the danger areas into which the people had been moved or had evacuated themselves. Sometimes the clergy had to arrange the billeting, for they had the local knowledge as to where strangers might most suitably be sent ; sometimes they had to supplement by their own efforts arrangements which proved inadequate for unexpectedly large numbers ; and they often provided centres of recreation and rest for town people who found themselves in an unfamiliar environment. In new and unprecedented ways the parochial system has proved its usefulness.

In the future social organisations which once were largely organised and run by the Church will be taken over and supported by the State. With the tax-payer and the rate-payer at their back, the local authorities will provide splendid community centres, with gymnasiums, baths and recreation rooms. It does not, however, follow that these will necessarily in all cases supplant the more modest accommodation which the Church can offer in its clubs. I once visited in a poor part of London a magnificently equipped club provided by some wealthy philanthropist: everything in it was of the best; but it was almost empty: there were a few well-dressed youths lounging about, but no boys from the district for which it was intended. A few nights later I was in a dilapidated and unattractive building crammed with lads of the district, all thoroughly enjoying themselves in various ways. There was a friendly atmosphere in this club which was absent from the more pretentious building. This will sometimes still be the case, and there will always be found some young people who will prefer a smaller and more homely club. But, whether the community centre started by the State is successful or not, the clergy and the laity of the parish should be ready to help in its work. Nothing would be more harmful to the influence of the Church than the existence in a parish of good social and educational organisations which were treated by the clergy as unfriendly rivals to their work. Even if the incumbent of the parish is given no official position in these organisations, he should be ready to visit them as a friend and to offer any help he can. If he shows himself both interested and capable, he will soon be asked to serve in an official capacity. While if he holds aloof from these centres he will miss a great opportunity of becoming acquainted with many of his parishioners who attend them, and of meeting them on neutral territory. The surest way of making these new organisations secular in spirit would be for the clergy and Christian laity to refuse to take any part in them. The clergy themselves with their own special work will often find it impossible to do more than visit occasionally these community centres; but they should encourage their laity to help in them.

From the Church there should go forth a body of workers, both clerical and lay, ready and eager to carry their churchmanship into all that concerns the life of the people. A Labour Mayor in the North of England recently said to a bishop: "Until I became Mayor I did not know that your people were

behind most of the social and philanthropic work of the city."
Wherever there is good work to be done, whether it is started
by the Church or not, churchmen should be ready to assist
in it. Into activities which are regarded as secular they should
carry their religious convictions. By the faithfulness and efficiency of their work they should show that Christianity has
a Gospel for the body as well as for the soul. By their
example and personal influence they will help to dissipate
prejudices which often stand in the way of the acceptance of
religion.

The Church, also, must take its part in the political life of
the nation. Its members in the various political parties—for
churchmen should be found in every political party—should
make their influence felt. The great danger to-day is that
religion may be forced by the State into a narrow groove, and
that churchmen may acquiesce in this position and attempt to
rationalise a reluctant retreat by claiming that they are with-
drawing to the catacombs. Unless the Church permeates with
its influence the political parties, they may become increasingly
indifferent to the claims of Christianity. Probably the greatest
political service which the Church can render in the near future
to the people will be through its insistence on the value and
freedom of each individual, against the demands of the industrial machine and the omni-competent State. Liberty is endangered by the ever-increasing encroachments of a Totalitarian
State. It is the Christian doctrine of the value of man as called
to be a child of God that is the strongest safeguard of his
freedom. And for a long time to come the Church must also
demand the abolition of the slums and the provision of decent
houses for the people. It must see that neither the State nor
the Local Authorities become slack in accomplishing what is
required by social justice.

But in the future, as in the past, the chief contribution which
the Church can make to the people is spiritual. In century
after century it has given to the men and women of this land
its message about God and His purpose for man; it has
ministered to them its sacraments; it has taught them the
Word of God; it has brought to them the certain hope of
another and better life than this; it has encouraged the dying
and comforted the mourner. In the days of darkness, which
may soon come, when the people find that their civilisation is

built on shifting sand, the need of God may once again be felt. It is then that the Church will be able to give to the people its special message and to offer them the spiritual help which it has at its disposal. It is not through its political or social witness, but through its Gospel and spiritual resources it will be able to give the best and truest service to the nation.

X

THE EXPANSION OF THE CHURCH OF ENGLAND

Three great obstacles have stood in the way of missionary work. Ignorance, hostility at home, and hostility overseas. Ignorance and indifference made Churchmen deaf to the call to convert the world. For a long period after the Reformation there was little thought of sending the Gospel overseas. This was partly due to the absorption in ecclesiastical controversies and in difficulties at home; partly through the accident that Great Britain of all the European nations is most distant from non-Christian lands. There was no real awakening until the Evangelical Revival. The noblest aspect of this movement is seen in its enthusiasm for the conversion of the heathen; it has given freely to this work, and has sent out a continuous stream of missionaries. The Evangelical clergy and laity have done more than any other party within the Church to break through the hard crust of indifference and ignorance.

X

THE EXPANSION OF THE CHURCH OF ENGLAND

Those who are inclined to be depressed about the Church of England with its numerous domestic problems should take courage when they look at its work overseas. The rapid expansion of the Anglican Communion has been one of the most significant signs of the vitality of our Church. For three hundred years there was justification for the charge that it was insular, mentally and spiritually as well as geographically. In 1800 there were seventy-five Anglican dioceses; of these only twelve were outside the British Isles. Now there are three hundred and twenty, of which two hundred and fifty-one are outside the British Isles. The Lambeth Conference was attended in 1868 by seventy-nine bishops; in 1930 by three hundred and eight. And the growth still continues.

It was natural that the first missionary work overseas should be among our own people who had migrated as settlers to distant parts of the world. As the British Empire expanded so did the Church. Those who had been Churchmen at home still desired the spiritual ministrations of their Church. Many who had had little to do with the Church while in England, missed its clergy and ministrations when far away : they wished their children to be baptised, their marriages to be blessed, and their relatives buried with the Church of England service. Chaplains and clergy gradually came out to the different settlements, either for a short period or to spend the rest of their lives among their inhabitants. Later the bishops came to confirm and to ordain, and with their arrival there were slowly built up the traditional Church organisations.

As Christians came into contact with the non-Christian world they soon found it was impossible to confine the ministrations of their Church to English-speaking people. Attempts to limit the chaplains in India to work among their own fellow-countrymen quickly broke down. Great Britain's responsibilities to negroes who—through the slave trade—had been transplanted from their homes, inevitably directed attention to their native lands. Above all, the gradual realisation of the full meaning of Our Lord's command to preach His Gospel in all lands inspired Christians to give both money and service, so that light and salvation might be brought to nations which were ignorant of the good news.

The Agencies of Expansion

The method used for doing this was through societies within the Church rather than by the Church itself. There have been three great lines of approach to the non-Christian world. Sometimes, for secular reasons, a State has used all its influence to convert to its religion the people it had conquered and the nations with which it traded. In the ancient world the victor often attempted to coerce the vanquished into the acceptance of his gods. Christians unfortunately sometimes followed this evil precedent. When Church and State were one this led to the persecution of the religion of a defeated foe. Religions have often been established by the sword, for it is false history to declare that the blood of the martyrs always prevails. The propagation of Christianity by force is contrary to the teaching of its Master, though unhappily this has sometimes been forgotten. In the struggles between nations at the time of the Reformation, Catholic and Protestant both used the coercive power of the State. Even to-day this policy has not been entirely abandoned. When Abyssinia was conquered by the Italians, the Roman Catholic Church made every effort to use the occupation for the purpose of proselytising, and many of the Abyssinian clergy were persecuted and murdered. Our Church at one time had prestige with the non-Christian world through its State connection, though it is doubtful if in the long run this has proved to be of advantage. It has, however, never asked in its missionary work for the help of coercive power, though it used its influence with the State in 1892 to prevent a withdrawal from Uganda which would have led to the revival of the Slave Trade in its worst forms. But when its missionaries were killed it appealed neither for punitive expeditions to avenge them nor for the infliction of heavy fines on the guilty.

Frequently, the work of evangelisation is undertaken by a Church. The most notable example of this is the Roman Catholic Church which has placed its missionary work under a central organisation—a "Sacred Congregation" of Propaganda which controls missionary work in all parts of the world. It directs from the centre the strategy of Christian expansion. It decides where new missions should be and on which missions support should be concentrated. It views the world position as a whole, and directs men and money to the countries where the need seems to be most urgent. It sends its delegates to visit and guide the various missions. The Religious Orders place at its disposal men and women who will go wherever they are sent. Its funds are largely supplied by the Society for the Propagation of the Faith, whose members help by their prayers and by gifts of money. The missionary organisation of the Roman Church, highly centralised and widely supported, is a great agency for the conversion of the world. Its missionaries have shown a devotion and self-sacrifice which call forth admiration from those who have come into contact with them. They go to the East or to the West as authority dictates, and they remain at their post until the end of their lives unless they are recalled by their superiors. We may criticise some of the methods used by the Roman Church in this work, but there can only be thankfulness for the single-mindedness and complete self-sacrifice of its missionaries, both secular and regular, both men and women.

On a smaller scale the policy of central direction in missionary work has been followed by some of the Churches of the Anglican Communion. The episcopal churches in the United States, Canada, Australia and New Zealand regard their missions as the responsibility of the whole Church. It is the Church which decides the places in which missionary work should be started and supported, and the general strategy of evangelisation. It works through committees, but their members are appointed by the Church, and their more important decisions must be reported to and approved by it.

The Church of England adopted, or possibly half unconsciously drifted into, a very different method. Its missionary work has been undertaken by voluntary societies within the Church; these have raised the funds, provided the missionaries, and for long have had the general oversight and responsibility for the work in the areas which had been opened up by its agents. First came the Society for Promoting Christian Knowledge in the Spring of 1698. A few years later the Society for the Propagation of the Gospel was founded : then at the beginning of the nineteenth century the Church Missionary Society : and subsequently various other societies and associations especially interested in the work of evangelising different countries. The work of these societies has been truly magnificent. They have the enthusiastic support of tens of thousands of Churchmen, and they have poured men and money into the areas for which they had undertaken responsibility.

As well as the societies there are Communities which carry on active work in many parts of the world. The nineteenth century saw a remarkable revival of religious Orders within our Church. Many of them have established missionary stations in Africa and Asia. They are kept, by regular exchange of visits, in touch with the Mother Houses, who support them by prayer, recruits and money. Those who, like myself, have had even a passing glimpse of the work of the Community of the Resurrection in its great schools and settlements in South Africa must feel profoundly thankful that the Orders are engaging in these evangelistic and educational enterprises.

There are many who hold that the Church ought to be its own missionary society, and that the policy of allowing societies to be responsible for missionary advance should gradually be superseded. In any case it would be a matter of great practical difficulty to abandon what has now been so successfully followed for a considerable period of time. Even more serious is the possibility that the enthusiasm called forth by the societies might be lost. The phrase " the Church its own missionary society " needs careful scrutiny. What agency would the Church use ? Would it be a committee ? Would it be appointed by the Church Assembly ? Would it mean the loss of those who have specialised in this subject ? Dr. Max Warren makes a powerful statement of the case for the societies when he writes : " The sanctification of all human life demands of necessity from the appointed leaders of the Church a very large part of their attention because the Church is a catholic society embracing all sorts and conditions of men. A Church so widely and properly preoccupied can only discharge her missionary task, as historically she has best succeeded in discharging it, by treating it as the specialised function of those within the ranks who have felt laid upon them the divine constraint. By according to its missionary societies its official recognition, the Church reserves to itself its own inalienable responsibility for the evangelisation of the world. At the same time the Church commits to those of its members who have the task particularly at heart the actual labours of prosecuting it."[1]

On the other hand, the societies should not become a substitute for the Church : they should be its agencies : and care should be taken both to co-ordinate their work with one another, and to secure that the policy they adopt is in accordance with the mind of the Church. For these reasons it was a step of great importance when in 1921 the Church Assembly formed its Missionary Council. Bishop Cash of Worcester goes so far as to say that the foundation of the Church Assembly Missionary Council is " the most outstanding event in the recent history of the Church."[2] The Council is composed of elected representatives from the Church Assembly and of the missionary societies. It has no power to raise funds and has no executive power for overseas missionary work, but it co-ordinates the work of the societies : advises the Archbishops and the Church generally on missionary problems : and gives guidance to the Diocesan Missionary Boards. No one has greater right to give an authoritative description of the work of this Council than its secretary, Canon McLeod Campbell, who writes that it has " taken its part in a substantial advance in the spirit and practice of co-operation, especially at Headquarters. In Area Committees of the Council, preparing annually a Unified Statement of the main events and problems within their respective spheres, representatives of all the Anglican agencies concerned have found an opportunity for common counsel. Team work between the officers of the societies and the Council has been characteristic of the missionary education movement, the missionary approach to youth, and the campaign for enlisting recruits."[3] The Council should be much more than a co-ordinating agency ; it should think out missionary problems, and should be the

---

[1] " The Calling of God," p. 61.

[2] " The Missionary Church," p. 171.

[3] " Christian History in the Making," p. 338. This is an important book and should be read by all who wish to know more about the missionary work of the Church of England.

centre which receives information from all over the world as to the progress or reverses of the missionary movement; it should be ready to formulate policies and strategy when necessary, and urge the Church as a whole and the societies to adopt them. While the Council must refrain from entering into competition with the societies in appeals for money, its work is hampered unnecessarily if it can neither receive money, appeal for it, nor distribute it. These limitations are yielding before the pressure of facts. The Archbishops asked the Council to distribute the generous gift made by the American Protestant Episcopal Church in the darkest days of the war to assist Anglican missions: and recently it was asked by the Archbishops to make itself responsible for an appeal for £100,000 to help the Church in China. There are occasions when an appeal in a special emergency can be made by the Council with greater force than by any of the societies. It should have funds to vote in special directions where the societies are unable to act. Moreover, it would be impossible to give money direct to the missionary work of the whole church, except through the dioceses and the societies, unless the Council is able to receive donations and legacies which it can distribute at its discretion.

Obstacles in the Way

Three great obstacles have stood in the way of missionary work. Ignorance, hostility at home, and hostility overseas. Ignorance and indifference made Churchmen deaf to the call to convert the world. For a long period after the Reformation there was little thought of sending the Gospel overseas. This was partly due to the absorption in ecclesiastical controversies and in difficulties at home: partly through the accident that Great Britain of all the European nations is most distant from non-Christian lands. There was no real awakening until the Evangelical Revival. The noblest aspect of this movement is seen in its enthusiasm for the conversion of the heathen; it has given freely to this work, and has sent out a continuous stream of missionaries. The Evangelical clergy and laity have done more than any other party within the Church to break through the hard crust of indifference and ignorance.

Indifference occasionally changed into bitter opposition.

Missionary effort was feared and derided. It was feared lest possible indiscretions on the part of the missionaries might make the work of administrators more difficult, or lest they should bring to light and denounce evils connected with the advance of Western trade into countries inhabited by backward races. It was derided on the grounds that there was so much to do at home that it was sheer folly to leave an unconverted England to preach the Gospel in distant lands : and that it was unreasonable to unsettle people who were content with their ancestral faith and to attempt to replace it by a religion which had its strongest citadels in the more civilised parts of the world. Sydney Smith vehemently attacked Indian Missions " if missionaries are not watched the throat of every Englishman will be cut," our administrators who favoured missionary work would " deliberately, piously and conscientiously expose our Eastern Empire to destruction for the sake of converting half a dozen Brahmins, who after stuffing themselves with rum and rice and borrowing money from the missionaries would run away, covering the Gospel and its professors with every species of impious ridicule and abuse."[1] Charles Dickens in " Bleak House " ridiculed the missionary enthusiast by his picture of Mrs. Jellyby who neglected her own family, for " she has devoted herself to an extensive variety of public subjects at various times, and is at present (until something else attracts her) devoted to the subject of Africa, with a general view to the general cultivation of the coffee berry—and the natives—and the happy settlement, on the banks of the African rivers, of our superabundant home population." While the vehemence of this hostility died away, prejudice still lingered on. Fifty years ago many of the clergy hesitated at inviting missionary preachers or arranging collections for fear of the opposition of a section of their congregations. Occasionally sidesmen refused to collect when the collection was in the support of one of the societies. Indifference as well as hostility at home have been largely dispersed through careful and intelligent missionary propaganda and through the high testimony borne to the value of missions in India and Africa by administrators and others who have had direct personal experience of them.

[1] Quoted by Canon McLeod Campbell in " Christian History in the Making," pp. 83, 84.

Frequently the missionary has met with strong opposition from the people to whom he went with the Gospel. Sometimes it was due to anger and fear at teaching which undermined the authority of the long-established religions. Sometimes it arose from prejudice against things that were new and unfamiliar. Sometimes from suspicion that the evangelist would be followed by the slave dealer or land grabber who would wrest the country from them. Often the missionary had to go in peril of his life from the sudden violence of the mob or the cold enmity of those who feared a rival religion.

There are no more glorious pages in the annals of our Church than those which record the sufferings, hardships and often the martyrdoms of those who preached Christ. In Africa Bishop Hannington was murdered. In 1885 three converts, Baganda boys, were burnt to death, though they had had the offer of their lives if they would deny Christ. The story of their death as told by an old chief is very moving. They were given the choice of life if they denied Christ. They chose death. They were bound and driven along the road to a swamp where they were to die. As they went they sang the hymn, " Daily, daily sing the praises." At the swamp they were burnt to death, faithful to the end.[1] The Universities Mission to Central Africa lost many of its staff through fever, and others—like George Atlay and William Douglas—were murdered. In China in various anti-foreign risings many missionaries and their converts were murdered, among them Robert Stewart and his wife, whose six children subsequently all became mission workers. Bishop Patteson and two of his companions met their death in Melanesia in 1871. And in country after country there are stories of the persecution, ostracism and sometimes the murder of converts. When the day comes for our Church to include in its Kalendar some of the names of those who have been its saints and martyrs since the Reformation, among them will be many of those who gave themselves ungrudgingly for the extension of Christ's Kingdom. In the recent war many of our clergy and laity remained at their posts in the Pacific Islands, though they knew this would mean a cruel death at the hands of the Japanese. A Roman Catholic doctor gave a vivid description of the courage of an Anglican priest, Father Vivian Redlich, in staying at his post in New Guinea when his mission

[1] " The Missionary Church " by William Cash, p. 81.

district was invaded by the Japanese. He was warned that he would be killed, but the next morning he celebrated the Holy Communion for his flock. " I do not think I have ever witnessed a more devout congregation. The fervour expressed in those faces would have equalled that of the early Christians assisting at Mass in some hidden catacomb. Like those early Christians, these New Guinea Christians were assisting at Mass at the risk of their lives. The dense silence of the jungle was broken only by the sound of the priest's voice praying for his people. Then came the rustle of movement as those bare brown feet moved near the altar at the time of communion. It was really edifying to witness each native present communicate in such a devout and reverent manner." He concludes the narrative by saying Father Redlich's decision to remain cost him his life. " As his head was struck from his body and the white sand of the beach covered with his blood, there died a missionary whom we in Papua shall never forget. He died because he remained true to his trust. When he might have fled he did not flee." To-day in all parts of the world there are to be found members of the Anglican Communion, both ordained and lay, who in remote and often unhealthy regions have devoted themselves to lifelong service among the non-Christian peoples. While our Church sends out year by year its sons and daughters to the mission field we need not fear about the future.

From Mission to Church

In due time the mission district financed and controlled from the home base became a diocese, and wherever possible Provinces have been formed, so that dioceses which would have been isolated are brought into a fellowship larger than they could otherwise have possessed. A mission with many converts, and with flourishing organisations outgrew its original tutelage and naturally asked for its own bishop and the right to manage its own affairs. Within a hundred years many of the missionary districts thus have become dioceses within the Anglican Communion. They have their own bishop who ordains and confirms, their Synods, their Canons and their Courts. The home base no longer controls the mission for which at first it was entirely responsible ; now it assists and advises, and accepts the fact that its son has become of age and can no longer be treated as a small child learning to walk. The transition is a dangerous and delicate stage in growth. There is the temptation of the child to assert unduly its independence ; there is the even greater danger that the parents may still wish to guide and control the son who has reached manhood. The natural development of a native Church will be fatally obstructed if it is denied autonomy. At a time when nationalism is strong, the Eastern or African Church which follows and imitates all the ways of its Western parents, will be viewed and suspected as a foreign intruder. In Japan shortly before the war prejudice against foreign elements led to the expulsion or withdrawal of most of the bishops and many of the missionaries. The dioceses in India which are part of the Anglican Communion will be regarded as alien unless they can prove they have an independent indigenous life of their own. The new Churches must increasingly be staffed by native bishops and priests, who will be responsible for the work of the diocese, though it is to be hoped that they will always welcome the assistance of Europeans.

The principle is not confined to matters of organisation or administration ; it must be applied to the statements of doctrine and the manner of worship. As the central doctrines of Christianity had to be re-stated when they passed from Judaism to the Hellenic world, so now they will often have to be re-interpreted in the terms of thought most natural to the Eastern or African world. It is even more urgent that the worship of China, Japan, India and Africa should be conducted with ritual and ceremonial most natural to the people. I was once greatly impressed in India by the contrast between two different churches with large native congregations. The Service in one might have been, but for the language, in a Victorian church in a respectable suburb of London ; we had the full Matins, settings by Stainer, and Ancient and Modern hymns, in a building whose architecture was a debased imitation of Gothic. In the other church the atmosphere was different—the architecture was Indian, the worshippers took off their shoes as they entered ; there were no seats, the people sat or stood where they could ; the hymns were sung to Indian tunes and went on interminably until the officiating priest clapped his hands as a sign for silence ; the collection consisted of rice, bananas and other kinds of fruit and vegetables, which with coins were thrown into a large sheet held at the chancel steps. The first service was intelligible to the few English people present, the other was the worship of the people of the country. An Anglican service as conducted in a parish church at home is as unsuitable for an Eastern congregation as an Indian or Chinese service would be for a suburban or village congregation here. This is now widely recognised : the new cathedral at Dornakal is Indian in its architecture ; the great cathedral in Cairo is Eastern ; the beautiful chapel at Trinity College, Kandy, clearly belongs to Ceylon, and is enriched with paintings by a Cingalese artist. Much has been done to develop native Christian art, with Indian, Chinese and Japanese interpretations in sculpture or painting of Our Lord, of the Madonna, and of the Gospel stories.

The Influence of Missions

The purpose of missionary work is to convert men and women to the knowledge and obedience of Jesus Christ : this is its primary object. But in doing this there follow various by-products of the utmost value. The missionary must teach, so very rapidly schools in connection with his work come into existence : often at first very primitive in equipment and method, but later developing into the great schools and colleges which are found in India, China and Africa. The Church in many lands has been the pioneer in education. The value of its work has been recognised frequently by Governments and Commissions. The Commission on Higher Education in East Africa stated : " It is impossible to praise too highly the devotion, courage, zeal, charity and wisdom with which the missionaries performed their task," and in the more recent " Report on Higher Education in West Africa," we read : " When one looks for the root from which West African education sprang, one comes back, everywhere and always to the missionaries. It was the Christian Missions who first came out to the Coast, without desire for fee or reward. . . . Finally it was, and still is, the Churches who have made it possible to talk of West African education, higher, middle or lower, as a fact and not merely as an ideal." These commendations are not directed exclusively to Anglican Missions, though they have played a notable part in the education of the African. Large numbers who receive their education in Christian schools in India, China and Africa are never converted to Christianity, but they carry from them into daily life the knowledge of a high standard of social and individual conduct. Shortly before the war I visited Kashmir and saw something of the remarkable work done by Dr. Tyndale-Biscoe. He has been here for over fifty years. He has founded great schools for boys and girls, both primary and secondary. They are like the best of our schools in England. There was alertness, physical fitness, and keenness apparent in all the hundreds of students. There have been very few converts, only a small handful after long years of devoted work. But boys and girls alike have carried into their homes and into the State ideals of conduct and life which before were unknown. Again and again I heard from Christians who had spent many years in Kashmir that these schools were gradually leavening the whole lump with a Christian outlook on life which later on might lead to the acceptance of Christianity.

Missionaries very quickly found that the healing of the body must be preliminary to the healing of the soul. They were appalled with the vastness of preventible disease and suffering. In the spirit of their Master they were eager to alleviate it and to bring some help to the sufferers. So medical work became closely associated with the preaching of the Gospel. Great hospitals were built in the cities and became pioneers in healing work—the description of the C.M.S. hospital at Hangchow shows how varied are the activities of these centres of healing : " Besides the work of the five-hundred bed hospital and its numerous departments, there have grown up sanatoria for tuberculosis patients, branch hospitals for the blind, the incurable, the lepers, and the mentally afflicted : a nursing school, ante-natal and child welfare clinics : the means of free vaccination and inoculation against smallpox, cholera, typhoid and meningitis."[1] The villages also have their medical service : they are visited by mobile units at regular intervals, a talk on health is given and then the patients are seen. At Travancore there is a floating dispensary which travels along the numerous waterways of that State. To these hospitals patients are brought from long distances. Visiting a hospital at Srinagar, I noticed a bearded tribesman sitting by the bed of one of the patients ;

[1] " The Wholeness of Man," by P. Garlick, p. 147.

on asking about him I was told that he was one of a group that had brought the sick man many hundreds of miles over the mountains of the Frontier, that the man's family had also made the journey, and that they all would wait there—the men making excellent medical attendants—until the patient either died or recovered. This was no unusual incident, for these long journeys on the part of a whole family to conduct one of its members to a hospital were quite common. Many of the Missions also teach the people improved methods of farming and cultivation. In some cases the village churches have become self-supporting through these means. The village, once squalid and poverty-stricken, has been changed into a centre of order and cleanliness and prosperity. In North India one of the Christian Colleges sends out regularly little companies of students to the villages in a large area to teach the people how to improve their cultivation and to develop local industries.

Missions to-day are thus not only centres of evangelisation, but also of education, medicine and agriculture. Here, for instance, is a description of the Community of the Resurrection's mission at Middelburg in the Transvaal : " The work has certain well-marked divisions. There is first the Jane Furse Memorial Hospital. It is a fairly large one for a mission hospital—with over a hundred beds. Consequently it ranks as a training ground for native nurses, and is State-aided. . . . On the other side of the hospital building is the primary school. Some three hundred children attend it (and children may be over twenty years of age). Thirdly, there is the farm. . . . It will be a great thing to teach the natives the elements of sound farming." This is characteristic of many of our Missionary Settlements in different parts of the world. Their work must be judged not only by the number of their converts, but by the Christian influence which radiates from them and which attracts those who are as yet unbaptised.

The Anglican Communion

The various Provinces and Dioceses of the Anglican Communion are as different from one another as the parishes in an English diocese. There are some in which teaching, ritual and ceremonial are predominantly Catholic ; there are others which are strictly Protestant, in their worship and methods. The varieties in Churchmanship are even greater than those found in an English diocese, for services are authorised and practices permitted which here are forbidden. These divergences quite obviously carry with them dangers ; they may become so great as to result in disruption. How are these Churches held together in one Communion ?

Historically there are two types of ecclesiastical organisation. On the one hand there is centralised Government : the Roman Catholic Church is the great example of this. It is governed by one person, the Pope : it is the Pope who makes the appointments to the different bishoprics and who regulates the worship and teaching of the Church. No one man unaided can perform such a huge task : he is thus helped by a great army of officials. The government and administration of the Church of Rome is by a highly centralised bureaucracy of which the Pope is the head. This system has great advantages. It makes for administrative efficiency and presents an imposing picture of unity. But it stifles liberty : it deprives the different churches of the power of managing their own affairs : and it tends to reduce the position of its bishops, to use George Tyrrell's phrase, to " marionettes " of the Pope.

The other type of organisation is the more primitive—namely that of a number of self-governing churches in communion with one another. This was usual in the first four centuries when the dioceses and Patriarchates were neither under a visible head nor held together by an administrative system. They were free and independent churches giving allegiance to the One Lord, holding a common faith, possessing the same sacraments, and one with the Apostolic age by the threefold ministry.

The Anglican Communion belongs to this second type of organisation. It is a fellowship of self-governing Churches in communion with the See of Canterbury. A resolution of the Lambeth Conference of 1930 defined as follows the nature and status of the Anglican Communion—" The Anglican Communion is a fellowship, within the One Holy Catholic and Apostolic Church, of those duly constituted Dioceses, Provinces or Regional Churches in communion with the See of Canterbury, which have the following characteristics in common :—

(a) They uphold and propagate the Catholic and Apostolic faith and Order as they are generally set forth in the

Book of Common Prayer as authorised in their several churches :

(b) They are particular or national Churches, and, as such, promote within each of their territories a national expression of Christian faith, life and worship : and

(c) They are bound together not by a central legislative and executive authority, but by mutual loyalty sustained through the common counsel of the Bishops in conference."[1]

The different Churches are united by common doctrines and ideals. The doctrines are those stated in the Apostles' and Nicene Creeds and confirmed by the Scriptures. The ideals " are the ideals of the Church of Christ. Prominent among them are an open Bible, a pastoral Priesthood, a common worship, a standard of conduct consistent with that worship and a fearless love of truth."[2] All these Churches are free, while they have no power to change the Scriptures, the Creeds, the Sacraments or the Catholic ministry, " they may regulate rites, ceremonies, usages, observances and discipline "[3] as they think best for setting forth to their people the Christian faith, and building them up in it.

Externally the Churches of the Anglican Communion are held together in three ways. First by the recognition of the Primacy of the See of Canterbury. Its Archbishop claims no Papal powers, and has no jurisdiction over the various Provinces. He has no right to interfere in their affairs. But through its historical position Canterbury has great moral and spiritual influence throughout the Anglican Communion. Successive Archbishops have done their utmost to make themselves familiar with the problems of the different churches. Information about them is always pouring into Lambeth, and the Archbishop is incessantly asked for advice and counsel by overseas Bishops. And most important of all he is responsible for the invitations to the Lambeth Conference over which he presides.

The importance of this Conference in uniting the Anglican Communion is very great. Every ten years (unless hindered by war), bishops from all over the world come together for mutual discussion and conference. Day by day for six weeks

[1] Resolution 49.
[2] Lambeth Conference Report, 1930, on the Anglican Communion, p. 154.
[3] " Church and Nation," Creighton, p. 212.

or so they pray and take counsel together on the matters which most concern their work. Before the actual date of the meeting there is careful preliminary preparation of the subjects to be discussed: during the Conference committees report and recommend on them: their recommendations are accepted, rejected or amended, and eventually appear as resolutions of the Conference and form the substance of an Encyclical Letter. On most of the subjects a common mind is reached. At the two Conferences I have attended only twice was there a serious division of opinion on matters of grave importance, though on nearly every question there was considerable debate. The resolutions are not coercive, the Conference has no executive powers, and they are only advisory: they have no binding force until they are accepted by the different Provinces; one Province indeed may accept what another may modify or reject. Their moral weight is however very great, for they are reached only after invocation of the Holy Spirit and after the fullest consideration by the assembled bishops. The guidance they give and the advice they offer cannot be lightheartedly disregarded.

A Consultative Body acts as a continuation committee of the Conference. It has no authority beyond that possessed by the Conference itself. Like the Conference it has no legal powers. Its authority is solely moral. It carries on work left by the preceding Conference and assists the Archbishop of Canterbury in preparing for the next to be held. It can be consulted by the Archbishop or by any bishop or groups of bishops on questions of faith, order, policy or administration. But it has always the right to refuse to consider any of these subjects. The existence of this Body might prove of great importance if in the period between the Conferences there should arise some problem or dispute which might affect the whole Anglican Communion.

Relationships between the Churches of the Anglican Communion have been strengthened during recent years by the more frequent interchange of visits between the Archbishops and clergy in different parts of the world. The Archbishops of Canterbury and York have visited the United States and Canada, and visits from the bishops of both those churches have been fairly frequent. Since the First World War visits by Anglican bishops have also been paid to India, South Africa and Australia, while many of their bishops have visited the home

Church. More rapid travelling means closer fellowship between the Churches.

The Anglican Communion is not unlike the British Commonwealth which now consists of self-governing States held together by common aims and ideals. They are no longer bound to the Mother Country by legislative chains : they are free to stay within, or to secede from, the Commonwealth. Frequent consultation and the exchange of visits by representative leaders strengthen and defend the ideals which they all hold. The Anglican Communion has developed its system quite independently but on the same lines as that of the British Commonwealth.

Tasks Ahead

While the story of the expansion of the Church of England is full of encouragement, it must not leave us with a mistaken optimism. The greater part of the world is still unconverted. Missionary maps often unconsciously give a false impression, for they show the world divided up into a network of Anglican dioceses, but they give no indication of the small numbers of priests and laity often within them. In China, for instance, only one hundredth of one per cent. of the huge population is a member of the Anglican Communion ! But in China, India and Africa the Church is growing. In one diocese in India 150,000 have become Christians in twenty-five years. In one area of Africa members have increased from 26,000 to 327,000 in less than forty years. At the Conference at Tambaram a medical missionary who had worked for many years in Arabia was asked how many converts he had made in that time. His reply was " Twelve, but we are not discouraged, we thank God and go ahead." In the same spirit of thankfulness and resolution and with far greater cause for encouragement the Church of England faces its responsibilities overseas.

XI

TOWARDS THE REUNION OF CHRISTENDOM

The Church of England has taken the lead in the movement towards Christian unity. It has special qualifications for this as both Catholic and reformed. Catholic in its very nature and origin, it meets the historic churches of Christendom on equal terms. Reformed it understands and appreciates the position of the Protestant Churches. By its wide sympathies and its special position it should show the way to the reunion of Christendom, though the road may be long and beset with obstacles before the goal is reached where all Christians are visibly one in Christ.

XI

TOWARDS THE REUNION OF CHRISTENDOM

IN the last half-century the Church of England has made a notable contribution towards the reunion of Christendom. At the opening of the century it had very little association with other Christian Churches. With the Roman Catholic Church there was open hostility, the efforts once made for a *rapprochement* by a small group of Anglicans and Gallicans had failed, and there was no kind of co-operation between the two Churches. The position with the Orthodox Churches of the East was more favourable, but there was comparatively little communication with them. With the Continental Reformed Churches we were better acquainted, and through royal marriages there was more sympathy with the Lutheran Church in Germany than with the other Churches. At home our relations with the Nonconformist Churches were most unhappy. There was much dislike and suspicion on both sides and this persistently broke out into bitter controversy, bringing scandal upon Christianity. The Anglican clergy looked down on the Free Church ministers as interlopers in their parishes, as unsound in faith, and as lacking a valid authority. Free Churchmen naturally resented this attitude, criticised the privileged position of an Established Church, and feared its Catholicism meant a movement towards Rome. Social and political differences widened the gulf. The Church of England on the whole was Conservative and connected with the land, Nonconformity was Liberal and commercial. Attacks on the Establishment and the Church Schools accentuated the bitterness. Historical causes had much to do with this conflict; Anglicans remembered the persecution of their clergy and the outlawry of their Prayer Book in Cromwellian days; Nonconformists recalled the ejection of the 2,000 Puritan ministers at the Restoration, and the series of Test and Subscription Acts which debarred them for long from taking part in public life.

It is difficult for those of a younger generation to realise how deep were the divisions between the Anglican Church and the Free Churches. The leaders of the Churches had no personal knowledge of one another, controversy was conducted at long range, either in the press or from the public platform. The clergy rarely knew the Nonconformist ministers who were working in their parishes. In the country districts the hostility— for no other word can describe it—was most marked, and charges of attempted intimidation and bribery were frequently heard. In Parliament the representatives of the Free Churches opposed or obstructed any Bills intended to improve the discipline and administration of the Church, usually on the ground that the less the Church was reformed the stronger would be the case for Disestablishment.

A number of different causes have led to a complete transformation in the relationships between the Church of England and the Free Churches. In the first place through the Student Christian Movement and other interdenominational movements there was more frequent intercourse between the younger members of the different churches. Men who had prayed, conferred and played together as laymen were ready to pray and work together when they were ordained. The Edinburgh Conference, the first of many of such Conferences, was the natural outcome of the wish to co-operate in the mission field. Then came the four-year war ; everywhere Englishmen were drawn closer to one another ; and national unity had its influence on Christian unity. Anglican clergy and Free Church ministers found themselves participating in great services of intercession and thanksgiving ; the chaplains of all denominations serving in the Forces were thrown together, and many of them returned to their parishes with an intense desire to promote Christian unity. When the war was over it was soon seen that all the Christian Churches were confronted with the common enemy of secularism. Compared to the gulf which separates Christianity from materialism, ecclesiastical differences appeared much less significant : stress was more frequently laid on the doctrines and practices which unite rather than on those which divide.

The Lambeth Appeal

It was in this more favourable atmosphere for Christian unity that the Lambeth Conference met in 1920 and issued its great

"Appeal to All Christian People." It commenced by acknowledging "all those who believe in our Lord Jesus Christ, and have been baptised into the name of the Holy Trinity, as sharing with us membership in the universal Church of Christ which is His Body." It called Christians to repent for their share in breaking the fellowship, and stated for the Anglican Communion "we desire frankly to confess our share in the guilt of this crippling the Body of Christ and hindering the activity of His Spirit." It described its vision of a re-united Catholic Church as of "a Church genuinely Catholic, loyal to all Truth, and gathering into its fellowship all 'who profess and call themselves Christians' within whose visible unity all the treasures of faith and order, bequeathed as a heritage by the past to the present, shall be possessed in common, and made serviceable to the whole Body of Christ." This visible unity would involve the whole-hearted acceptance of the Holy Scriptures, the Nicene and the Apostles' Creeds, the Sacraments of Baptism and the Holy Communion, and a "ministry acknowledged by every part of the Church as possessing not only the inward call of the Spirit, but also the commission of Christ and the authority of the whole body." The Appeal went on to claim that "the Episcopate is the one means of providing such a ministry." It closed with the practical suggestion "that if the authorities of other Communions should so desire, we are persuaded that, terms of union having been otherwise satisfactorily adjusted, bishops and clergy of our Communion would willingly accept from these authorities a form of commission and recognition which would commend our ministry to their congregations, as having its place in the one family life. . . . It is our hope that the same motive would lead ministers who have not received it to accept a commission through episcopal ordination, as obtaining for them a ministry throughout the whole fellowship."

The Appeal made at once a great impression. It was sent to the heads of the different churches. There was widespread discussion of its terms and proposals. Conferences were held with the representatives of the Free Churches in this Country and discussions were initiated with Churches on the Continent. But though the Appeal had an immense moral and spiritual influence its immediate visible results have been comparatively small. The Pope acknowledged the receipt of the Appeal.

Many of the Orthodox Churches gave it sympathetic consideration. The Old Catholic Church has established full intercommunion with us, each Church acknowledging that the other was sound both in faith and order. With the Church of Sweden there has also been mutual recognition of Orders, and we take part in the consecration of their bishops as they do in ours. The non-episcopal Churches have recognised how much of the Faith we hold in common, but have not seen their way to accept the proposals for re-ordination and re-commissioning of their ministers. But though the tangible results as yet are small, with the issue of the Appeal the whole question of reunion was launched upon a new and more hopeful phase. This will become clear if we consider in greater detail the movements towards Christian unity in which the Church of England has been especially active.

The Non-Episcopal Churches

The improved relationships with the Free Churches and the willing co-operation with them on many matters of religious, social and moral interest have been most marked. A great step forward was made, though sometimes misunderstood by Free Churchmen, when a responsible committee with the two Archbishops and ten diocesan bishops among its members stated in 1923 in a memorandum that the Free Church ministries " as ministries which imply a sincere intention to preach Christ's Word and administer the Sacraments as Christ has ordained, and to which authority to do so has been given by the Church concerned are real ministries of Christ's Word and Sacraments in the Universal Church." It is true that discussions for corporate reunion have not yet led to any result. The proposal for Ordination *sub-conditione* was rejected by the Federal Council of the Free Churches, while the Baptist Union in 1926 stated that " union of such a kind as the Bishops have contemplated is not possible for us." But these rejections have not hindered the continuous growth of fellowship. Successive Archbishops, Davidson, Lang, Temple, and now Fisher, have done everything in their power to encourage friendship and co-operation. Of Archbishop Davidson the then Editor of the *Christian World* wrote in 1923 : " One might almost say that Dr. Randall Davidson is the first Archbishop for whom the English Nonconformists have a real affection. . . . It can assuredly be said that more Nonconformists have found a welcome at Lambeth Palace in the last twenty years than in the preceding two hundred years. . . . Not tolerance but good will has been ushered into ecclesiastical relationships during Dr. Davidson's régime at Canterbury."[1] This change has shown itself in several ways. There has been an almost entire cessation of angry and contemptuous controversy, Churchmen and Nonconformists no longer rush into the fray; when we have to make clear our differences we do so with restraint and courtesy. The controversy over Disestablishment has died away, though the majority of Nonconformists are still opposed in principle to an Established Church : strife over education has given way to co-operation. When Mr. Butler's Education Bill was presented Anglican and Free Church leaders had reached agreement on its religious policy—though minorities on both sides were dissatisfied. There have been frequent consultations and often united public pronouncements on matters of national importance. Co-operation has not been confined to social and moral questions, united services on days of national prayer are usual : on Armistice Day Churchmen and Free Churchmen meet together round the war memorials or in the parish churches and join in prayer : the Religion and Life Weeks, such a feature of the closing years of the war, were organised and supported widely by clergy, ministers and their respective laity. And in most of the large centres of population there are Christian Social Councils, representative of all the Churches. We no longer regard our divisions as inevitable or as beneficial, we now know that they are sinful and pray that they may be healed. The British Council of Churches, presided over by the present Archbishop of Canterbury, is the most striking manifestation of the new spirit. Anglicans have taken an active part in its creation and are well represented on it. More important are resolutions passed by the Southern and Northern Convocations approving under exceptional conditions of the admission of baptised communicant members of other Churches to the Holy Communion celebrated by our priests ; and in certain other cases permitting Free Church Ministers to preach in our pulpits and the clergy to accept invitations to preach in Nonconformist chapels.

[1] Quoted in " Randall Davidson," by George Bell, p. 1124.

Negotiations with the Church of Scotland proved disappointing. Both our Churches hold so much in common, and both insist so strongly on Church Order that there was good hope that some agreement towards mutual recognition and intercommunion might be reached. Moreover it is generally recognised that in interdenominational conferences the Anglican and Presbyterian representatives usually find themselves in close agreement on many of the matters under discussion. Four sessions of a Joint Conference were held at the invitation of the Archbishop of Canterbury to consider the Appeal, but they came to an end in 1934, when the General Assembly of the Church of Scotland instructed its representatives to make plain " that any agreement with regard to the Orders and Sacraments of the conferring Churches can only be based on the recognition of the equal standing of the accepted communicants and ministers in each."

In the Mission Field more than anywhere else the need for Christian unity is felt. The spectacle of Christians separated from one another in the midst of a vast non-Christian population is a grave hindrance to the spread of the Gospel. The Hindu and the Moslem contrast the unity of their religion with the divisions of Christendom. No wonder that Gairdner of Cairo once wrote : " It takes faith, believing in Christ, His Church and Ministry here in this Moslem city. But on my word it takes more faith to believe in these when one thinks of the Church itself as it exists here, sect upon sect, each more intolerant than its neighbour. Each practically ex-communicating the other in the name of the One Lord, and that in the face of an Islam which loathes all alike."[1] It is not therefore surprising that it is in the mission field that the most strenuous efforts have been made in the cause of union. This is notably so with the South India Scheme by which four dioceses and the chief non-episcopal Churches of South India will unite ; if this comes into effect the new Church of South India at first will be outside the Anglican Communion, and its bishops will not be invited to the Lambeth Conferences ; but it is hoped that within thirty or forty years admitted irregularities will have been removed and that the new Church will take its place within the Anglican Communion.

The discussions on the South India Scheme have made clear

[1] " Life," p. 266.

that reunion in one quarter might threaten unity elsewhere. Any scheme of reunion which ignored the definite Anglican position as Catholic in doctrine, worship and ministry, would result in disruption. The South India Scheme would be unacceptable to a large body of Church people, both clergy and laymen, if it followed that during the experimental period the new Church remained in full communion with the Church of England. Its position during this period was described by the Encyclical Letter of the Archbishops and Bishops present at the Lambeth Conference in 1930 in which they state : " The fact that the Church in South India will not be a member of the group of Churches called the Anglican Communion will inevitably impose on our brethren a temporary severance of close and treasured relationships in council and synod, with their brethren in North India. But these are sacrifices which we believe they will make cheerfully in the hope of achieving a union between episcopal and non-episcopal churches such as has never yet been effected, and of building up a real and living Church in India." Those who agree with the Lambeth Conference in the wish " that as soon as the negotiations are successfully completed the venture should be made and the union inaugurated " hope that eventually from this great experiment there will emerge a Church which gives the Indian expression to the faith, worship and ministry of the Catholic Church.

The Œcumenical Movement

The Church of England has taken an active part in the Œcumenical Movement. In 1910 it sent representatives to Edinburgh for the World Missionary Conference : it did so on the understanding that the Conference did not deal with questions of Faith and Order. But a bishop of the Anglican Communion, Dr. Brent, urged the Protestant Episcopal Church of the United States to promote a world conference on these excluded subjects. The first of these Conferences was held at Lausanne in 1927 ; with the exception of the Church of Rome and the Baptists all Christian Churches were represented at it. The second Conference was held at Edinburgh in 1937 and was attended by three hundred and forty-four delegates representing a hundred and twenty-three Churches. Their purpose was to affirm the underlying unity of the churches which springs from loyalty to Christ and to study how best to overcome the obstacles in the way of full unity. International conferences also met on Life and Work at Stockholm in 1925, and on Church, Community and State at Oxford in 1937. Immediately before the war in 1939 an international Youth Conference was held at Amsterdam. From these various movements there came the British Council of Churches and the proposed World Council of Churches, now in process of formation. After preliminary hesitation the Church of England sent to the conferences some of the strongest of its leaders and has made a most valuable contribution to their success. Archbishop Temple from Lausanne onwards was one of the pioneers of this movement; he more than anyone else is responsible for the importance it has acquired, and all who attended its meetings recognised in him—to use the words of a Quaker—" a unique man in a world-wide movement."[1] He presided over the conference at Edinburgh, was Chairman of the British Council of Churches and was elected President of the provisional Committee of the World Council of Churches.

The Œcumenical Missionary gathering at Edinburgh in 1910 was followed by similar conferences at Jerusalem in 1928 and at Madras in 1938. I was present, as Bishop of Winchester, at Madras. There were 471 delegates, and nearly half of these were from the younger churches. The Anglican Communion was well represented, though it was in a small minority; its members had every day an early morning Celebration of the Holy Communion in the Anglican Chapel in the college at Tambaram. Then after breakfast there was a united devotional service in the large assembly hall, conducted by a selected delegate on the lines to which he was accustomed. Sometimes I think the Anglicans were as startled by the freedom and unconventionality of these services, as the non-Anglicans must have been chilled at our greater formality and liturgical correctness. The morning was spent in conference, broken up into different committees. In the late afternoon and in the evening there were meetings and conferences for all the members, and the day closed with an act of worship. There was a remarkable spirit of unity and fellowship; we prayed, conferred and fed together. Differences of Church, nation and race did not hinder free and unrestrained discussion. Personally I never

[1] Carl Heath in " William Temple : An Estimate and Appreciation," p. 83.

found a trace of resentment when occasionally at a full session I stated quite uncompromisingly the Anglican position. On Christmas Day the Holy Communion was celebrated in the Conference Hall by Bishop Azariah at a temporary altar furnished with candles and a cross; he was assisted by bishops from America, Africa, China, Japan, and myself, and we administered the Holy Sacrament to Africans, Indians, Cingalese, Germans, Chinese, Japanese, Burmese, Americans, Fillipinos and members of the British Commonwealth of Nations. Japanese and Chinese while their countries were at war, knelt side by side. It was a most moving and unforgettable experience. I have dwelt with some detail on this conference, the only one of this nature I have ever attended, to make it plain that Anglicans without any loss of principle can take part in these conferences, and make their special contribution to Christian fellowship.

In many other ways the Church of England has been able to assist in the Œcumenical Movement. Before the war steps were taken towards intercommunion with the Church of Finland, though as that Church had lost since 1884 its Apostolic succession, this was not so simple as in the case of the Swedish Church which had retained its succession unbroken. Agreements were made with the Churches of Latvia and Estonia to admit to communion members of their Churches. During the war friendliness between our Church and the Churches of Denmark and Norway increased, through our sympathy with them in the dark hours of their occupation and our admiration for the resistance made by their Church leaders. Since the war the Primates of these two Churches have visited England and have had conversations with the Archbishop of Canterbury and other Anglican leaders, but there does not appear to be any desire in their Churches for the Apostolic succession. After the defeat of their country the German Lutherans in various ways have looked to the Church of England for assistance; there has been considerable intercourse between their pastors and some of our chaplains, and the Bishop of Chichester has done much to keep contact with German Church leaders. The dangers of a totalitarianism which destroys individual freedom and responsibility, and of a civilisation which is secular in its aims and methods are drawing Christians together in defence of their common heritage. And now that civilisation itself is threatened with collapse through famine and want, while in the background there is the menace of destruction through the atomic bomb, the call for closer co-operation between all Christians becomes even more urgent.   The witness and warnings of a single Church have little influence upon the world, but the weight of the united witness of Christendom will have far greater effect.   With hope we can look to the future of the Œcumenical Movement. Archbishop Temple's words at his enthronement are prophetic : " a Christian fellowship which now extends into almost every nation, and binds citizens of them all in true unity and mutual love—almost incidentally the great world-fellowship has arisen : it is the great new fact of our era. . . .   Yes, here is one great ground of hope for the coming days, this world-wide Christian fellowship, this Œcumenical Movement."

The Roman Catholic Church

The Roman Catholic Church takes no part in the Œcumenical Movement, its title Œcumenical is really a misnomer while the great Church of the West is not included in it.   Beyond a courteous acknowledgement the Roman Catholic Church has made no response to the " Appeal to all Christian People."   It is not fair to say that this is due to its lack of interest in Christian unity, but to a different conception as to the means by which it should be brought about.   While we think of the united Church as one in which the various churches would retain their identity, and, accepting the Catholic Scriptures, Creeds, Sacraments, and Orders, would bring into it their special gifts and contri- butions : the Roman Catholic Church demands submission and absorption with possibly a few minor concessions to make more easy the way of surrender.   In his Church the Roman Catholic already sees the One Holy Catholic Apostolic Church in all its perfection and completeness ; its numbers will be increased, but its character will be unchanged by the return of those whom he regards as now disobedient to it.

In recent years two attempts have been made to bring about a *rapprochement*.   In 1894 this was made by the late Lord Halifax and the Abbé Portal, but the overtures came to an end with an Apostolic letter from the Vatican declaring Anglican Orders to be null and void.   From 1921 to 1925 meetings were held at Malines under the chairmanship of Cardinal Mercier between a small group of Anglicans and Roman Catholics. The initiative was taken again by Lord Halifax who in his old age was devoted as ever to the cause of Reunion. These conversations were of greater importance than those which had taken place thirty years previously, for they were held with the knowledge of both the Pope and the Archbishop of Canterbury. Later on it was made public that they were being held, and both the Archbishop and the Cardinal received many protests, those addressed to the Archbishop were often hysterical in their vigour. But the Archbishop approved of the continuance of the discussions, though by then it had become clear that any report or statement issued would have to contain not only a summary of the matters on which there was agreement but also of those on which there was disagreement, especially on the Primacy of the Pope. But Cardinal Mercier died before the final Conversation was held. A few months later Cardinal Bourne delivered a vehement attack on the Church of England, and on January 6th, 1928, Pope Pius XI issued an Encyclical reasserting in uncompromising terms the doctrine of the Papal Supremacy, declaring that true believers must hold the dogma of the infallibility of the Roman Pontiff in the sense defined by the Œcumenical Vatican Council with the same faith as they believe the Incarnation of Our Lord. It condemned various movements towards Christian unity and pronounced " that it is not in any way lawful for Catholics to give to such enterprises their encouragement or support." From these Conversations no immediate practical results have followed, but Dr. Bell is surely right when he says : " There has been progress in understanding, in charity, in desire. So far as the longed-for *rapprochement* was concerned, the funda-mental difficulties remain unsolved. But channels of thought and methods of study have been started, from which perhaps in later days some great gain may result."[1] In the diocese of York there are two reminders of the part played by Cardinal Mercier in these Conversations : set in one of the chalices used in the Minster is the ring he gave on his death-bed to Lord Halifax : and in the little Church of Kirby Underdale, the present Lord Halifax has given a window in which the Cardinal is shown.

The difficulties in the way of close co-operation between the Church of England and the Church of Rome in this country are very great. There is still deep and widespread fear and

---

[1] " Randall Davidson," by George Bell, p. 1302.

dislike of the Roman Church, and this has been increased through the failure of the Pope to denounce the atrocities committed by the Italians in Abyssinia, and by the Nazis in the countries they occupied. Its insistence on the re-baptism (or conditional baptism) of converts from the Anglican Church, the re-ordination of any of its priests who secede, and the rigidity of our marriage laws are continual causes of irritation.[1] The condition its hierarchy often makes that there should be no prayer at any united meetings in which their priests or laymen take part is too heavy a price to pay for their co-operation. An equally formidable obstacle is the policy of Roman Catholics in the Mission Field where they often enter deliberately into competition with other Christian Churches, confusing by their claims the minds of converts, and enticing away those discontented or under discipline.

Nevertheless some slight progress has been made towards a better understanding. Much of the old bitterness of controversy has passed away: and violent and abusive denunciation is rare. We recognise more freely the strength, extent and devotion of the Roman Church. There are more frequent friendships between individual Anglicans and Roman Catholics. The chief Roman Catholic paper in this country " The Tablet " sets a high standard of Christian scholarship and courtesy when it deals with religious controversy. For a time Anglicans took some part in the Sword of the Spirit movement; and occasionally Anglican, Roman Catholic and Free Church leaders issue joint statements on matters concerning national and international affairs.

The Orthodox Churches

With the Orthodox Churches of the East the relationship of the Anglican Church is more happy. Although it is always difficult for the East and West to understand each other, and the rich ceremonial and ritual of the East far exceed anything which is customary in the West, there are many reasons for friendship between our Churches. We are united in repudiating the Papal claims, we reject the Pope's infallibility, his claims for jurisdiction, and his demand to be regarded as the Vicar of Christ.

---

[1] Since 1908 a Roman Catholic who has married an Anglican in one of our churches is regarded by his Church as living in sin.

The theology of both the Anglican and the Eastern Churches has been deeply influenced by the Greek Fathers. On many doctrinal questions we avoid the over-definition so characteristic of the Church of Rome. The Eastern Churches like the Churches of the Anglican Communion are independent, self-governing Churches, respectively recognising the priority in dignity of Constantinople and Canterbury, but claiming freedom from their jurisdiction. The Roman Catholic Church has always endeavoured to undermine equally the influence of the Church of England and of the Eastern Churches and to proselytise their members. Union under a central bureaucracy chiefly consisting of foreigners is alien both to the Anglican and Eastern conceptions of the Catholic Church.

The appeal to all Christian People met with a sympathetic response from the Orthodox Churches. The ground had been prepared by the writings and friendship of men like Bishop Collins and Mr. W. J. Birkbeck, and more recently by Canon J. A. Douglas. A delegation had been sent from Constantinople to confer with the Lambeth Conference Committee dealing with Christian unity. There was much discussion then and subsequently on Anglican Orders and doctrines. In July, 1922 the Patriarch of Constantinople declared on behalf of the Holy Synod that " the ordinations of the Anglican Episcopal Confession of bishops, priests and deacons, possesses the same validity as those of the Roman, Old Catholic and Armenian Churches possess, inasmuch as all essentials are found in them which are held indispensable from the Orthodox point of view for the recognition of the ' Charisma ' of the priesthood derived from Apostolic Succession." Later on the Patriarchs of Jerusalem, Cyprus and Alexandria also recognised the validity of Anglican Orders. Thus was paved the way to closer friendship, though actual inter-communion is still far off, but by the exercise of the principle of economy the members of our Church are allowed to receive Communion in Orthodox Churches when away from the ministrations of their own priests, while similarly we allow their members to communicate at our altars.

Before the Revolution there were many friendly contacts with the Russian Orthodox Church. In 1896 Bishop Creighton, and and in 1897 Archbishop Maclagan, visited Russia and were received with every courtesy by the Church and State. I had always wished to visit Russia, for whose Church and people I had a great admiration, so when at a Bishops' meeting in January 1943, Archbishop Temple passed me a scrap of paper on which he had written : " There is some suggestion of an interchange of visits between Anglican and Russian ecclesiastics, what do you think ? " I at once replied that I would gladly go to Russia if this would help. To this he wrote : " If you go it will make all the difference." It was not possible however to make the visit until September of that year. I flew by Cairo, Teheran and Stalingrad to Moscow, and I was greeted with the greatest cordiality by the Patriarch Sergei, who a week or two before had been elected to the restored Patriarchate, and by the archbishops and bishops he had with him. At the Liturgy I was always given a place by the altar. I was formally welcomed by the Patriarch at the first Liturgy I attended, and the people thundered forth the hymn of welcome to a bishop. I shall never forget the vast crowds in the Cathedral pressing forward to touch my cope and ask for my blessing. Though I had many conversations with the Patriarch and his Synod we did not discuss Anglican Orders, it would have been premature to have done so : but in every kind of way the Orthodox authorities expressed their friendship to the Church of England. It was a memorable visit, as it was the first time since the Revolution that a representative of any Church from outside had visited the Russian Church. In 1945 a delegation of Russian ecclesiastics visited this country, and were received by the Archbishop of Canterbury at Lambeth ; they came to York for the Sunday and were welcomed formally to the Minster, where they presented me with a touching gift, the blue enamelled pectoral cross which had been worn by the Patriarch Sergei who had died since my visit : I wear it with my robes, as a sign of our friendship with the Russian Church.

Elsewhere, too, I have experienced the readiness of the Eastern Churches to show friendship with our Church. On a visit to Athens in 1945, Archbishop Damaskinos spoke frequently of his wish for a closer co-operation with us, though always recognising that there were serious difficulties which would have to be removed before inter-communion is possible. In striking contrast to the Roman Catholic Church in Belgium and France which had refused the use to our chaplains even of the ruined churches our men had restored for worship, the Greek Orthodox Church offered its churches freely to us for the worship of our forces. Once when I was out in the country near Athens, a chaplain followed me with a group of sailors who had missed their Confirmation the previous day, I proposed to confirm them under the shade of a large tree ; but I was at once told that the Orthodox priest of a church close by would be glad for me to use it for this purpose : so in a simple country church with brightly painted eikons and without seats of any kind I confirmed the men, the Greek priest and some of his flock standing by. When I thanked the Archbishop Regent for the kindness he and his priests had shown to our soldiers his reply was " Your soldiers, they are our sons, our children."

The Bishop in Jerusalem keeps in close touch with the Patriarchs of the different Churches resident there, and holds a key position for work for Christian unity. Many who have visited Jerusalem have been much struck by the influence he has gained among the representatives of the various Churches. Both the Greek and the Armenian Patriarchs are especially interested in, and closely follow, all that concerns the Church of England.

The same is true of the Patriarch of Alexandria ; he uses every opportunity of welcoming Anglican representatives who are passing through Egypt. He has told all of these who have visited him how anxious he is to see strengthened the bonds which already exist between our Churches. The Bishop of Egypt, Dr. Gwynne, has done remarkable work in Cairo in bringing together the different churches in Egypt for common counsel and action. In Khartoum his successor carries on this noble tradition. In 1946, during my visit to our Forces in the Middle East, I was invited to preach at a Service of Unity in the Cathedral at Khartoum : only at Tambaram have I ever seen a more impressive manifestation of Christian fellowship— Anglicans, Methodists, Presbyterians, Greeks, Armenians and Copts all took part in a service in which prayers and hymns were said or sung in different languages.

With the smaller Eastern Churches there are the same friendly contacts. In 1939 I met at Kottyam in Travancore the Syrian Christians ; they are tragically divided among themselves, and their internal quarrels weaken their Christian witness, but they all expressed friendliness to our Church. It is much to be hoped that these groups of Syrian Christians who have been so faithful during long centuries in the midst of a vast Hindoo population may attain peace among themselves, and in God's good time be used as one of His instruments for the conversion of India.

Away in Abyssinia, an island of Christianity surrounded by Mohammedanism, the Church of Ethiopia recognises and welcomes the friendship of the Anglican Communion. It suffered persecution at the hands of the Italians during the invasion, but the Roman Catholic Churches stand as deserted shells, while the round Ethiopian Churches are crowded. In 1946 I took to the Emperor and his Church messages of goodwill and friendship from the Church of England. I was assured by the Emperor and by the acting head of the Church that neither Abyssinia nor its Church would ever forget the sympathy shown by the Church of England during the dark years of the invasion and occupation.

Future Prospects

Some of the above acts of friendship and goodwill may seem trivial in themselves, especially when it is remembered that usually they have been on the part of the leaders of the Church while the great mass of their people have been uninfluenced and sometimes even unaware of the movements towards Christian unity; this is as true of the Anglican and Nonconformist Churches at home as it is of the vast body of the priests and laity of the Eastern Churches. But these Christian courtesies and exchange of greetings, the discussions and occasional united action by the Christians of different Churches, are something entirely new contrasted with the iron curtains which separated the Churches only half a century ago. The progress which has been made in this comparatively short period augurs well for the future.

I myself see no immediate hope of complete and formal intercommunion, and still less of reunion in this country. The day for this is hidden in the mists of a distant future. We who are members of the Church of England have no intention of surrendering either our Catholic heritage or the freedom we gained at the Reformation. Not even for the sake of unity can we give up, or compromise on, the Catholic creeds, Sacraments, Scriptures, and the threefold Apostolic Ministry : nor are we prepared to surrender our appeal to the Scriptures as the test and standard of what is necessary for eternal salvation, nor the right of a particular or national Church " to ordain, change and abolish ceremonies or rites of the Church ordained only by man's authority." On the other hand, Rome refuses to abandon or modify the claims of the Pope : the Orthodox Churches need reassurance about Anglican soundness in doctrine ; while the non-episcopal Churches, though sometimes prepared to recognise episcopacy as the most ancient and convenient form of Church Government, show great reluctance to agree to any form of re-ordination even *sub-conditione*. Moreover, should the leaders of the Free Churches agree to this, there would still remain great differences between the rank and file of Anglicans and Nonconformists in their attitude to the Sacraments, the Creeds, and Church Order. These are only some of the obstacles which stand in the way of reunion : it is folly to ignore them with a light-hearted optimism or to attempt to evade them by ambiguous formulas which later on would only lead either to charges of bad faith or to disappointment.

On the other hand, I look forward with the utmost confidence to growth in Christian friendship and co-operation. We shall dwell more than we have in the past on the fundamental beliefs we hold in common. They are far more important than anything which separates us. When we have to speak on the questions of faith and order which divide us, we shall do so with charity as well as with firmness. We shall meet together more frequently for prayer and discussion. Through the World Council of Churches and the British Council of Churches we shall bear united witness on the moral and political problems of the day. As we learn to pray, confer and work together, the sin of Christian disunion will become more evident. Precipitate and rash steps would ultimately hinder rather than promote reunion, but with prayer and patience we shall wait upon God until He shows us the way to the complete union which is His Will. The Church of England has taken the lead in the movement towards Christian unity. It has special qualifications for this as both Catholic and reformed. Catholic in its very nature and origin, it meets the historic churches of Christendom on equal terms. Reformed it understands and appreciates the position of the Protestant Churches. By its wide sympathies and its special position it should show the way to the reunion of Christendom, though the road may be long and beset with obstacles before the goal is reached where all Christians are visibly one in Christ.

Note

In 1933 the Archbishops of Canterbury and York formed a Church of England Council on Foreign Relations. This has taken, since it was constituted, an important part in the movement towards Christian unity with foreign Churches. The Council exists to do work, and to offer advice when required, in relation to the different Churches both Catholic and Reformed. It has acquired and circulated much useful information, and it has arranged various services and conferences in the promotion of Christian unity. Its activities are steadily increasing, and it is doing much to bring together representative members of different Foreign Churches.

XII

YESTERDAY AND TO-DAY

I was ordained nearly fifty years ago. During that time great changes have taken place in every direction. The Church, like every other society, has been profoundly affected by them. How great they have been will be at once obvious if I give some account of the Church as I remember it both at my ordination and during the years immediately preceding it.

XII

YESTERDAY AND TO-DAY

Fifty Years Ago

I was ordained nearly fifty years ago. During that time great changes have taken place in every direction. The Church, like every other society, has been profoundly affected by them. How great they have been will be at once obvious if I give some account of the Church as I remember it both at my ordination and during the years immediately preceding it.

The most striking of the external contrasts between then and now is over the observance of Sunday. It was kept as a day of worship and rest. There were no Sunday excursions or amusements. The motor car had scarcely been heard of, so the great majority of people remained all day in or near their homes. There were no cinemas to open either on Sunday or any other day. The demand for the opening of museums and art galleries had not yet been successful. Occasionally there were concerts, but usually under the excuse that they were performances of " sacred music." The wireless was still in the future. Sunday games were forbidden or frowned upon, though there were villages in which out of the hours of Church Service there was cricket on the green with the approval and often on the initiative of the incumbent. My recollection as a child of Sunday in the country consists of best clothes, church-going, Sunday school, and groups of lads standing about the village whistling at the girls as they passed, or of couples courting in the lanes. We as children were fortunate ; we were allowed on Sunday to have our best toys, and to play in the garden as long as we did not shout too loudly. But many children were expected by their elders to keep the day without games and with Scripture picture books as their only solace.

Almost everyone who was able to do so went to church at least once on Sunday : in the morning the people from the big houses, the farmers, some of the women folk of the cottages, and the children from the Sunday School: in the evening, or the afternoon—for often the service was at three—the villagers, the servants and most of the growing lads and girls. There were some who went to chapel; there were the men in charge of the cattle who were unable to come to church: there were a few who deliberately stayed at home: and there were little gangs who chose the time when landlord and farmer were in church to poach for hares and rabbits in the fields or in one of the chalk-pits. Both morning and afternoon the church was well filled. There was a good choir with many men and boys, and there was no difficulty in filling vacant places. On Ash Wednesday, Good Friday and at the Harvest Festival there were large week-day congregations. Most of the country parishes near my home had good congregations on Sundays. We used sometimes to walk to neighbouring churches, and to be sure of a seat it was necessary to be there in good time.

The Holy Communion was celebrated on most Sundays, either early in the morning or, more often, after Matins—"the second Service," as this was generally called. Though Communion was much less frequent than it is now, there was, I think, greater care in preparation for it. Those who intended to receive usually kept the Saturday evening quiet, and abstained from social amusements. Baptism was administered once a month at the afternoon service, and in the presence of the usual congregation. Confirmations were held at the neighbouring church some miles distant, and the candidates used to drive there in a wagon drawn by two cart-horses lent by one of the farmers.

As a boy I was taken for holidays to Worthing and Southsea, when older I went to school at Portsmouth, and occasionally spent a Sunday in London with friends. Everywhere there were large congregations: in some of the more fashionable churches with rented pews the visitors had to stand in the aisle or at the back until the five-minute bell started, and then there was a general post for places in the pews still unoccupied. When I was first ordained there was a congregation of a thousand at Matins in Portsea Parish Church, and nearer two thousand in the evening. Dr. Lang's gifts as a preacher had something to do with this, but the greater part of his large congregation was inherited from his predecessor, Dr. Jacob: and with a few exceptions most of the churches in Portsmouth and Southsea were well filled, both morning and evening.

At that period church-going was general : though in the great towns there were large numbers who never thought of attending either church or chapel, and only a small minority of those who lived in the slums were in touch with the church. But Society of that day was on the side of church attendance. For many it was only a conventional and irksome habit : but the pressure of their social environment to appear once a week in church was difficult to resist. In the country even more definitely popular opinion expected church attendance. The mistress of the house required it of her domestics, and there were farmers who, when they engaged labour, made Sunday church-going a condition of employment. In some villages the farmers paid the men for their time in church both on Good Friday and at Harvest Festival, and deducted their pay if they were absent.

It is more difficult to describe the standard of morality in those days. There was far more drunkenness, both in village and in town, than at present. On Saturday nights and on the holidays, from the public houses there poured out a stream of men, and occasional women, the worse for drink. Sometimes the roads were made dangerous through their presence. There was not so much gambling, though sweepstakes were popular, but they were not organised anything like to the extent of the Pools. Illegitimacy, especially in the country, was common, though the boy who " got a girl into trouble " was expected to marry her, and many unhappy marriages were the result. The unmarried girl with a child, and still more her parents, had a sense of shame and disgrace which is now almost entirely absent. Village opinion condemned the man who was unfaithful to his wife ; if this was notorious his neighbours showed their disapproval by gathering some dark evening outside his house banging trays with pokers, and ringing bells, and making other noises. Divorce was rare ; it was unknown among the poor, and in Society a man or woman who re-married after divorce suffered a minor form of boycott, the county people expressing their disapproval by refusing to call. There was a high standard of honesty. Theft was regarded uncompromisingly as wrong, and the term " scrounging " had not yet been invented to excuse it. While the landed classes looked upon poaching as a serious crime, village opinion was always strongly on the side of the offender.

The great majority of the clergy both in town and country felt assured of their position. Anthony Trollope's description of them was still true. Most of them had been educated at one of the old Universities, and took their place naturally with the members of the landed and professional classes in their parishes. Their vicarages were well kept and great care taken over their gardens. The smooth lawns, the flowers in formal beds, the lilacs, laburnums and laurels always rise to my mind when I think of the parsonage houses of those days. There was a good deal of hospitality, and as many of the clergy had large families there were frequent children's parties. In our neighbourhood many of the clergy had some special interest or hobby in addition to their work : my father was both a gardener and an astronomer ; our next-door neighbour was a geologist ; yet another was a collector of moths. Most of them knew their people of all classes, and diligently sought out among the children those who were not yet confirmed. They were punctilious in their Sunday duty, their sermons carefully written out and read ; but there were very few services in the week, and the church was usually kept locked. The town clergy had little time to spare from their parishes. All of them that I knew would have said without hesitation that pastoral visiting was more important than any amount of organisation. There was little understaffing ; Charlotte Brontë's remark was still true, " Of late years an abundant shower of curates has fallen upon the North of England : they lie very thick upon the hills." There were plenty of assistant curates for both town and country, usually they remained several years in the same curacy ; their stipends were small—I was given for my first year £20 and board and lodging, and for ten years I was a curate at Portsea. Marriage for most was not possible nor contemplated until some years after ordination. Two strong impressions I retain of the clergy, both beneficed and un-beneficed, of fifty years ago. They were confident of their Church and of their own position. They felt secure in their faith. They admired and followed the Prayer Book. They had no misgivings about the place of their Church either in Christendom or the nation. And with this confidence there went great gladness in their work. Before my ordination I was attracted by the happiness of so many of the clergy, both old and young. And when I was one of a large staff of clergy this impression was strengthened. We all—and this was true of the curates apart from our clergy house—were really happy in our lives and work. It was not until much later that I came across ordained men who were disgruntled and unhappy.

Ecclesiastical controversy had little part in the lives of the majority of the clergy. They disliked extremes. In their churches they took the Eastward position, with cross, flowers and candles on the altar, but the candles were lit only in the evening; they observed the seasons by changes of colour, and a cross or banner sometimes was carried in procession before the surpliced choir. They wore black scarves for the services; if they were inclined to be "High" they might instead wear coloured stoles —this for many years was our custom at Portsea. The party disputes which filled the correspondence columns of *The Times* and the pages of the Church newspapers only slightly affected the ordinary parish. There was a lull after the more violent disputes of a previous generation. The Benson Judgement was received by most of the clergy with quiet approval as a victory for common sense and toleration. There was considerable anxiety over *Lux Mundi*; it was reported that in it there was a dangerous essay by a Mr. Charles Gore: but one of the few of my friends among the clergy who had read it told me it would soon be forgotten! A good deal of annoyance was expressed over Sir William Harcourt's denunciations of ritual, even those who agreed with his opinions felt that they came inappropriately from him. But only the clergy who read the Church papers were interested in party disputations.

The Church had considerable influence in social and political life. It was strongly Conservative as opposed to the Liberalism of the Nonconformists. The Labour Party at that time was hardly known. I heard from the Strangers' Gallery of the House of Commons, its solitary representative, Keir Hardie, a sturdy, stocky figure, making his protest, amid great uproar, against a resolution congratulating the Crown on the birth of the future Duke of Windsor. As a rule the Conservatives could still rely on the Church vote being cast in their favour, but there might be wholesale abstentions if its interests were disregarded. The views of the Church on education and other matters had to be treated with respect. The bishops attended the House of Lords fairly regularly, and by their speeches and votes made their influence felt. Some of them were asked to sit on Royal

Commissions or at any rate to give evidence before them. The Charges of the leading bishops were widely read and discussed, and considerable importance was attached to any public utterance they made on subjects of the day. To sum up, half a century ago the Church of England had large congregations ; it was well staffed with clergy, its bishops and clergy were confident of its place in the nation, and its political and social influence was generally recognised.

Fifty Years Later

Since that time change after change has taken place. There have been inventions which have had a great influence on everyday life. I remember so well as an undergraduate spending an afternoon with the inventor of one of the first motor cars ; we had driven from his house to the end of the short drive, and then laboriously had to push back the ungainly machine. His neighbours regarded the inventor as half mad with his prophecies that oil-propelled cars would take the place of horse-drawn carriages, and as somewhat of a danger to the public when he was fined by the magistrates for driving his car to the market town without a man walking in front of it with a red flag. But to-day motors, cinemas, the wireless and the aeroplane are everyday objects. They have transformed many of our social customs. They have brought new interests to the lives of multitudes, opening to them new horizons. Education is now universal, and its standards are steadily being raised ; and with the spread of education the Press is no longer for the few who could read and write, but for the masses. There has been a general improvement in culture and comfort. Democracy has entered into its own, and now with the strength of a giant is rapidly acquiring economic as well as political freedom and equality. Two great wars have destroyed empires and nations, altered the balance of power, and from widespread ruin a new world begins to emerge.

The effect of these changes on man's mental and spiritual outlook has been very great. Victorian stability and security have gone, the future is uncertain, and over it there hangs the menace of the atomic bomb. An atmosphere of strain, excitement and restlessness has replaced the optimism and self-complacency of our forefathers. Progress is no longer a confident watch-word. The sudden and catastrophic changes of revolution now seem more natural than slow advance through evolution. There is no respect for the past or confidence in the future. Man has become scientifically minded, and is sceptical of all assertions and claims unless they can be proved by the accepted methods of experiment by trial and error. The younger genera-tion is mechanically minded ; it understands mechanism, inter-prets the world and human nature by it, and the spiritual and mystical make little appeal to it. In the midst of material advance man is in danger of losing his spiritual faculties. This life now appears to be all that he is offered—religion is rejected as wishful thinking when it speaks of that which is spiritual and eternal. The threatening possibilities of the future and the loss of faith in God make men and women greedy to get for themselves and for others the utmost pleasure out of this life, before all their hopes and fears are buried for ever in the silence of the grave. Only in the light of this changed mental and spiritual atmosphere is it possible to understand the contrast between the Church of England to-day and fifty years ago.

Losses

Sunday is now generally observed as a holiday rather than as a holy day. An unending stream of cars pours out from the towns early in the morning to the nearest seaside resort. Those who have to stay at home have the wireless turned on for the greater part of the day : and in the evening the cinemas are crowded. As a consequence, churches which once were full have now smaller attendances both morning and evening. Like all general statements this is subject to considerable qualifica-tions—there are some churches as full as ever, while most on special occasions have large congregations. But the average congregation in the ordinary church is considerably smaller than it would have been fifty years ago. This is true of the village as well as of the town. Sometimes the congregation consists of a small group of elderly people and children, while the majority of the parishioners are in their homes, or in their gardens, or on a day's excursion, and the bare possibility of attending church has never crossed their minds. There are to-day many adult men and women who have never attended an ordinary service either in church or chapel. It is, however, not true to say that the younger generation is never found in church : this is a popular cliché, repeated without examination : as a matter of actual fact, in most of our churches there are to be found a number of adolescents and groups of young men and women. The smaller choirs and Sunday schools are partly to be accounted for by the falling off in the birth-rate, which has resulted also in the closing of many of the day schools. Sometimes the clergy are blamed for the decline in Church-going : it is said that the people would come if the services were brighter, the sermons more eloquent, and parochial visitation more frequent ; that changes in ceremonial or in the hour of the service have alienated the people. Occasionally these have been contributory causes, but the real reasons for smaller congregations are the loss of faith in the spiritual and the change in social customs. The social atmosphere is now as unfavourable to Church-going as once it was favourable, but this by itself would not be sufficient cause if there were still the belief that attendance at public worship is a duty owed to Almighty God. An American writer states : " People would go to Church if they were certain they would find God there." For the fundamental cause of the falling off in Church attendance is both ignorance and rejection of the Christian faith. It is often difficult to distinguish them ; there are many who, when they say they reject Christianity, are in reality repudiating some strange misunderstanding of it. But it is very difficult for a mechanically-conditioned mind to grasp the spiritual or supernatural. Large numbers regard the claims of Christianity as inconsistent with modern ways of thought. Phrases like the " Fatherhood of God," " Salvation through Christ," " Life after death " seem to them meaningless platitudes. Belief in God seems irrelevant to the man in the street. His faith is in political ideals, social rights, or economic claims. For them he is often ready to fight and die, but faith in God makes to him no appeal. The difference between the success of famous missioners in the past, and the failure of the modern evangelist to make any impression on the outsider is due to the fact that once the missioner and his hearers held in common certain beliefs ; there was general acceptance of belief in God, in the

reality of sin, and the judgement after death. To these fundamental convictions an appeal could be made, and often would
awaken a response from the conscience of an audience. To-day
if a mission preacher addresses a crowd in the open air, probably most of his hearers treat God as a mere name, sin as an
exploded superstition, and the judgement after death as a myth
disbelieved by all intelligent men. And where there is no
deliberate rejection of Christianity, there is widespread ignorance of the most elementary facts on which it is built. Masses
of Englishmen could not say what is meant by Christian faith,
and neither read their Bibles nor say their prayers. England
is still influenced by past centuries of Christian life and teaching,
but very many of its people know nothing about Jesus Christ,
and few accept Him as their Lord and Saviour.

It used to be stated by agnostics of the Victorian age that
even if the Christian faith were discarded, the Christian ethic
would still be generally accepted. Men like J. S. Mill, Tyndal
and Huxley all regarded it as the highest known to man. But
with the rejection of Christian dogma has gone the rejection
of Christian morality. For centuries the Christian moral ideals
were treated with honour, even when they were not realised
in practice. They were still accepted for moral judgements,
even by those who disbelieved in their source. To-day they
are openly criticised and scorned. There are some writers who
attack the Christian ethic as false and mischievous. This change
of outlook is seen on a large scale in the relationships between
nations, when national necessity is now treated as sufficient
reason for breaking treaties. It is seen in ordinary social life,
when the solemn pledges given " in the sight of God " by husband and wife for life-long loyalty are lightly set aside when
convenience or pleasure dictate. Marriage is not regarded as a
sacrament, but as a contract which can be broken by mutual
consent. Adultery is treated even more flippantly on the stage
and in the novel than it was by the playwrights and courtiers of
the Restoration, while fornication is excused as a harmless pleasure
condemned only by the old-fashioned. Honesty and truthfulness
have lost the high place they once held in national life. Magistrates, police and teachers speak with anxiety about the spread of
dishonesty and falsehood among the young. With the decline of
religious conviction moral standards have gravely deteriorated.
The Church and the World are now in open opposition.

There is, of course, another side to this. There has been a great and welcome awakening of the national conscience against social injustice. This is, perhaps, the most striking moral advance of the last fifty years. Wrongs which were once tolerated or ignored are now generally recognised as such and condemned. Strenuous efforts have been made to improve the housing and nutrition of the people, to abolish unemployment and poverty, and to open wide to the poorest the doors of the secondary schools and universities. There is much less drunkenness; this is partly due to education, partly to the increase of various forms of recreation, and possibly also to the reduction in strength, and increase of price, of alcoholic drink. Two wars have proved to what heights of heroism and sacrifice the ordinary man and woman can rise. But the condition and habits of children evacuated during the war to the country from the poorer parts of the great towns show how much still has to be done.

The neglect of organised religion, the repudiation of the old moral standards, the rise of new interests and opportunities have affected adversely the position and influence of the Church and its ministers. They are fewer in number and have neither the political nor social power they once possessed. This is not altogether a cause of regret, especially as its clergy and laity are now found in the Labour as well as in the Conservative party, though on account of historical reasons few are supporters of the Liberal party. Representatives of the Church are rarely asked to sit on Government commissions or committees. In the parish the position has also changed: the school is probably State provided; clubs, institutes, recreation of all kinds are organised independently of the incumbent. A popular incumbent may be welcomed as a member of their committees; he may even through his special gifts become chairman and leader, but this will be for personal rather than for official reasons. No longer is the vicarage regarded as by right and custom the centre of the charitable and social activities of every village, though as a matter of actual fact this is often still the case: the parish has a life of its own, independent of the Church. This is even more so with the urban parishes, where the incumbent rarely has time to occupy himself with local affairs, though the incumbents of Mother parishes, especially in the North of England, are usually expected to take an active part in civic life. Both in town and country parishes are under-staffed, and the shortage of clergy is serious. The clergy also have suffered by the changes in money values. The cost of living has steadily increased. Higher income tax, rates, wages have reduced the value of incomes which were never high. In most of our parishes the incumbent and his wife without servants struggle to cope with a large vicarage. The smooth lawns have gone, the paths and the flower beds of the once neatly-kept garden are overgrown with weeds, and part of the parsonage house is permanently closed. The incumbent would gladly move to a smaller house, but none is to be found, and with building restrictions it is difficult to obtain a licence to erect a smaller and more convenient vicarage. Various attempts have been made in every diocese to augment the smaller incomes, much has been done in this way by the Ecclesiastical Commissioners, but the cost of living increases more rapidly than the rise in stipend.

There is another marked difference between conditions to-day and fifty years ago. Money raising has a much larger place in the work of the clergy and laity. In the past the parish, through collections and donations, met its ordinary expenses and the claims of the sick and poor : and occasionally there were special collections in church or at meetings in response to missionary or other appeals. In most of the parishes the money required was easily and simply raised. This is no longer the case, and much thought and time have to be given by the clergy and the laity to the raising of money not only for the needs of their own parish, but for the various outside claims made upon them. The Central Board of Finance asks each diocese to make a definite contribution for central work, and the Diocesan Board of Finance has to obtain this from the parishes with the addition of the sum required for diocesan purposes. The growing needs of the Church make this unavoidable, but the ever-increasing demands upon the parishes become a heavy strain. The contributions in theory are voluntary ; they cannot be enforced by law, but they are regarded as a moral obligation both to the diocese and to the Central Board, and the parish which fails to raise the amount allotted to it throws an additional burden upon its neighbours. There are frequent appeals from the Archbishops for causes both at home and overseas : and many dioceses have committed themselves to the raising of very large sums of money for their own purposes. These incessant appeals for money are due to the growing activities of the Church; there seems to be no way of dispensing with them, but they throw a severe burden upon the poorer parishes, and much anxiety is caused by the necessity of raising the required amounts. Central bodies in London acutely conscious of the need of money for the extension and maintenance of Church work, do not always realise the difficulty of raising it, nor the burdens laid upon the clergy in responding to these appeals.

It is never easy to admit unpleasant facts. It is always tempting to try to conceal them by evasive rhetoric. But facts are facts, and things are what they are, and it is both useless and dishonest to attempt to deny them. The hard facts of the present position are that there is widespread indifference to and ignorance of Christian faith and ethics, that Church attendance is far less general than it was fifty years ago, that the Church has less influence on national life than once it had, and the work of the clergy is exceptionally difficult. B. K. Cunningham, the much-loved Principal of Westcott House, towards the end of his life used to say: " Once my students came back from their parishes saying they could not meet all the demands made upon them, or use all the opportunities open to them: now they come to me disheartened and perplexed, for they say no one seems to want them."

But in its long history the Church of God has had to pass through many fierce ordeals and disappointing periods. Our Church—and this is true of other Christian Churches—is passing through such a period. It is a stern testing time. But if it endures faithfully, it will in the years to come be able to serve its Lord more truly and effectively. The Church of God is still the anvil on which many hammers have been worn out.

Gains

Against losses in numbers and influence there must be set positive gains. There has been advance as well as recession. Three of the most remarkable gains of recent years have been described in previous chapters : namely the increased part taken by the laity in the life and work of the Church : the spread of the Church overseas : and the contribution made by our Church in the promotion of Christian unity. These are gains which do much to compensate for disappointments elsewhere. There are five other directions in which there has been definite progress :

(1) There has been steady and growing recognition that the Church of England is a living spiritual society, the Catholic Church in this land. There was a time when Churchmanship in the popular mind consisted simply of preference for a certain type of service, which was neither Roman Catholic nor Non-conformist : there was little thought of the Church as a fellow-ship. Many looked upon it as so bound up with the State that Disestablishment would be fatal to it. Very few now regard the Church as a department of State. The long con-troversy over the Prayer Book made it plain that though Parliament's consent was necessary to make the prayers of the Church statutory, yet it could use an Order of Worship which had been approved by the Convocations even though it had not been legalised. The creation of the Church Assembly by the Church itself, the greater interest taken in the meetings of Convocation, and in the various diocesan and other conferences have helped Churchmen to become more conscious of their membership of a society with a spiritual life of its own. If Disestablishment should come, the Church of England would still be the National Church through its long and unbroken connection with the nation, and through its widespread organi-sation. Clergy and laity alike are now aware that they belong to a spiritual and corporate society, with its life independent both of the advantages and restrictions due to its State connection.

(2) There has been improvement in the training and in the efficiency of the clergy. Never before have the clergy been selected so carefully and submitted to such a thorough training. And never before has there been such a high standard of devo-tion, character and efficiency among them. In an earlier chapter I have already written of this. This statement may be questioned by some of an older generation who contrast the clergy of to-day with those they knew when they were younger. It is possible that there are not so many individuals of outstanding personality as there were half a century ago. I can recall many incumbents both in town and country who were recognised by their parishioners and their neighbours as distinguished in character and force, and I do not think I see so many of the

same calibre to-day. Possibly this may only be due to the unavoidable difference in outlook between a junior curate and an elderly archbishop ; the one sees lofty peaks where the other sees only the gentle hills ! Both in the Church and the Nation there has been of late a dearth of great men, though the names of William Temple and Winston Churchill contradict this statement. But if to-day there are not so many outstanding clergy as there were fifty years ago, the general level of priestly and pastoral ideals and work is distinctly higher. The Church, like the State in secular matters, is determined that neither the social nor financial position of the parents shall stand in the way of their sons receiving the best education if they are accepted for Ordination, and its clergy are drawn from a larger field than in the past.

(3) There have been remarkable developments in the administration of the affairs of the Church. Central organisations are stronger and more numerous than they were at the beginning of the century. Under the Church Assembly, as well as independently of it, there have come into existence Boards and Councils which assist and co-ordinate Church work in the different dioceses. The Central Board of Finance, the Central Advisory Council of Training for the Ministry, the Moral Welfare Council, the Central Council for Women's Church Work, the Church of England Youth Council are some of the central organisations which did not exist fifty years ago. More frequent Bishops' meetings help towards united action on the part of the episcopate. Central organisation has become so strong that there is some danger that it may interfere with the independence of the local and diocesan organisations. This is especially true in connection with the Northern dioceses which cannot easily send their representatives to attend the meetings in London, so inevitably those who live in the dioceses nearest London have a predominating influence in central affairs. The dioceses have been gradually organised on the same lines ; and have strong central boards dealing with matters which concern the whole diocese. The parishes are no longer as isolated as once they were ; greater facilities in travel have brought them in closer touch with one another and the centre. The creation of new and smaller dioceses has made episcopal supervision more possible : and though complaints are sometimes heard from the clergy that the bishop does not visit their parishes sufficiently, the improvement is great compared with

the past. My father, vicar for twenty-five years of a parish within four miles of Farnham Castle, had only two visits during the whole of that time from his diocesan. While the clergy far too often receive inadequate incomes and pensions, considerable improvements have been made in both respects. A Dilapidations Measure has removed some of the most serious defects inherent in the old system, when an incumbent at retirement or his widow on his death might be liable for a large amount impossible to meet. Through the Union of Benefices Measure many small parishes have been united, so that an incumbent has more work and a larger income. And the hateful system of the sale and purchase of benefices is rapidly coming to an end as the result of Church legislation. The financial system of the Church has also been greatly improved, and though the quotas required of them often prove a burden both to the diocese and the parish, they enable the Church as a whole to make itself responsible for work which could not be undertaken by any single diocese : and the diocese to give necessary support to the poorer parishes.

(4) In the last fifty years religious communities have grown both in number and in influence. For over three hundred years after the Reformation they were unknown in the Church of England. But in 1841 the three vows of poverty, chastity and obedience were taken by Marian Rebecca Hughes. This was the beginning of a remarkable revival. Within a few years more than twenty Anglican Communities were founded, and in the earlier part of this century their numbers rapidly increased. To-day the religious Orders have an honoured and recognised place in the Church of England. Their great contribution has been towards the deepening and strengthening of the spiritual life of both the clergy and the laity. " Varying much in details of organisation and method of work, religious Communities have this in common : that they are bodies of devoted persons who have given their lives in complete sacrifice as a supreme act of worship to God, and for His immediate service. They represent a spiritual energy, showing itself in a consecration of the whole life, with all its powers, to the Glory of God and the benefit of His Church."[1] Their houses are centres of prayer and intercession, frequently not only for their own members but also for many visitors who come to

[1] Report on the Lambeth Conference 1930. Page 184.

them from time to time for retreats. The Communities have also taken an active part in the life and work of the Church. From some of them there go forth trained preachers and evangelists conducting missions, retreats and quiet days. Some of their members have written useful books on theology and devotion. Mirfield and Kelham are doing valuable work in the training of ordinands. Many of the Sisterhoods have flourishing schools for girls. Others have some of their members working in the poorest parishes of crowded cities ; while yet others are well known for the contribution they have made to church needlework and embroidery. Moreover in their zeal, some of these communities, both of men and of women, have spread far beyond their homes in England, and have founded and maintained great missions both in Africa and in Asia.

The value of the contribution made by the Orders is so great that those who are in authority must do all they can to act in accordance with the recommendation of the Lambeth Conference, and recognise " with thankfulness the growth of religious Communities, both of men and women in the Anglican Communion, and the contribution which they have made to a deeper spiritual life in the Church, and their notable services in the mission field." The resolution goes on to advise " the establishment, by Canon or other means, of closer co-operation between the episcopate and the Communities." The first step towards this has been made by the creation of an Advisory Council on Religious Communities, consisting of members nominated by the Archbishops and the Communities.

(5) Another sign of vitality can be seen in the number of new organisations which have sprung into existence during the last fifty years. The Industrial Christian Fellowship (the offspring of the Navvy Mission and the old Christian Social Union) : the Christian Workers Union, an adaptation of the Jocist movement : the Anglican Evangelical Group Movement : the Seven Years Association, a society for younger Anglo-Catholics : the Anglican Young People's Association : the Servants of Christ the King : the Bible Reading Fellowship, with a membership of many thousands : are only some of the associations which have come into existence. In addition there are inter-denominational societies which have been founded by Churchmen, notable among them is Toc H founded by " Tubby " Clayton, a priest of the Church of England. These supplement

the older societies and unions which in most cases are still active. Though there is a danger from the over-multiplication of these various organisations, they are an expression of abundant vitality within the Church.

Against therefore the decline in Church congregations and influence there must be set a more vigorous and better organised intensive life. The temporary decline in numbers has compelled the Church to concentrate more on the quality of its members. There is good hope that by a deepening of spiritual life with a raising of the standard of its clergy and laity, the removal of anomalies, and with more efficient administration the Church will be the better equipped to undertake the work of the evangelisation of England.

For the pessimists overlook the possibility of a spiritual revival which would once again fill our churches. There have been periods in ecclesiastical history when Church influence has reached a very low ebb, when its leaders have deplored the decline in Church-going, and when its enemies have rejoiced prematurely over what they regarded as the impending doom of the Church. Then unexpectedly there has come the revival and the Church has gone forward with renewed strength. The failure of material civilisation to secure a new order under which men can dwell in peace and harmony has come as a great shock to our contemporaries. This disillusionment may turn the minds of men once again towards God. We cannot organise a religious revival ; too often this has been attempted and disappointment has followed. But we can place ourselves in an attitude of readiness to recognise and welcome its first signs. We shall not do this if we believe that the golden days of Church life and work have gone for ever, and that now we must sadly await further decline in the years to come. This is in effect a denial of the power of the Spirit of God. The supreme task in front of the Church to-day is to win the people of the nation to the service of God. Incomparably the greatest contribution the Church can make to the people of England is to convert them once again to the Christian faith. The most precious gift the Church in the past brought to the people of England was the Gospel of Jesus Christ : it is both the responsibility and duty of the Church to declare the same Gospel under new conditions, but in the language and terms which will be most easily understood and appreciated by those to whom it is addressed.

XIII

TO-MORROW

The Church will not be able to meet the great claims of to-morrow unless in its own life there is holiness. It is the holiness of a Church which proves the authenticity of its claims to be the Catholic and Apostolic Church. There is a great need for the deepening of the spiritual life of both clergy and laity. Soundness in theology, efficiency in organisation, the external splendour of worship will count for little with the world if holiness is absent. But if shining through the life of our Church men see something of the holiness of God, shown in justice, self-sacrifice and love, they will be the more ready to acknowledge that the Church of England is indeed the true and authentic representative in this land of the Catholic Church of Jesus Christ.

XIII

TO-MORROW

THE immediate and vital work before the Church of England is that of evangelisation.[1] Successful missionary work overseas will not compensate for the loss of the home base. But the re-conversion of England has difficulties which were not present in the past. The good news will not be addressed to a nation hearing it for the first time, but to a nation which once heard and accepted it, and has now largely forgotten or rejected it. And the older methods are not applicable; great crowds will not easily come together to listen to the preaching of a mission, however widely advertised it may have been; and if the fame of some evangelists or the novelty of his methods should collect a crowd it will consist chiefly of those who are already members of some congregation. Shock tactics, widespread advertisements, a nation-wide campaign, are unlikely to result in genuine conversion.

Sound Teaching

First there must be a renewed study and more systematic preaching of theology. In the Convocation of York in May, 1946, it was resolved "that a renewal of Christian theology is the necessary antecedent to evangelisation." We must be theocentric rather than anthropocentric in our teaching. We are too ready to concentrate upon the needs of man, rather than on the claims of God. At the beginning of the century Man was enthroned in the place of God, but the wars have cast him down from the high place he had usurped, and now it is questioned if he is of any value at all in the Universe revealed by modern science, or in a world of Totalitarian States. There is a tendency to dwell on his present misery and to comfort and reassure him by bringing theology to his rescue. What

[1] See " Towards the Conversion of England," 1945.

is first necessary is to set forth the Vision of God. The writers in both the Old and the New Testaments concentrate their teaching on God. In the Old Testament we are shown Him in His Power as Creator and Holy making absolute claims upon the obedience of man. In the New Testament we see Him also as Redemptive Love in action revealed in and through Christ. The Majesty, the Holiness and the Love of God must be proclaimed rather than the sinfulness and weakness of man. This was the Bible method. The more clearly God is seen, the more certainly will man recognise his sinfulness and weakness. God is too often assumed in modern teaching and we pass on rapidly to the doctrines which result from faith in Him. The very term God has lost its meaning to most of our contemporaries who hear or use it. It has a different content from what it had in the past. The flippant way in which the Name of God is now used on the most trivial occasions shows how far we have moved from the reverence which once made men shrink from uttering it. Discoveries of the extent of the Universe should have heightened our conception of the Majesty of God. History should have revealed more clearly the judgements of an All Righteous God. And humanism, which rightly understood must not be despised, should have led to a further compre-hension of the goodness, truth and beauty of God. It is only the reassertion of the Majesty and Supremacy of God as Creator, Sovereign, Judge and Father which will bring man-kind to recognise that He demands absolute obedience to His Laws. It is only the Vision of God in His Righteousness and Love which will create a sense of sin and the need of forgiveness.

With our Anglo-Saxon emphasis on what is regarded as practical there will be with some an element of impatience with this emphasis on theology. But a sound theology, possessed not by the few but by the great mass of Church people, will have far reaching results. For it is only on a sound theology that the true doctrine of man can be built. In the nineteenth century man exalted himself as the Master of all that he surveyed ; to-day he has swung to the other extreme, and despises himself as a helpless atom in the Universe he has discovered, or as the slave of the State he has created. It is the Christian doctrine of God rather than philosophical theories about the nature of man which will enable him to understand his true nature. To quote

the Bishop of Southwell : The Gospel of God coming into
that world had claimed man for a human destiny more exalted
than Sophocles or even Plato dreamed of. It restored the
consciousness of divine vocation, the infinite worth of human
life and so much that demoralised and threatened it, because
God had come into the life of man. Human life was saved.
Man is precious because the Father loved him and Christ died
for him and was raised from the dead by the glory of the
Father that man could walk in newness of life. It is that
aspect of human life which is supremely needed to-day. . . .
Telling people that they are children of God and heirs of
eternal life would be found in the days ahead to be the only
effective bulwarks of liberty against the ever mounting pretensions
and encroachments of secular totalitarianism.[1]

With a sound theology there must go sound ethical teaching.
Christian dogma and Christian morals cannot for long be
separated. With the abandonment of Christian faith there has
been a general deterioration in social and personal morality.
Not only are the Christian standards broken or ignored, but
there is widespread confusion and doubt as to the existence of
moral standards which are binding on all. It is not really true
to say that all men instinctively know what is morally right,
and that their conscience condemns them when they do wrong.
This oversimplifies the modern position. While there are many
who know what is right conduct and deliberately challenge it
by their behaviour : there are also many who fail to see the
distinction betweeen right and wrong, and sometimes genuinely
accept as right what the Christian condemns as wrong. The
Christian Church must uncompromisingly declare that dishonesty, hatred, intemperance, pride, envy, falsehood and the
other sins are contrary to the law of God : that they are sins
wherever and whenever they are committed. It must insist
clearly and emphatically that cruelty and falsehood are always
evil, whether committed by the individual or the State. But
something more is necessary. It is not sufficient to proclaim
God's commandments, men must be convinced that they are
in accordance with reason and with the well being of both society
and individuals. And still more is required—precepts originally
given to small rural communities must be applied to the changed
circumstances of an international and industrial society. With

[1] Speech in the Full Synod of the Convocation of York, May 23rd, 1946.

the Industrial Revolution and the creation of the Totalitarian State new moral problems have arisen. In every direction to-day there have appeared complex moral situations unknown to our forefathers. The Christian Church has thus a two-fold duty—to insist uncompromisingly on the binding nature of the traditional moral values and on the condemnation of their breach, and at the same time to apply and relate them to the special circumstances of our time. " There is an obligation on the Christian to be conservative in so far as the essence of Christian experience of life goes, and, on the other hand, to be very progressive as far as the understanding of changes in the modern world are concerned."[1]

The Church of England as the national Church has the right and duty to give guidance to the nation on moral problems. Thomas Hardy recognised this when in 1922 he wrote : " What other purely English establishment than the Church, of sufficient dignity and footing, with such strength of old associations, such scope for transmutability, such architectural spell is left in the country to keep the shreds of morality together." In carrying out this duty the Church should provide the theologians and moralists who can restate the old doctrinal and ethical truths both in relation to the new environment of the twentieth century and in terms which can be understood by the ordinary man. The Universities should take the lead in this. The Church should encourage the establishment of strong theological faculties in all the newer Universities. These are steadily increasing their influence, and many of them through their geographical position are more alive to modern problems than the older Universities. Unless there are Christian teachers of first class intellectual ability in the new Universities the faith will often suffer through default. But it is of equal importance that the parochial clergy should be kept in close touch with the latest theological thought. It is easy for men who are overwhelmed with the pressure of practical duties to give up all study and thought. It is disastrous in the case of those who week by week are called upon to teach others. Their message becomes stale and lifeless. Their hearers soon feel they are listening to an oft repeated form of words, which has no direct bearing on their immediate questions and problems. Sir Richard Livingstone says that we are all familiar with men of forty years and over who hold positions of

[1] " Diagnosis of Our Time," by Karl Mannheim, p. 143.

responsibility and "should be the pumps to drive the water of progress onward, and are at any rate the pipes and conduits through which it must pass, but who are in fact so furred and fossilised that they prevent its flowing at all. They may be men of ability and goodwill, they may have had an excellent education. But they are living in the world as it was when they were in their twenties, they have lost the intellectual and imaginative vigour which would have enabled them to move with the movement of the times : the pace is too much for them, it frightens them : routine, which is another name for action divorced from thought, gets an increasing grip on them : and the younger generation grumbles impatiently : 'When will they retire or die, so that we can get on ? ' "[1]

Sir Richard Livingstone argues that adult education is the best antidote against middle aged staleness. And in support of adult education he claims that experience of life is necessary for the fruitful study of literature, history, politics and economics, and to these subjects I would add theology and ethics. After some years of ordained life a man is much more qualified to appreciate both theology and ethics than he was at his theological college. In many dioceses for some years past those recently ordained have been given courses of study to follow. In some of them schools for older men have been arranged, when for five or six days lectures are given followed by discussion in groups. In the Northern Province in the last three years a successful school of theology has been held in the summer at York, attended by a hundred and thirty clergy selected by their diocesan bishops. It would however be a great gain to the clergy and the whole Church if there were theological courses which lasted for a term instead of a week. When the parishes are more adequately staffed than they are at present it ought to be possible for many of the parochial clergy to attend one of these full term schools after they have been in orders for ten or twenty years. I should like to see two colleges, one in the South and the other in the North, well endowed and staffed, situated in attractive surroundings, to which the clergy could come for intellectual refreshment. What a boon it would be for the Church if in York with its great history and splendid buildings there could be one of these colleges ! If a wealthy man wished to help the Church of England I can think of few contributions

[1] " The Future of Education," p. 91.

of greater value than the presentation of a house with an adequate endowment for this purpose. The clergy in their turn would instruct the laity, and for them also courses of instruction in the Christian faith should be more frequently arranged. We shall make little progress towards the reconversion of England until the teaching office of the Church is so strengthened that clergy and laity both know what they believe and how they can best commend it to thoughtful men and women. Useful work has already been done among the laity by the Church Tutorial Classes and other adult movements. But their work should be spread and strengthened. For the laity should be given the opportunities of attending courses of instruction for the strengthening of their faith. The layman within his factory or workshop has special opportunities of bearing intelligent witness to the Christian faith, which are not equally open to the parish clergy.

The Life of Fellowship

No amount of preaching and teaching by themselves will convert in these days many to Christianity. Realism calls for life rather than words, and the claims of Christianity will never be accepted unless they are seen in action. In the early days the convert was admitted by baptism into " the common life in the Body of Christ."[1] They became members of a fellowship, which drew its life from Christ its Master. The Church was a society in the world, but not of the world. Its members were distinguished and separated from the heathen who lived around them. To-day fellowship in a world divided by hate and fear has more than ever an attractive power. The ordinary man will not believe in Christianity unless he sees it expressed in a genuine fellowship. Preaching apart from community life is a vain beating of the air. Already the fellowship is in existence in the Church, a fellowship which is universal and international, but it will not be recognised unless Jack Smith and William Brown find it in their own village or in connection with the city church close to their homes.

Every Church should be the meeting place at the centre of

[1] The phrase is taken from the title of the great book on this subject by L. S. Thornton.

a fellowship. This is already the case with many of our congregations. I can think of genuine communities which have been built up round the worship and life of the Church. In my early days as a curate I had personal experience of this corporate life. I was in charge of a district, within the Parish of Portsea, in which the streets were still unfinished. At first a small group met in an old shop : as the district increased we moved to an iron church which after a year had to be enlarged : a few years later we had a permanent Mission Church, holding about five hundred, with its halls and rooms for Sunday School, Bible Classes and Clubs. The buildings were the expression and result of community life. The district they served was occupied by a working class population, most of them employed in the dockyard. Those who attended the church from the first were conscious that they were members of a fellowship and not only of a congregation. They knew and helped one another in sickness and in health. They made themselves responsible for the work of the different organisations and collected money for the building of their church. Most of them were communicants and members of one of the Bible Classes. And best of all they were always increasing the numbers of the fellowship by bringing into it their friends and their neighbours. From the outset a new member learnt he had responsibilities and duties to the whole of the fellowship. I have never experienced so vividly the meaning of Christian fellowship as during my ten years in that working-class district. There are hundreds of parishes where the community life is as strong or stronger. Often it centres round the parish Communion. But there are also parishes where there is no fellowship, and the congregation disperses as separate individuals uninterested in one another. There should however be no parish so weak that it cannot show the common life in Christ. In the smallest of parishes there could be formed a group or cell of half a dozen or more communicants who would meet together for prayer and instruction and who would confer together as to how best they might extend the Kingdom of God in their midst. In the larger parishes several such groups might easily be formed. The Church Council itself should be such a group. The purpose of all these cells would be to show the Christian life in fellowship and for their members to witness to Christ among their neighbours. Often the condition of the parish is such that large organisations are impossible, but it should be possible to form a group, which however small would be the fellowship to which the newly confirmed were welcomed, which gave the hand of greeting to the Churchman who had newly arrived in the Parish, and which showed in actual life the warm-hearted fellowship of the Christian society. It is impossible to exaggerate the influence these groups would have on the whole Church if they were in existence in every parish. Everywhere there would be found communities of praying and instructed Churchmen and Churchwomen pledged and trained to bear their witness to Christ. To many this will seem a slow and dull method of evangelisation, contrasted with emotional gatherings with large harvests of converts, but it is a following of the Lord's example who at first concentrated on a chosen few so that trained and consecrated by Himself they might presently give His gospel to man.

The Strengthening of the Parishes

The success of this method will depend upon the strengthening and supplementing of the parochial system. This is no longer sufficient for the needs of our times. It was adequate for the days when most of the parishes were rural. It is now impossible to staff all the parishes and equally impossible to pay their incumbent a stipend on which he can live. Sheer necessity had led to the union of many small benefices. But there remain many in which there is neither sufficient work nor income for a man of vigour. It is wasteful and foolish to attempt to preserve in its entirety a system inherited from days when villages were separated from one another by dangerous forests and moors, when robbers and wild beasts made travelling dangerous, and when there were rough tracks instead of roads. More parishes will have to be united, and in many cases small parishes should be grouped round some central parish : possibly in some cases the Rural Deanery might be treated as a unit for the purpose.

In the towns the position is different. Here large parishes have been repeatedly sub-divided, though usually each parish has a population of several thousand. If a fair proportion attended church the congregation would be large : but in most cases the church is large and the congregation is dishearteningly small. Here the Vicar is overworked and not underworked as he might be in a small country parish, but probably the stipend he receives is as insufficient as that which goes to his brother in the country. There is a strong case for more town parishes like Portsea, where the Vicar and sixteen assistant curates living together in a clergy-house worked a parish of forty thousand with a great central church and four district churches. Parishes of this type are great training schools for the newly ordained, and the young deacon or priest is spared the loneliness he might otherwise have to endure. The destruction of so many churches by the raids and the passing of the Re-organisation Measure afford an opportunity of regrouping parishes and of revising parochial boundaries. Where before the war there were a number of weak parishes each with its small congregation there should be built up a strong central parochial life. Both the Church and the State have been given an opportunity for replanning which they should use to the full. New towns are also soon to be built : the State will see that in each new town there is a community centre for the social life of its citizens, the Church must see that equal prominence is given to a building for worship. The churches must be there before the towns are complete, if they are built long after the people have settled into their new homes, a great opportunity will have been lost. Occasionally it may be possible to demolish a church no longer needed through the removal of the population which it once served, and to transfer its furniture and endowments to one of the new cities : the price obtained for the sale of the site of the demolished church would be applied to the building of a church where it is most needed. In the suburbs on both sides of the Thames there are churches which were provided in this way, and which carry the name of the older church and possess its Communion plate.

The parochial system will need reinforcement from without. Fewer clergy, longer interregnums, and parishes without a resident priest necessitate help from external agencies. In three directions this supplementary help should be strengthened and developed :

(*a*) First through the preaching and missionary work of religious Orders. Their revival has proved a source of spiritual help to hundreds of parishes. Not only have their houses been centres of prayer, but from them have gone forth men trained both in the spiritual life and in preaching, to conduct missions, retreats and quiet days. Almost inevitably so far the members of these communities have belonged to one school of Churchmanship, and definite Anglo-Catholics are not always acceptable to parishes where the Churchmanship is Central or Evangelical. In any case the demands for help made upon the existing communities are greater than they can meet. I should like to see an experiment of community life conducted on different lines : namely the formation of small groups of priests under vows of celibacy, poverty and obedience for a short period—say three to five years. They would live together in a community house, under the bishop or some senior priest appointed by him ; they would go where they were sent and would undertake work of a special nature. They would take charge of parishes during vacancies, assist a new vicar in the visitation of his parish, conduct teaching and evangelistic missions, and would preach courses of teaching sermons in various churches : some of the members of the community would be set apart for work of a special nature ; one would concern himself with the students of a diocese, another would be sent as chaplain to the great industries, another would do his best to keep in touch with the workers in docks, or the lorry drivers : each man would be given work for which he was specially qualified. When the period for which they had taken vows ended, they would be free to marry and to engage on any parochial or other ministerial work to which they felt called. If in addition to the recognised Orders there were a number of small communities of this nature the work of the Church would be greatly strengthened. Funds for their support might be obtained by the diversion of endowments from churches no longer required.

(*b*) It will be necessary to use to a larger extent lay help in the conduct of services and in pastoral work. During the absence of so many of the chaplains on active service many of the churches would have been closed if it had not been through the help given by laymen. Sunday by Sunday they are still responsible for public worship in many churches. The lay readers' boards of the dioceses have raised the standard of the men who are licensed for this work and the congregations have now become accustomed to their ministry. Their ranks require replenishing and an appeal should be made to younger Churchmen to come forward and help in this way. As most of the lay readers are fully occupied with their own work in the week it is often difficult, if not impossible, for them to undertake parochial visitation. But lay work suffers from a serious weakness when it consists of preaching and the taking of services apart from all pastoral work. The value of the lay reader to the Church would be greatly increased if he could give at least one evening of the week to visitation.

(c) Many more women should be recruited and trained for Church work. Some of them should be admitted to the Order of Deaconesses, an Order formally restored by the Convocation of Canterbury in 1923, and two years later by the Convocation of York. In their resolutions they declared that " The Order of Deaconesses is an Apostolic Order of Ministry in the Church of God." There are about four hundred deaconesses at work in various parts of the Anglican Communion. Diocesan Bishops can authorise deaconesses to read the services of Morning and Evening Prayer and the Litany, and to instruct and preach, except during the Holy Communion.

There are large numbers of women who are neither deaconesses nor sisters, but who have passed appropriate examinations and are now licensed or given permission to conduct various kinds of Church work. The whole tendency is to give them work of greater importance and responsibility. Some teach, others are almoners, others organise the work among women and girls, more are active in parochial visiting.

Our Church has been very slow in the past in recognising the importance of the work which can be done by women. Timidity and hesitation were shown in restoring formally the Order of Deaconesses. This was partly due to the fear that this might lead to the Ordination of women to the Priesthood. There is no possibility that the Church of England would approve of such a grave departure from the traditions of the Catholic Church. When under the stress of war an overseas bishop ordained a woman to the priesthood, the Archbishop of Canterbury publicly expressed disapproval and the Province of which the bishop was a member disavowed his action. But uncertainty about the status and the future of the Order discouraged many who might have come forward to Ordination. The same hesitation has characterised the attitude of the Church to unordained women workers ; it has paid them inadequate stipends and has been slow to give them responsible posts. Lately there has been a change ; successive committees have made recommendations for the better training of women and for giving them greater opportunities in Church work. Women who have shown themselves efficient in administrative posts in the war, and who in education, medicine, politics and other departments of life have proved that they are at least as capable as men, should be afforded far larger opportunities of service in the Church. They must be trusted with more responsible posts, given larger stipends, and assured of permanence of work until they reach a pensionable age if the Church is to take full advantage of their gifts. It will be impossible to re-evangelise England without their help, and it will be equally impossible to maintain and extend pastoral work in understaffed parishes unless within them there are found capable and fully trained women workers. In many parishes a fully trained and capable woman is of greater use than an additional curate on the staff. But women of ability will not be found for Church work if irrespective of years of experience they are treated as of less account than the youngest curate who has just come to the parish.

Evangelisation

So far I have written as if evangelisation concerned mainly the internal life of the Church. But evangelisation means proclaiming the good news to those who have never heard it. How is the Church to-day to teach the Christian faith to the multitude who never come to public worship ? Side by side with the deepening and strengthening of the inner life of the Church there must be a going forth to reach the masses. There are many ways in which this can be done. There are four which are of special importance :

(1) First the old and long tried method of pastoral visitation. The regular systematic house to house visitation does more to win people to the Church than great evangelistic missions. The parish priest through personal friendship prepares the way to give his message as the ambassador of Christ. Where such visiting is possible, and the most hardly pressed incumbent should always find it possible to visit every month a few non-Churchgoers, quiet evangelistic work is taking place.

(2) Full use should be made of the opportunities afforded by special occasions. In every parish there are days in the year when the church is well filled. At one time in the towns many of the churches were crowded for the midnight service on New Year's Eve. Harvest Festivals and Remembrance Day Sunday usually fill the churches. And in addition in most of our churches, especially in the Mother churches, there are Sundays when the church is thronged by some parade or by some organisation holding its festival service. These are days which should be most carefully used. The service should be arranged so as to be intelligible to those who do not usually attend church, and the sermon a simple statement in non-technical terms of some fundamental Christian doctrine with its practical application to the special occasion. Through the welcome given and through worship and sermon, many may learn that the Church cares for them and has a message for them.

In addition to special occasions such as I have just mentioned, there are the special events in the lives of those who live in a parish—a baptism, a wedding, a burial. To those concerned these are great occasions, and are remembered when days of national prayer have long been forgotten. Often they bring the non-Churchgoer into contact for the first time with the parish clergy. They are given an opportunity of which they should make full use. In the desire to assert the discipline of the Church nothing must be said or done which will hide the Master's love of the sinner and the careless. The friendship and charity shown by the parish priest on these occasions may have a lasting influence on the lives of those who hitherto have kept far from the Church and its ministrations.

(3) The Church should use the press, the wireless and the cinema to reach the non-Churchgoing public. These are the three great instruments of popular education.

The Press is as a rule ready to accept short articles on religious subjects. In every diocese care should be taken to help and encourage the local press to publish good articles clearly written in a popular style. Replies should be made at once to any attacks on Christianity or the Church. The Church has its Press and Publications Board which is doing very useful work in circulating information about the Church : but its resources are insufficient, and the scope of its work too limited. We need a strong central Publicity or Propaganda Agency which would circulate not only ecclesiastical news, but supply the press with statements about the Christian faith and articles which from time to time might be inserted, especially if they bore upon current events. Ill informed criticism is partly the result of the negligence of the Church in letting people know more about its work and achievements. Our dislike of publicity is often carried too far. Both in London and locally there should be individuals ready to write at once to the press to correct mis-statements or to reply to attacks on religion.

The B.B.C. since its foundation has carried on most remarkable work on behalf of religion. It has given in its programmes great importance to worship and religious teaching. It has had very able men at the head of its religious work. The debt which Christians owe to the B.B.C. is very great. Sometimes it is criticised both for its services and for the character of some of the sermons it broadcasts. But defects in these are negligible compared with the immense influence the B.B.C. has had in keeping millions in touch with the Christian faith. It has day by day brought religion into homes which otherwise might have been deaf to its appeals. Many look upon Dorothy Sayers' broadcast plays " The Man born to be King " as the greatest evangelistic appeal made in our time. All encouragement should be given to listening to the addresses on religious subjects, and much more serious attempts should be made to link up teaching in the parishes with some of the broadcast series of lectures. Groups for discussing these lectures and addresses might attract non-Churchgoers to a more serious consideration of religion.

The Cinema so far has not been used to any large extent by the Church. Most of the religious films have been below standard, and their cost is very great. The Church has its Council which issues lists of films it can recommend, but much more serious thought should be given to the problem as to how the cinema might be used more fully for religious purposes. It is at present the most powerful of all agencies for influencing both the thoughts and habits of millions of men, women and children, who at least once a week, and often more frequently, find recreation in watching the films.

(4) More should be done to promote popular Church literature which in simple language sets forth the Christian faith and the reasons for accepting it. In addition there should be books and

pamphlets making plain and defending the position of the Church of England. Many of our railway bookstalls are crowded with attractively produced literature of the Rationalist Press ; some of it consists of reprints of books now long obsolete, but there are also more modern books which vigorously attack the Christian religion. The Church of England has many theologians and religious writers who have produced valuable works, but very often these are expensive, sometimes difficult to obtain, and usually written in technical language. The Penguin series has already on its lists definite Christian books ; but what is needed is a whole series of volumes sold as cheaply, written as simply, produced as attractively, and as accessible to all as the books in that series. There are many who will not listen to the Christian evangelist for they assume he will speak of what is incredible : they have read some book which criticises or rejects Christianity, and they take it for granted that this is the verdict of all intelligent men. A spate of good but inexpensive Christian literature brought before the traveller or the casual purchaser, will lead many to read books which may not convert them, but which will soften the resistance which otherwise they would instinctively offer to the claims of Christ and His Church.

Church Reform

The Church will be gravely handicapped in its evangelistic efforts unless it shows in its organisation and administration that it is indeed the Body of Christ. It is because of its high claims to be the divine society through which Christ carries on His work that it is judged more severely than a society committed solely to secular aims. While Church reform by itself will never convert England, a Church marked with blemishes which all can see will never carry conviction that it is supernatural in its origin. Frequently in the previous chapters Church reforms have been mentioned. Here even at the risk of some repetition is a summary statement of three groups of reform which seem to be both urgent and essential.

Re-adjustment in the relationship between Church and State is overdue. The Church should be given statutory power to alter its worship and to restate its doctrine without reference to Parliament. In actual fact the Church already has considerable freedom in these respects : imperceptibly some of its doctrines have been restated both by theologians and general consent, and its worship has been enriched without any reference to the State. But to make these changes legal an appeal to Parliament is at present necessary, and a House of Commons in which Churchmen may be in a minority can veto alterations demanded by the great majority of Church people. While this position remains the Church is open to the accusation that it is controlled by Parliament both in doctrine and worship. And this charge finds some justification in the appointment of its archbishops, bishops and deans on the nomination of a Prime Minister who need be neither a Churchman nor a Christian. In principle the present position is indefensible and fraught with practical dangers. No spiritual society should be content that its chief officers should be appointed solely by the State and changes in its worship be only legalised by Parliament. The present position cannot continue indefinitely. It is humiliating that the Church, by allowing variations and changes in the statutory services, should be open to the charge of contempt of the law. The Church should make strenuous efforts for some change in its relationship to the State. If no solution can be found acceptable both to the Church and the State, disestablishment will be inevitable as the result of action either by the Church or the State.

Reform is also necessary for the restoration of order within the Church. The extent of ecclesiastical disorder is often greatly exaggerated. But a small minority is now able to break away from all accepted standards of Anglican worship and to defy with impunity their bishop and to alienate their congregations. There is great uncertainty as to which of the laws of the Church are still binding on the clergy, and as to the nature of the " lawful authority " which can sanction departures from the Prayer Book. This also is a humiliating position. To remedy this the Prayer Book should be revised, emphatically not as an instrument of ecclesiastical discipline ; the primary purpose of revision must be to make the worship of the Church more worthy of Him to Whom it is offered. But a new Prayer Book would incidentally make more plain the law of Church worship. Even more important is the provision of a new code of canons. Our Church alone among the Churches of the Anglican Communion is without a body of canons amended in the light of modern conditions and accepted as authoritative by its members. A revised body of canons has now been prepared for submission to the Convocations. But behind the canons there must be ecclesiastical courts spiritual in their origin and nature, whose judgements will commend themselves to the consciences of loyal Churchmen.

Thirdly, there is a large group of administrative and financial reforms. These include patronage reform, limitation of the parson's freehold, and the regrouping of the parishes : larger stipends for the clergy, and the sale or modernisation of unsuitable parsonage houses : a fixed age for retirement, with an adequate pension. It also is necessary that the payment of the lay workers of the Church of both sexes should be placed on a more satisfactory footing. Large sums of money will be required for most of these reforms, and these can only be found by the redistribution of the existing funds of the Church, and by larger contributions on the part of the laity. The Church should limit the number of its clerical and lay workers by the funds it has at its disposal, and it should fix the standard of payment at a figure which, while it would not bring wealth to its servants, would be sufficient to keep them secure from financial anxiety.

For years past many of these reforms have been recognised as necessary. They have been reported upon by various committees, they have been discussed at length, but very few of them have been carried. Everywhere else the rate of change has greatly accelerated. Parliament has legislated at a pace which would have astonished politicians of the last century. The Church cannot afford to be dilatory in a rapidly changing world. Its sincerity will be doubted and its witness will be prejudiced if it does not prepare itself for an age of crisis by drastic self reform.

But the machinery of the Church is ill adapted for the work of reform. The approval of Convocation involves four different Houses—the Upper and Lower Houses of the South and of the North. It is difficult to arrange for the four Houses to keep in step, notwithstanding frequent telephonic communications between Lambeth and York when the Convocations are sitting. Archbishop Lang sometimes compared himself to a man trying to drive four horses abreast, and never knowing when one might lie down or another kick out at its neighbour. Official and older elements predominate in the Convocations, and though there is always readiness to pass general resolutions and to ask for committees to consider special problems, there is greater reluctance to act upon their recommendations. If, however, a reform is approved by the Convocations, and a Measure is required, resort has to be made to the Church Assembly. This means further discussion, and when the Measure has received final approval from the Assembly it has to undergo the scrutiny of the Ecclesiastical Committee before it can be submitted to the two Houses of Parliament for their decision. This intricate and lengthy procedure gives almost unlimited opportunities to those who dislike change, and who, though they are living in the midst of days of revolution, steadily resist all reform. Sometimes their opposition is open, but more often the proposed reform is received with Christian sympathy, and then eventually smothered by postponing its consideration to a more opportune occasion, or until some committee remotely concerned with its subject has produced its report! Until the Convocations are reinforced by younger men, zealous for reform, there is little possibility of making changes which in principle are generally approved, and are widely regarded as overdue.

An Age of Crisis

The signs of the time indicate that for years to come the human race will have to pass through a series of tremendous crises. The old order is breaking up and the new order has not yet come to the birth. The great changes which have transformed the Continent are already making themselves felt in an island which in the past has been immune from revolutionary storms. We shall experience still greater social, political and economic upheavals in the next few years. The rate of movement shows no sign of slackening. In the international world the outlook is dark and menacing. Unless there is a change of heart in the nations another and even more ghastly war is inevitable, and the use of the atomic bomb will bring to an end Western civilisation. The Church of God must be ready for any catastrophe which may strike it and the society within which it exists. The early Church survived the destruction of Jerusalem and later the invasion of the barbarians because it was organised for a time of crisis. Though in the world it was so detached from the world that the crash of civilisations around it left it standing amidst the general ruin.

We must face the possibility of the worst. What would this be? It is conceivable that opinion might become hardened against all forms of religion : a Totalitarian State might openly reject it : there would be no physical persecution, but the social and mental atmosphere might become so hostile to and scornful of Christianity that the followers of Christ would have to endure a time of fierce spiritual trial. There would be a sifting of the half-hearted from the faithful, a falling away of many, and the certain Disestablishment of the Church. In the goodness of God His Church in this land may be spared the trials which elsewhere it has to suffer. But it must be ready for whatever may come. It must strip itself of all that encumbers it, as an athlete before the games. It must see that it is built so firmly on the rock which is Christ that it stands foursquare and strong however wildly the winds and storm beat upon it. But it may have to pass through a more devastating experience. It is not impossible that within fifty years the nations may in angry madness use the atomic bomb in warfare. If they do civilisation as we know it will perish. Our cathedrals and churches will be destroyed in the universal ruin. If the human race survives it will be impoverished and homeless, uprooted from its old environment, living from day to day with no confidence in the future. But amidst the devastation, stripped of its wealth, its privileges, its buildings, the Church of God will survive if it is loyal to its Master. We must see that our Church is so true to its Catholic heritage, so strong in its faith, and drawing so fully and freely on the spiritual resources which God has given it that it will endure when all that is around it disappears. " The removing of those things that are shaken, as of things that are made, that those things which cannot be shaken may remain."

These disasters may not come, but the Church should prepare itself to meet them. It must call the nation to penitence, but it must first show penitence in its own life. It must call for the removal of injustice in the national life, but it must see that in its own life and organisation injustice has no place. It must show quiet confidence and trust which will help and reassure the despondent and bewildered, for it has its eyes ever on Him Who is invisible.

In these days of crisis the Church must not however be self-absorbed in its own life or its own concerns. It must not hide itself in the catacombs. It must proclaim the truth of God openly and aggressively. It must boldly challenge the World. It must go out into the everyday life of the nation, taking to it the revelation which has been committed to its keeping. Its Gospel is good tidings about God as Creator, Father and Redeemer. It has also good news about man, that he has been redeemed by Christ, that he is called to be a child of God, and is an inheritor of a Kingdom which is eternal.

The Church will not be able to meet the great claims of to-morrow unless in its own life there is holiness. It is the holiness of a Church which proves the authenticity of its claims to be the Catholic and Apostolic Church. There is a great need for the deepening of the spiritual life of both clergy and laity. Soundness in theology, efficiency in organisation, the external splendour of worship will count for little with the world if holiness is absent. But if shining through the life of our Church men see something of the holiness of God, shown in justice, self-sacrifice and love, they will be the more ready to acknowledge that the Church of England is indeed the true and authentic representative in this land of the Catholic Church of Jesus Christ.